stolen images

stolen images

lumumba and the early films of raoul peck

Raoul Peck

Foreword by Bertrand Tavernier

Translated from the French
by Catherine Temerson

Featuring the screenplays
Haitian Corner
Lumumba: Death of a Prophet
The Man by the Shore
Lumumba

Seven Stories Press

NEW YORK

A Seven Stories Press First Edition

Introductions to individual films created in conversations between Raoul Peck and Dan Simon in New York City, August 8, 9, and 10, 2010.

Book design by Jon Gilbert

Library of Congress Cataloging-in-Publications Data

Peck, Raoul.
[Screenplays. English. Selections]
 Stolen images : Lumumba and the early films of Raoul Peck : featuring the screenplays, Haitian corner, Lumumba: death of a prophet, The man by the shore, Lumumba / Raoul Peck ; foreword by Bertrand Tavernier ; translated from the French by Catherine Temerson.
      p. cm.
 Includes an introduction for each individual screenplay, based on conversations between Raoul Peck and Dan Simon in New York City, August 8-10, 2010.
 isbn 978-1-60980-393-3 (pbk.)
 I. Temerson, Catherine. II. Title.
PQ3949.2.P32A2 2012
842'.92--dc23
                                        2011052214

Printed in the USA

9 8 7 6 5 4 3 2 1

Contents

Foreword by Bertrand Tavernier   **7**

Haitian Corner (1988)   **13**

Lumumba: Death of a Prophet (1991)   **111**

The Man by the Shore (1998)   **163**

Lumumba (2000)   **207**

Foreword by Bertrand Tavernier

Imagine if cartographers drew maps and regularly forgot provinces, regions, or even countries. Well, in the cinema world this happens very often—in articles, overviews of festivals, or yearly roundups, for example.

The filmmaker Raoul Peck isn't "mapped" as often as he ought to be. Despite a nice recent two-page spread here in Libération, it is almost as if Peck didn't exist. Yet he has devoted two films to Patrice Lumumba—a documentary in 1992 and a "fiction" film, cowritten with Pascal Bonitzer, in 2000—and has dealt with the tragedies of Haiti in *Haitian Corner* and *The Man by the Shore* (an official Cannes Festival selection in 1993). There is also *Sometimes in April*, about events in Rwanda; *L'Affaire Villemin* (co-written as well with Pascal Bonitzer), the terrific, exemplary French television miniseries [on the 1984 case involving the tragic death of a four-year-old boy that caused endless blunders and miscalculations within the judiciary and in the media]; and another television film, *L'École du Pouvoir*, about the graduating class of the highly competitive École Nationale d'Administration (or ENA) that trains and warps the elites destined to govern France.

Think of the career of this eternal exile, who does not see himself as an exile though he was uprooted from his country at the age of nine, and carted around, from Haiti—where he returned twenty-five years later—to Africa, to the United States, to France. And then think of everything that came out of these wanderings, of being uprooted, of the culture shocks—all the films he directed that seize reality and grapple with it. There is a physical side to his work, the sense of violent confrontation. A confrontation between the director and his subject(s), but also perhaps confrontation in the inner depths of a man torn amid several cultures and several kinds of cinema, using each one of them as a secret weapon. A man who digs down deep in order to put up with Rimbaud's rough embrace of reality, thereby fulfilling Jean Vigo's call for French cinema to make documented fictions, while at the same time fulfilling the perennial appeal of certain enlightened and demanding French critics to make movies as courageous and aware as the films of American filmmakers.

In fact, Raoul Peck did make American movies. In *Sometimes in April*, financed by HBO—the cable television network that has given a number of American filmmakers the opportunity to tackle highly topical and controversial subjects (John Frankheimer's *Path to War* was an HBO movie)—he delved into a subject that was by and large ignored by his American colleagues and went much further than *Hotel Rwanda*, showing himself to be considerably more radical and analytic (and was therefore blamed for being didactic by people who can't bear to face up to their responsibilities). He overtly accused the American government of blindness and inertia with regard to the genocidal Hutus ("We don't want another Somalia," says a government official to Debra Winger), facts that have been confirmed by recently declassified documents. The administration knew, but did nothing; this is seen in the film and some viewers were shocked by it. Nor is France exonerated for its heavy responsibility for what happened.

We dare not think that this partial absence, this silence, is due to the fact that Raoul Peck is Haitian and black. No, it must be due to the fact that Raoul Peck is constantly darting from country to country, from America to France, shifting from politics (he was minister of culture in Haiti for two years, from 1995 to 1997), to documentary filmmaking, to fiction films. His camera leaps from the Congo to the French provinces, from an Africa devastated by civil war, to the corridors of government offices. How can we make sense of it? How can we put a label on it and categorize it? It's not nice to make life so complicated for exegetes and taxidermists. You move around too much, we can't keep up. It would be so much simpler if you would do what we expect you to do. You should be more sensible, more sober: sober writers are the counterparts of sensible voters, according to Victor Hugo.

Above all, Raoul Peck commits the ultimate sin: he constantly moves back and forth between Cinema and Television. I am deliberately using capital letters as in France there seems to be a kind of Berlin Wall between these two disciplines, these two audiovisual fields. In the United States, many directors between studio productions—Frankenheimer, Mike Nichols—shoot one or more films on personal or daring subjects for HBO or another channel before returning to cinema. But in France, aside from a few rare exceptions, there is no bridge between the two. No interaction.

One important turnaround though, a dramatic change still in line with Peck's turbulent career, further blurs the picture: on January 10, 2010, just two days before the catastrophic earthquake that shattered Haiti's capital, Peck was called to preside as chairman of the board over the very prestigious Parisian cinema school, La Fémis, thus now serenely looking over the future of French cinema. What a splendid and ironic occurrence!

Let's talk cinema. I've kept a vivid memory of Lumumba played—brilliantly—by Eriq Ebouaney, as a proud, haunted man, of great oratorical skills, whose stubbornness worked against him. Peck doesn't hide Lumumba's faults, his lack of diplomacy and strategic vision. But he brings home to us the strength and tenacity that sustained him in his daily fight against evil, corruption, and despotism, qualities that enabled him to impose two months of democracy. (To paraphrase Virginia Woolf, there is no greater passion in the heart of man than the desire to have his faith shared.) Before the collusion of the colonial powers, the United States and Lumumba's rivals (including Joseph Kasa-Vubu, whom he had known when he sold beer) executed him in shameless fashion. Roger Ebert summarized it perfectly: the film is "powerful, bloody and sad." And he refers to a passage that had struck me too: Mobutu's speech at the second anniversary of Independence and his request for a minute of silence in honor of Lumumba. During this silence, Raoul Peck shows shots of the execution, the burial and the dismemberment of Lumumba, and the burning of his body, a montage worthy of Kozintsev or Pudovkin. As John Dos Passos said in *State of the Nation*, "You can tear a man away from a country but you can't tear a country away from a man's heart."

And in a way, *Sometimes in April*, which some people have cleverly described as a "feel bad movie," is an extension of that film, for it is about the relationship between the present and the past and shows us, as Faulkner said so well, that "the past is never dead. It's not even past." And it tells us that filmmakers shouldn't show us an exit door, they have no right to let us to sneak away as in so many pseudo-progressive works; they ought to refuse to give answers or solutions that might relieve the conscience of the viewer, an irritating flaw in Hotel Rwanda. "There is no last word in this story, it's up to you to write it," said Samuel Fuller at the end of *Run of the Arrow*. Let us add that Raoul Peck insisted on shooting the film on location:

> This film could only make sense for me in this country; the story could only be told ethically with people who had been its main actors otherwise I would have felt like a voyeur, a usurper. That said, how do you tell an "untellable" story?

With what images? With what stories? Every draft seemed too limited, too incomplete, too restricted. Hence the idea of choosing among real-life accounts, of combining them in one family and finding dramatic interconnections over a period of ten years—from 1994 to 2004—and writing a fragmented story on parallel temporal levels.

This kind of idea—unity of family, or of place, or of time—haunts the greatest documentary filmmakers from Marcel Ophuls to Ken Burns.

But here, some readers will object, you're discussing subject and theme. What about the actual filming? First of all, we're struck by the intelligence and acuity of his castings: how well he directs his actors and how perfectly they incarnate their characters. Add to this quality the justness of the milieus, of the atmospheres, of the sets, never ostentatious or overdrawn: a café, an investigating magistrate's office, the edge of a river, a country road. Never anything spectacular or falsely cinematic, never anything that smacks of a preconceived vision propping up the authors' intentions, that condemns or absolves the characters. We have the feeling that the filmmaker is discovering his characters at the same time we are; we enter places with him and are horrified along with him by the practices of the investigating magistrate, his idiotic stubbornness, and the uncontrolled blunders of the press. Uncontrolled like the prewar tabloids whose primary motive was to grab attention and defile at the expense of the human beings involved, sometimes blatantly incriminating them, even if this meant manipulating the investigation. It is easier to accuse and condemn the guilty than it is to look at them, said Marcel Pagnol.

Raoul Peck also pays meticulous attention to feelings, small details and behavioral characteristics that many directors eliminate because they feel they don't carry the action forward. But for Raoul

Peck the action consists in X-raying power relationships, and the human and social damage they cause. His is a cinema that wants to show, simply and unostentatiously, which is not so common, that the first revolutionary principle consists in saying, like George Orwell, that 2+2=4, in the hope that the rest will follow.

—Translated by Catherine Temerson

Haitian Corner (1988)

My first feature came about in the midst of great turmoil. I had no real model for the kind of film I would make, at least none that described the world I saw around me. Much later, I became aware of filmmakers like Hailie Gerima and Charles Burnett, who would both become dear friends, and in the case of Hailie, the nearest person to a mentor that I would have in my life. All I knew, all I had been taught, was the dominant cinema of that time. There was no Spike Lee, no John Singleton yet. There were no black actors either, except in typecast roles. So I felt I had to uncode our own cinema, invent it out of whole cloth. I had essentially studied European filmmaking while growing up with American cinema. What was "Haitian" cinema?

Haitian Corner was very low budget; it was shot in Brooklyn with a mixed crew of mostly unprofessional actors—Haitians, Americans, and even German and Swiss friends from my film school in Berlin, Deutsche Film- und Fernsehakademie Berlin (DFFB). My director of photography and my eye was Michael Chin (*Chan is Missing*, Wayne Wang's first film). Both of my producers were women: one Korean-American, Christine Choy (later Chair of NYU's graduate film program), and one Japanese-American, Renée Tajima-Peña. Was I unknowingly making sure not to be influenced in one particular direction? In a way, the title of this book, *Stolen Images*, is meant to convey the same idea. I was "stealing" images that didn't exist, that were not supposed to be. More than twenty-five years later, I still feel that the only reason to make films is to keep on "stealing." We are stealing images in the sense that we are creating images that are not supposed to be, that are not already considered legitimate, whether aesthetically, dramatically, or even economically. The dominant worldview Hollywood had imposed on me wasn't the world I'd experienced so far. I knew from the start that there was something wrong with it. If I was to restore the complexity of the world around me, I would have to go behind the curtain into the kitchen, use the merchandise, borrow the cooks and helpers, mix the ingredients, change the flavors, break some glasses and cook, as James Baldwin wrote, "a kind of pungent missionary stew—a funky dish of chitterlings."

I began writing *Haitian Corner* in New York in the early eighties. I had already studied engineering and economics in Germany and was driving a cab in New York while I waited for a career-type job I was hoping was going to open up at the UN. While the job failed to materialize, I had plenty of time to think about the choice I was going to make. It was a decisive moment: I was to abandon the prospect of a well-paid job and probably an interesting career in development policies, or . . . nothing. To give up the comfort of having a profession, family, and credibility in order to become a *saltimbanque*. After a month of indecision, I decided to return to Germany, this time to attend film school, where I could work more on the *Haitian Corner* script.

In 1986, Reagan had begun his second term. In Haiti civil society had begun the last stage of its rebellion against Jean-Claude Duvalier, which would culminate in his leaving the country. I remember that when my handwritten screenplay was done, my mother typed the first draft for me. That must have been around February, because it was the month when Baby Doc was overthrown, and also because my mother died shortly thereafter.

To me, *Haitian Corner* is all about asserting our Haitian identity. As Creoles, imposing the language, and as a class, struggling to exist in the American melting pot. It is a way of saying, "We Exist!" The mood is one of defiance. *Haitian Corner* is a film for *us*, for Haitians, at a time when the struggle against the American-backed dictatorship was bloody, and the making of this film a way to acknowledge all those who died in that fight. By the time the script was complete, vengeance had emerged as its strongest theme.

Haitian Corner was inspired by two women, Denise Prophete and Laurette Badette, whom I met during my research. Both had spent eight years in Fort Dimanche, the darkest place in Haiti during the Duvaliers' reign, a prison they sent you to die, a place where few prisoners lasted more than a year. Yet these two women had each beaten those odds: they were freed as part of an exchange for the kidnapped US Ambassador to Haiti, Clinton Everett Knox, in 1973. Both were living in Europe—one in Brussels, the other in Paris—and I went to meet each of them. I felt that without the visits I couldn't make this film. I remember sitting in a public square in Paris talking to Laurette, who had become a librarian. She was so calm, so poised, and possessed of a complex mixture of great compassion and understanding along with the ability to comprehend a world that was so violent and brutal.

These two women gave me the film's soul; they allowed me to understand deep down what being tortured meant, what the scars were and what you had to overcome. Neither one appears in the film, but the testimonies at the beginning of the film are all real stories. And since then, in all my films there is always a "witness" sequence with real people.

—RP

Haitian Corner
A film by Raoul Peck

CAST AND CREW

Main Cast

JOSEPH CAJUSTE	Patrick Rameau
SARAH	Aïlo Auguste-Judith
JEAN	Jean-Claude Eugene
HEGEL	George Wilson
THEODOR	Emile St. Lot
JOLICOEUR	Jean-Claude Michel
FELICIA	Toto Bissainthe
WILSON	Hegel Gouthier

Main Crew

DIRECTED BY Raoul Peck
WRITTEN BY Raoul Peck
PRODUCED BY Klaus Vokenborn, Christine Choy, and Renee Tajima
ORIGINAL MUSIC BY Mino Cinélu
CINEMATOGRAPHY BY Michael Chin
FILM EDITING BY Aïlo Auguste-Judith
PRODUCTION DESIGN BY Charles McClennahan

TITLE OVER BLACK: HAITIAN CORNER

CUT TO:

TITLE CONTINUES OVER BLACK AND WHITE
STILL PHOTOGRAPHS

Music begins. Photographs of President Jean-Claude Duvalier tak-ing power. The first "tonton macoutes" (militia) appear. We see fear on faces in the crowd. A public execution in the cemetery. The death of the tyrant after twenty-three years in power. His 18-year-old son, Jean-Claude Duvalier, becomes president for life. Jean-Claude's sumptuous marriage years later. Repression and poverty continues . . .

EXT. PORT-AU-PRINCE—DAY

Black and white photographs are replaced by grainier photos, inter-spersed with Super 8 movies of Caribbean-style wooden houses.

A neighborhood in Port-au-Prince: modest houses, almost shanty-like, except for the clearly traced streets and sidewalks. We feel boredom more than poverty under this heavy sun.

EXT. PORT-AU-PRINCE—DAY

A backyard. A deserted water fountain. Two children are playing.

FADE OUT:

The music continues as we hear the sound of falling rain.

FADE IN:

INT. CAJUSTE APARTMENT—DAY

A tilting window throws traces of the morning light against the shabby walls. The music stops, but the rain continues. Outside the window is Brooklyn, New York. A heavy summer rain spatters the window. We look around the room. It is sparsely furnished. On the wall: an ancient calendar advertising beer and a rusty medallion hanging from a crooked nail. Dusty pulp novels on a shelf lean against a plaster bust of Martin Luther King. Furniture: a folding card table with a rococo plastic lamp. Two men sleeping on cots.

Joseph, 30, darkly handsome, with close-cropped hair and sharply cut features, is gripped by a tormented sleep. He is still fully clothed. He opens his eyes suddenly and wipes the sweat from his brow and face. He is afraid to move. He stares fearfully at the ceiling. His attention is diverted by the sound of someone crying. He closes his eyes.

CUT TO:

EXT. HAITI (DREAM)—DAY

Port-au-Prince. In an impoverished area, a dirt road leads to a public fountain. Abandoned by their owners, jugs in all shapes and sizes wait to be filled with water. A metal pail is under the dripping pipe of the fountain. Two tiny hands grip the bucket, then are joined by two larger hands; a fight for the bucket begins. A small girl, about 8, struggles with a boy about 15, but the children are smiling at each other. The boy splashes the girl and the girl splashes back. They chase each other around the fountain laughing and laughing.

OLD WOMAN'S VOICE

Joseph! Sarah!

Suddenly, the square is deserted.

CUT TO:

INT. APARTMENT—CONTINUOUS

Joseph can't sleep. He opens his eyes, turns his head, and sees his brother—Brunel, 17, scrawny, but muscular in a speedy kind of way— across the room, jump up out of bed. Brunel is in a panic.

BRUNEL
(in English)

Shit! Shit! Goddamnit!

He grabs the alarm clock by his bed and stares it straight in the face.

BRUNEL
(to the clock, in Creole)

Your Godmother's cunt!

He taps it violently. The alarm starts to ring. Joseph turns over, ignoring the whole rampage. The room is silent for a moment. Then we hear the burst of a pop radio station and static as Brunel searches for a song he likes. Joseph is now definitely awake.

INT. APARTMENT—BATHROOM—SHORT TIME
LATER

Joseph stands at the bathroom sink looking into the mirror. He tries to catch enough water from the erratic faucet to splash his face. From the other room comes the frantic sound of Brunel's continuing search for the perfect radio station. As we watch Joseph, we also hear the radio and its disjointed announcements:

RADIO
... How old should your child be before you buy him a computer? ... (*music*) ... (*static*) ... Hey Dad! Look at Harold's new Japanese car!— Son, that car's not Japanese, it's Korean ... (*static*) ... (*music*) ... A personal relationship with God can be yours for the asking. Just $4.95, plus shipping and handling ... (*music*) ...

Under this sonic barrage, we see Joseph open the medicine cabinet and select a bottle of pills. He spills two of the pills into his palm and pops them into his mouth. He cups his hands to get water from the tap. Swallowing the pills, he closes the mirrored cabinet, revealing Sarah, 24, dark like Joseph, beautiful and sultry, framed in the mirror. They look at each other in the mirror. She has caught Joseph, and he looks embarrassed by her playful, scornful frown.

SARAH
You're still here.

JOSEPH
I dreamt about you last night, Sarah.

SARAH
Hope you slept well. Here.

She hands him a pearl necklace and turns around. He strings it around her neck and takes his time fastening it. When he's done she turns for him to see.

SARAH

Well, how do I look?

From his expression, we can see he honestly admires her beauty. But because he is not looking at the necklace, there is an awkward moment between them. She raises her eyebrows to hurry his response.

JOSEPH
(in Creole)
You could not be more beautiful.

She is quiet. He takes advantage of the moment to kiss her on the neck. She doesn't stop him.

BRUNEL
(off-screen)

Sarah!

SARAH
(to Joseph)

Idiot!

She exits. Joseph smiles.

INT. APARTMENT—KITCHEN—LATER

Felicia Cajuste, 50, a short and formidable woman with a slight build, is preparing coffee. She is dressed in her morning coat and shawl.

With alert, lively movements she completes the ritual, pouring hot water over the coffee. Joseph is leaning against the greasy yellow walls.

JOSEPH

Mother!

But she only turns part way to give him a disapproving glance. Her irritation forces him to stare at the floor.

FELICIA

(in Creole)

It has to be done. The hospital has sent your father's papers.

JOSEPH

Speak English, mother.

FELICIA

(in Creole)

Is that all you have to say?

Joseph sits at the table and waits for his coffee. Brunel enters and sits. Brunel knows not to enter into the argument. He just watches it, like a tennis match.

JOSEPH

I know you'll do what's right.

FELICIA

(in English)

It's not your problem, is it?

(in Creole)

If your father dies, you won't escape your share.

Joseph is silent. Felicia serves Brunel coffee, but not Joseph. She slams the pot back on the stove.

FELICIA
(in Creole)
You don't care, do you?

Joseph gets up and pours himself some coffee. He stands at the stove sipping it. His mother continues.

FELICIA
(Creole and English)
As if the rest of the world didn't exist. None of your business. Why don't you just wait in here until the day your father jumps out the window?

JOSEPH
That's enough!

FELICIA
(English, then Creole)
How dare you!? Thunder!

She smashes an empty cup on the floor. As the pieces fly all over the kitchen, the sound continues into next scene.

CUT TO:

INT. IMAGINARY PLACE—DAY

An empty room. The sound of the shattering cup fades. The room is narrow, flooded with light. The floor is damp, made of stones that have been scratched with metal. The stone walls are damp. The sound of running water. It is a prison cell.

CUT TO:

INT. APARTMENT—LIVING ROOM—SHORT TIME LATER

Joseph and his cousin, Pastor Mondestin, 36, who is excitedly reading out loud from the New York Post in a voice of dismay, sit with their coffees at a wooden table. Between them is an old man, about 65, with a vacant stare, looking inward toward eternity. The deeply etched lines of his face suggest a hard life with many memories and stories now lost in a permanent silence. This man, Hyppolite Cajuste, is Joseph's father. Felicia sits in the background next to her sewing machine, surrounded by tissue patterns and fashion magazines, and folding children's clothes. Pastor folds the paper.

PASTOR
(to Joseph)
People live on lies. Look at this . . .

Joseph takes the paper.

PASTOR
Little pig says to his mother, "Mother, you are
so sad, why does your tail get so long?" His mother
says, "For you, my son. You are getting bigger. You
will see."

JOSEPH
(completing the thought)
... and ten days later he gets eaten.

Both men laugh. Sarah enters and first gives her aunt a kiss.

SARAH
Morning everyone.

She kisses Hyppolite on the head. Then she goes to a mirror on the wall to check her makeup. Felicia gives Sarah a small package.

FELICIA
Take this to Claryce for me.

SARAH
No, please! I have a date after work!

Honking outside. Sarah hurries to leave.

FELICIA
Sarah!

JOSEPH
(to his mother)
I'll do it.

Sarah turns in the doorway and mouths the words "Thank You" to Joseph. She hurries downstairs. Joseph goes to the window. He sees the waiting car below.

FELICIA

(to Joseph)

Ask her to try to pay me a bit sooner . . . the
last time . . . and the sizes four and five . . . don't
forget to tell her . . .

*Joseph isn't listening. He watches a young man in a business suit get
out of the car. Sarah skips down the stairs to the street. The young man
ushers Sarah into the car and slams the door.*

EXT. STREET—DAY

*A row of small stores: a shoe vendor selling second hand shoes, repairs,
and shines; a dry cleaner; a dilapidated real estate office. On the street
are an overturned trash can and, occasionally, some chairs posted at the
stoops. The busiest place, though, is the café/grocery store. We can see the
counter inside lined with men talking, yelling animatedly. Books are
displayed in the window of the store. Above the door is a wooden sign;
painted on it in bright colors: HAITIAN CORNER.*

INT. HAITIAN CORNER—CONTINUOUS

*Joseph sits at the counter drinking beer from a can. The package for
Claryce is on the counter in front of him. Behind him is a book rack,
where the complete writings of Che Guevara are keeping company with
the latest novel by Jean Cau. Behind the counter, a bulletin board promi-
nently displays political pamphlets next to small advertisements and articles clipped from the papers.*

Cesar strolls behind the counter. At 50, he is a lost, displaced philosopher, sardonically alert to the world. He owns and runs Haitian Corner. Cesar brings Joseph a coffee.

CESAR
Ah, the sleepwalker!

JOSEPH
I don't want coffee.

CESAR
In a bad mood and it's not yet nine o'clock . . .

Joseph takes his beer and a newspaper to the store's only armchair. Cesar follows him.

CESAR
Ignorance, Joseph: it is worse than cancer. It doesn't let you die in peace, but kills you and displays you for all the world to see: a zombie, a walking dead.
(picking up a dusty book)
The Secret Life of Catherine de Medici, volume two. Of course I will have to find volume one, but even if I did, who will read this? Huh? What a waste. Instead, my walls are lined with paper that shouts.
(waving his hand to the bulletin board and shaking his head)
. . . So many voices. What a loud room.

JOSEPH
I have a parcel for Claryce.

CESAR
You have legs. She's upstairs.

Shouts from outside distracts Cesar. He journeys out to the street where Jolicoeur, a gangly, hawk-nosed Haitian, has jumped out of his gypsy cab to argue for a parking spot with a Puerto Rican woman. French, English, and Spanish epithets are flying.

Joseph is rising when we hear a latch unlock; the door to the upstairs quarters opens. Claryce, an attractive woman about 36 years old, poised in dress and posture, enters. She is wearing a striking dress with deep cleavage. When she sees Joseph, she smiles warmly.

CLARYCE
So early?

JOSEPH
What is it with everybody? Is it a miracle that
I get up in the morning?

CLARYCE
I was just saying hello . . .
(beat)
So . . . ? How are you, Joseph?

JOSEPH
You know how it is . . . I have this for you.

He gives her the package.

JOSEPH
. . . From my mother . . .

CLARYCE

Oh, I see. Where's Cesar?

She goes behind the counter and puts the package in a safe place.

JOSEPH

. . . She'll send the rest later.

Claryce approaches Joseph and brushes some imaginary dust from his shoulder.

CLARYCE

You'll have to bring that to me as soon as it's ready, won't you?

(beat)

Well, I'll see you then.

She leaves. Cesar returns from outside, all worked up.

CESAR

Joseph? You know what is worse than being ignorant? Being ignorant and stupid.

Jolicoeur enters with a sheepish grin and his arms outstretched, pleading forgiveness.

CESAR

Jolicoeur, you are a fool. You are dumber than President Lescot!

JOLICOEUR

But it's not my fault!

INT. CAJUSTE APARTMENT—LIVING ROOM—
AFTERNOON

Hyppolite sits at the same table, in the same position as when we saw him earlier. Without looking down, he runs his fingers over the frayed and yellow pages of a worn file before him. Coming from the kitchen, Joseph enters the room. He walks up quietly behind his father and puts his hand lightly on the old man's shoulder, but the old man just keeps turning the pages. We see newspaper articles about unions, strikes, police battles, elections, and photographs of groups of men. Touching the past, his eyes light up for a moment. Dusk and darkness overcome the room. Hyppolite is having trouble seeing the pages. Joseph turns on the light as he leaves the room.

INT. MUNICIPAL BUILDING STAIRWAY—
CONTINUOUS

Joseph climbs the last flight of a narrow wooden stairway two steps at a time. At the top is a door marked: HAITIAN SOCIAL AND CULTURAL CENTER/CENTRE SOCIAL ET CULTUREL HAITIEN: HSCC. Joseph rings the bell. Footsteps. A peephole in the door is opened and shut. The door is cracked open, but remains locked with a chain. Wilson, a young man between 20 and 25, peers suspiciously at Joseph.

> **WILSON**
> *(officiously)*

Yes?

> **JOSEPH**

Hegel.

WILSON

He's working. It's after five. We have classes
right now. Come back later.

He shuts the door. Joseph bangs on the door.

JOSEPH

Tell Hegel it's Joseph, please.

*The door opens again and Wilson takes a second look at Joseph. The
door closes. The chain is undone and Joseph admitted. Wilson locks the
door again. He leads Joseph down the corridor.*

WILSON

He told me not to let in anyone who was not
in the class. But, I'll tell him you're here.

*Wilson leaves Joseph in a small communal room: a combined kitchen
and library. Five people sit at a table practicing English with a teacher.
Joseph looks down the hall after Wilson and sees Hegel through the small
radio studio's window reading text into a microphone. Joseph walks
down the hall to the studio. Wilson greets him, putting his finger to his
lips for quiet.*

*Hegel is 36 and a large, muscular man. He has the air of a wounded
fighter. Hegel waves to Joseph, then continues reading.*

INT. STUDIO—CONTINUOUS

HEGEL
(in Creole)

Divorces, immigration, work permits. Go to the

specialists! When you need a lawyer, go to Senechal.
212 Flatbush Avenue, Flatbush, Brooklyn.

Hegel cues a record. The red light goes on. Wilson rushes in, but Hegel waves off the boy's concern. Hegel stands and takes his cane. He hobbles out of the room to greet Joseph. Hegel gives Joseph a bear hug.

HEGEL
What are you doing here?! Man, I thought you were in hiding!

JOSEPH
Factory job.

HEGEL
Same thing. Same thing. Come on in . . .

He ushers Joseph into a small office. Wilson watches them a moment, then goes into the radio booth.

INT. HEGEL'S OFFICE—CONTINUOUS

Hegel takes a cup of water from the fountain in his office. Throughout this scene, a small speaker in the office monitors the station. We hear music, then Wilson reading the news as the scene progresses. Hegel adds rum to his water.

HEGEL
Sit down. Tell me how you are. Tell me how's your father.

JOSEPH

He's . . . well, things are the same for him.

HEGEL

Life is cruel only to the great men. But your father . . . Fighters deserve to die in battle. That chance is gone now. My dear Joseph, please sit down.

Joseph presents Hegel with a notebook-sized packet.

HEGEL

What's that?

Hegel looks at Joseph for an answer, but Joseph only pushes the packet toward him. Hegel takes it and sits down in the chair behind his desk. He opens it. It's a manuscript. Taking the top page, he reads it twice. He looks briefly at the other pages. Then he looks up slowly.

HEGEL

You have gotten much better. It . . . Well, you seem older, finally. Very nice. You should do something with it.

JOSEPH

I didn't come here for a critique.

Hegel realizes what Joseph wants, then scoots the packet back over the desk to Joseph and shakes his head.

HEGEL

I can't help you.

JOSEPH

I want you to read it over the air. You read other works. Read mine.

HEGEL

There are so many problems right now.

JOSEPH

It's good and you know it. Don't give me shit.

HEGEL

You were always slow to grasp the reality of a situation. It's not your writing; it's what you write about.

JOSEPH

People should know about these things, too.

HEGEL

Look, you may think there's an interest out there in this kind of stuff right now, but I don't. Man, you live in a different time zone. This is now. That—
(flicking the ear of a page)
—is over and there's no time for romantics.

Joseph looks hard at Hegel, challenging him. Then Joseph looks around the room. He runs his finger over the edge of the desk as if to check for dust. He walks around the room looking at the books and newspaper clippings. Finally, he turns to Hegel . . .

JOSEPH
(smiling)
From one cell to another.

Joseph crosses the room and reaches for the packet. Hegel slams his cane across it. The two men lock onto one another.

HEGEL
All right. I owe you more than this.
(beat)
But, under one condition . . .

Joseph smiles and looks ready to sell his soul.

INT. STUDIO—LATER

Joseph sits nervously in front of the microphone. Hegel sits next to him and nudges him.

JOSEPH
This is a new poem that I wrote a long, long time ago. It is about a place where I lived when I was dead: "Wounds": "... A too long absence which does not/replace the hidden thoughts ..."

INT. OUTSIDE THE STUDIO GLASS—
CONTINUOUS

Wilson watches Joseph reading. Hegel appears moved by the slow, steady rhythm of Joseph's work. Joseph has entered a trance state. As he reads, he reenters the land of his dreams.

INT. FACTORY—DAY

We hear hammering, machines roaring. The din is pervasive.

Joseph stands before a machine. His face is dirty and the sweat forms black streams down his cheeks. He performs the monotonous, repetitious job in a trance. But this is a different kind of trance from the reading: it is a deadly, numbing emptiness.

INT. FACTORY—LATER

Joseph enters a freight elevator. He presses a floor button. The engine kicks in with a whine. The cage door slides shut and the elevator starts up with a lurch. Two floors up and suddenly everything stops. Silence. The elevator light goes out. Darkness. Joseph panics. He turns in useless circles, looking for a way out. He scratches at the gate, at the elevator walls. It's no use. He can't breathe. He starts to bang on the door when he passes out.

FADE OUT:

Shouts and laughter.

FADE IN:

INT/EXT. HAITIAN CORNER—DAY

The place is jam-packed. Mecilus, a ward nurse from the nearby hospital; Justin, a salesman of bibles and religious relics; François and Jolicoeur, owner and driver of a gypsy cab, respectively. Other people come and go, crowding the store, adding to the sounds of shouting and laughter.

Justin has the floor. He is a small man with fair skin and a pencil-thin moustache.

He wears a felt hat over his shiny, slicked-down hair. He looks like a pimp. As he talks he gesticulates wildly. A cigarette dangling from his lips bounces up and down.

JUSTIN
I have my feeling about this place.
(laughter)
I ring the bell.
(acting out standing tall)
A beautiful woman answers the door.
(laughter; forming her shape with his hands.)
She asks me to sit down.
(laughter)
I am more used to being thrown out!
(laughter)

Joseph enters. Everyone turns and applauds. Men slap him on the back.

JOLICOEUR
Our national poet! A radio star! I always said
one of us would make it big.

FRANÇOIS
(to Jolicoeur)
Careful: you'll give him a big head.

JUSTIN
It's too late. Look at it.

Joseph orders a coffee and a beer from Cesar.

JOLICOEUR

Justin, do you see yourself as a famous poet?

JUSTIN

My poetry is the poetry of God . . .

FRANÇOIS

. . . and beautiful women!

Laughter. Joseph takes his coffee and beer and sidles his way through the men crowded in the store. When he reaches the door, he turns and bows. Applause.

JOSEPH

Good day, you creeps.

And he goes outside. Joseph sits in one of the chairs outside and alternately sips coffee and beer. Across the street, a brown station wagon pulls up. Wilson gets out. He takes a pile of papers from the back and carries them into the Haitian Corner. Joseph finishes his coffee and, bringing his beer, follows Wilson. Wilson tacks a pamphlet to the bulletin board. The men in the bar each take a copy from the pile on the counter. Justin reads one aloud.

JUSTIN

Blah blah blah . . . So-called "Liberalization,"
"New Idea of the Regime"—hah!
(playing to the men)
The Artistes!
(to Wilson)
Did you write this?

Joseph watches Wilson.

WILSON

Do you have any comments to make?

JUSTIN

Yeah, I do.

Justin comes face to face with Wilson.

JUSTIN

It's shit.
(turning to harangue the crowd)
You make me sick with all these words. You're so
smart, so *intellectual*, and you will never be satisfied!
You don't have the balls to do what has to be done.

FRANÇOIS

Is that true?

JOLICOEUR
(to François)
It's true. This man really has no balls.

JUSTIN
(to Wilson)
You fuck up honest people with your leaflets . . .
all these promises.

Joseph goes behind the counter and gets a second beer.

FRANÇOIS

We're getting into the same old argument. Useless politics. We have enough problems with
America; do we have to take care of Haiti, too?

JUSTIN

We don't need this asshole dumping this bullshit on us.

WILSON

At least I'm not selling holy candles for dildos.

*Justin jumps on Wilson and the men have to break them apart. Joseph
pops the top on another beer and, coming over to Justin, offers it to him.
Justin knocks it out of Joseph's hand with a backhand sweep.*

JUSTIN

It's too early for me.
(beat)
You know, you're no different, Joseph. You want
a fight? Get a gun. Find an army. At least your father knew how it was really done.

*Silence. Justin stands free of the men holding him back. He straightens
himself and leaves.*

EXT. FLATBUSH AVENUE—EARLY EVENING

*The street is crowded with shoppers and people returning home from
work. Joseph walks through the crowds lost in thought. People shop at
sidewalk stands, a record store, a Caribbean fruit and vegetable market,
Woolworth's. Joseph stops to consider coffee cups. We see him bargain with
the saleswoman, but the price is too high. Turning around, something
across the street catches Joseph's eye. Brunel is wheeling a car tire down
the sidewalk. He rolls it up to the trunk of a sparkling white Oldsmobile
with darkened windows. He looks around to see who's watching, then
he raps the trunk. The trunk flies open. Brunel hoists the wheel inside*

and slams the trunk shut. He walks up to the driver's window. It slides down a crack. Twenty dollars in singles are slipped out. Brunel pockets the money and the car drives away. Joseph crosses the street. When Brunel sees his brother, Brunel looks scared and searches his brain for a good cover story.

BRUNEL

Hi, Joseph. What's going on?

JOSEPH

(coolly)

Hi.

BRUNEL

What are you doing? Can I offer you a beer? What do you say?

JOSEPH

Your game is on the wrong side of the fence.

BRUNEL

Who is going to decide that? You maybe?

JOSEPH

(Creole, at first)

You have a big mouth. But you're going to have to tighten your ass like everybody else.

BRUNEL

Bouch off, Joseph, don't give me no Haitian morality. Just stay out of my business and don't fuck with me! Don't!

In his anger, Brunel lets slip some of the bills he was holding. Joseph bends down to pick them up.

JOSEPH
(handing Brunel the cash)
Do you still have enough for two beers?

INT. BAR—LATER

A quiet, almost empty bar. We hear "Ti Paris" on the jukebox. An elderly Haitian man is getting sadly drunk.

BRUNEL
(over)
See that guy? He's lived like that for three years. Every day he gets up, he gets dressed, he checks his suitcase under the bed, he goes to the travel agency on the corner and asks the price of a ticket, then he comes here. Every day he thinks, "I will go home."

Brunel takes a drink of beer.

BRUNEL
(to Joseph)
Everyone here is living like that.

JOSEPH
Except you. You don't have that problem.

BRUNEL
I have other problems.

Brunel goes over to the jukebox and pumps a handful of quarters into it. Joseph orders one more beer and two shots.

BRUNEL

The other day . . . at the garage . . . we found this guy. His Jaguar was there. He was at the wheel, slumped over, like he was asleep or something . . . There were packages from every store imaginable on every seat of the car . . . The guy was like Santa Claus and there he was . . . alone, dead, like that. All those packages . . . for nothing . . . that motherfucker just died there.

JOSEPH

An overdose of conspicuous consumption.

BRUNEL

You don't get scared, do you? You never think, "Today I'm gonna die." Didn't you think about it in prison?

JOSEPH

That was different.

BRUNEL

But they tortured you.

Silence.

BRUNEL

You don't want to talk about it. You know, we're not in Haiti now. Look where we are. They cannot torture you here.

JOSEPH

Can't they?

The room and the music fade into echo. Brunel does not know the answer.

EXT. BAR AND STREET—CONTINUOUS

It is dusk. Shots of the bar, and, higher up, the street, dead and empty.

INT. HATCO—WAITING ROOM—CONTINUOUS

At the Haitian American Transfer Co. (HATCO). Children are playing between the rows of chairs. People are arguing. Workers are illogically moving parcels around the room. In one corner of the room is the cashier's office, surrounded by bars as if in a cage.

Sarah brings a client to the door. Joseph enters.

SARAH

(to client)

Don't worry. The crate will be picked up, then sent directly to the freight department. It should get there in one week. Everything will be fine, so please don't worry, madam.

The client leaves.

SARAH

(to Joseph)

Come on back. I have your things.

She leads him out of the waiting room and down a hallway toward her office.

JOSEPH
Where have you been? How come you haven't
been home the last few days?

They are interrupted by Jean, the young man who picked up Sarah the other day. He is a proper-looking, overly formal man who tries to convey a debonair, authoritative demeanor.

JEAN
Sarah, I have . . . Hello.

SARAH
Jean, have you met my cousin, Joseph? Joseph—
Jean Celstin, my boss.

JEAN
Sarah talks about you often. How do you do?

JOSEPH
Bonjour.

JEAN
How is it going? You should have come earlier.
I could help you. I have contacts.

JOSEPH
(ignoring Jean, looking around)
It's not bad here . . .

JEAN

You like it? It cost a lot of gray hair, but it was
worth it. I can't complain.

Silence. Sarah takes Joseph's arm.

SARAH
(to Joseph)
I want to show you something, now.

*They all nod goodbye. Sarah leads Joseph away. Jean exits. Sarah
pulls Joseph into her office, a cubicle separated from the other desks on
the floor by brightly colored standing partitions. On her desk is a plaque:
SARAH CAJUSTE, ASSISTANT MANAGER. The space is decorated
generously with plants.*

JOSEPH
(teasingly)
I'm impressed. Looks great! Moving on up!

SARAH

Just sit down.

JOSEPH

Of course, ma'am!

*Sarah takes her seat at her desk. They sit looking at each other, sepa-
rated by the desk. They start to find the situation funny and burst out
laughing together.*

SARAH

Psst! Not so loud!

JOSEPH

Have you finished my papers?

Sarah takes a folder out of her desk.

SARAH

Here. I've had all of it typed . . . except for the
spelling errors. It's not a criticism: it's just that I
think you should learn to spell a little more carefully.

JOSEPH

I am playing with the language.

SARAH

I hope I didn't screw anything up.

JOSEPH

Well, you can always do it over.

SARAH

I hate you.

He quickly surveys the texts.

JOSEPH

(emotionally, with gratitude)
Thank you, little sister.

Silence.

*A man's voice from the next partition catches Joseph's attention. He
tries to ignore it and continues to read, but it nags at him, like a buzzing
wasp. He puts down the manuscript and listens to the voice. It is a deep,*

raspy voice. It clearly belongs to an authoritative older man. Joseph is entranced. Sarah starts to talk, but Joseph shushes her. She watches him, thinking he is acting strangely. She eases herself into her chair. Joseph's rapt attention confuses her. The voice stops.

SARAH

If you could get these published, maybe you
could quit the factory. If you want, I have money
now; I could help you, you know, kind of take care
of you.

He raises his hand to silence her. She's stunned. We hear a chair being pushed back and footsteps walking away. Joseph is frozen in his chair with an expression of fear on his face.

SARAH

Joseph? Joseph?

(beat)

Wait here, I'll get you some water.

She leaves. Joseph, after a moment, steps carefully out into the main office. He sees the back of a large man in a black coat just as the man is exiting the office. Joseph follows him.

Sarah returns to the empty office with a cup of water. She sees the manuscript on the floor.

EXT. BROOKLYN STREET/HATCO—CONTINUOUS

Joseph stumbles down the stairs out onto the street. He looks for the man in the dense crowd. Vanished. Joseph half runs a few yards on a hunch. Nothing. He turns back. The man is coming out of a store. Joseph catches himself and drops back, staying in the crowd, but keeping sight of the man. The man crosses the street and makes a call from a payphone. Joseph crosses the street, still keeping out of sight. The man finishes the call. He stands outside the booth, checking his watch. Soon, a brown station wagon, exactly like the one Wilson was driving earlier that morning, pulls up. The man presents a yellow envelope to the driver of the car. We can't see the driver, who takes the envelope, rolls up the window, and pulls away. The man looks around to see if he is being watched. Joseph steps back, out of sight. The man starts down the sidewalk toward Joseph, who ducks back out of sight. The man recrosses the street and walks down into the subway station.

INT. SUBWAY STATION—CONTINUOUS

Joseph descends as a train is in the station. The brakes hiss. The doors are about to close, but Joseph hops in and starts to travel from car to car looking for the man. Joseph stands between two cars, and the door to the next one is jammed. Then, he sees the man, whose face is turned away from Joseph. Joseph can see that the man is wearing sunglasses and that he is bald. Joseph freezes. He tries the door again. Locked. He starts to go back, but suddenly feels trapped. The locked door, the roar of the subway all take him back to a place he has never left. The train pulls into a station and the man exits. Joseph is still too afraid to move. The train doors close and the train starts to leave. Joseph summons all his strength to bolt the chains between train cars and jump to the platform. He has to stop to breath deeply. Looking around he sees the last person to get off the train descending the stairs to the street. Joseph hurries down the stairs, dodging in and out of other passengers. When he hits the street, the man is gone. The man has vanished in the sea of people.

EXT./INT. HATCO—NIGHT

Lights are still on inside the office building. Joseph forces open the unlocked metal shutters over the entrance. Entering the office, Joseph is stopped by one of Sarah's colleagues, a woman.

WOMAN
I'm sorry, we're closed.

She starts to usher Joseph back out. Joseph is in a haze, then suddenly . . .

JOSEPH
I need to see Sarah.

WOMAN
Come back tomorrow. Now, sir, I'll have to ask you to . . .

JOSEPH
Sarah! Sarah!

We hear running footsteps approaching. Sarah enters.

SARAH
Joseph!

WOMAN
You know this idiot!

SARAH
(tenderly)
Yes, I know this idiot.

(to Joseph)
Come on, calm down, come with me.

He follows her back to her desk. He feels safe inside her partition. She returns to her work.

JOSEPH

There was a man here. A guy in a black suit. Do
you know him?

SARAH

Why?

JOSEPH

I need to know who he is. I need to be certain.
Do you know where he lives? Anything?

SARAH

I don't.

JOSEPH
(desperate)
Well couldn't you ask someone?

SARAH

I suppose. But not now. Everyone's gone home.

Joseph sinks into a chair despondently. Sarah doesn't know what to do with him.

SARAH

I have an idea. I'll be right back. Don't run away
this time, okay?

Joseph sits alone with his eyes closed. Sarah returns with a large date book. Sarah goes to her desk and spreads it before her. She runs her fingers down the lists of names.

SARAH
Where did you see him? What office was he in?

Joseph points to the one next door. Sarah searches the book.

SARAH
Here he is. No name, though. That's strange.
Money order to a relative.

JOSEPH
What's the relative's name?

SARAH
They don't list that here.

Again, Joseph looks like everything's lost.

SARAH
But I know where we can find it.

She crooks her finger to get him to follow, then leads Joseph to the office next door. She motions him to stop at the doorway and keep a lookout. Sarah then searches the out bin on the desk. When she finds the document, she waves it like a prize. She reads it. She joins Joseph at the door and looks both ways in case the woman might see them.

SARAH
(whispering)
Mimose. The relative's name is Mimose.

He doesn't recognize the name. The disappointment sends Joseph deep inside his own mind and the painful memories there. Standing in the office doorway, they share a suspenseful intimacy. Sarah touches Joseph's face to draw him back to reality. They are alone. She holds his head in her hands, trying to comfort him. He looks down into her eyes.

EXT./INT. HSCC—LATER SAME DAY

Joseph enters the building. Carrying an armload of toys, Wilson is descending the stairs that lead to the office. Without warning, Joseph swings at Wilson, knocking him flat. The toys go flying. Wilson starts to get up, but Joseph hits him again.

WILSON
What the fuck . . . !

Joseph picks up Wilson and runs him up against the wall.

JOSEPH
Where is he?

WILSON
I'm gonna break your skull, man!

Wilson struggles to break free, and Joseph renews Wilson's association with the wall.

JOSEPH
I want him. The man you met this afternoon.
Theodore.

Wilson suddenly stops struggling. Joseph recognizes that the name has rung a bell and lets Wilson free.

WILSON

Now listen, man, if this is a joke . . . I'm not laughing.

JOSEPH

Sylvain Theodore.

Wilson starts to pick up the toys.

WILSON

What are you talking about?

JOSEPH

Tell me where he is and we'll forget the whole thing.

WILSON

First, I don't know what you're talking about. I never met anybody . . . I've been here all day. All fucking day, man. I don't know what drugs you've been taking but you're seeing ghosts.

Wilson exits. Joseph goes down the empty corridor. The offices are empty. At the end of the hall, we see a crack of light under a closed door. We hear distorted music. It stops and starts. Joseph pushes open the door. He finds Hegel sitting on a barstool in front of a wooden xylophone. On a tripod next to him are blank music sheets on which he is composing. Joseph's entrance causes Hegel to turn. He signals Joseph to wait a moment. Hegel plays the tune he's been composing, finds the note for which he was looking and . . .

HEGEL

Imagine: I've been looking for that damned note for ages. Just kept missing it, over and over.
(pointing to the score sheets)
Theoretically, this note doesn't exist. The instrument's too primitive for that.
(continuing playing)
However, as you can see . . .
(seeing Joseph is upset)
What's wrong Joseph? You don't look too good.

JOSEPH

I'll be okay in a moment.

HEGEL

Wait.

He leaves Joseph alone in the room. Joseph goes to the xylophone and plays distracted notes. Hegel returns with two glasses and gets a bottle of rum from a shelf. Hegel points to the xylophone.

HEGEL

A friend from Zaire gave it to me.
(handing Joseph the rum)
Chin Chin . . . It belonged to his grandfather. Drink, Joseph.

JOSEPH

I just had a fight with Wilson.

HEGEL

(laughing)
No! Over a woman!

Hegel sits down. Joseph takes up Hegel's walking stick and tries using it to walk around the room.

JOSEPH
How long have you needed this?

HEGEL
You know exactly how long.

JOSEPH
Isn't it strange we weren't caught at the same time.

HEGEL
We were together enough, that's true. But I was caught after curfew. You had the privilege of house arrest. Door-to-door service.

JOSEPH
Who caught you?

HEGEL
Soldiers.

JOSEPH
Then what?

HEGEL
What do you mean? Then they beat me—for fun—but I didn't think it was funny so they tried to impress on me the importance of a sense of humor. That's how I got the stick. A relic of the punch line.

Silence.

JOSEPH

Sylvain Theodore is here.

Silence. Hegel looks shocked and stunned.

JOSEPH

I followed him. He wasn't trying to hide. He was doing business as usual on the street. Just like you or me, in broad daylight. He's changed, perhaps more impatient. He's even gotten a little bald.

HEGEL

Sylvain Theodore?

JOSEPH

He met Wilson's car.

Pause.

HEGEL

Wilson?! Wilson was here all day! Anyway, what would Wilson be doing with Sylvain?

JOSEPH

It was Wilson's car.

Hegel pours himself another drink, takes the cane from Joseph, and starts to pace the room.

HEGEL

There are lots of cars just like Wilson's.

(beat)

You didn't get the license plate number, did
you?

JOSEPH

I didn't think of that.

HEGEL

See, what can you do? So, where's Sylvain now?

JOSEPH

I lost him.

Silence.

HEGEL

Maybe you saw someone else. Maybe it's only
a mistake.

(beat)

Sylvain, here? In a Sunday suit!? I doubt it! I
think you should forget Theodore and the whole
thing.

JOSEPH

(out of control)

How can I forget him! He killed us! We are the
dead men! He took away our lives. All for the
pleasure of his torture.

*Pause. Joseph is nearly in tears. When he sees Hegel's patronizing look
of concern, he tries to pull himself together.*

JOSEPH

Okay, okay, you don't believe me. Look, do me just one more favor: help me find him.

(beat)

At least prove to me he is not still alive, that he is not here.

HEGEL

All right, Joseph. I'll look into it. It won't be easy, but I will help.

INT. FACTORY—DAY

Joseph's face is covered with sawdust. Joseph and Jeff are pushing a large beam through a circular saw. The two men are careful to keep a fixed gaze on the saw. There is a deafening cutting noise. A siren wails. Everything stops. Another day ends.

INT. CAJUSTE APARTMENT—DAY

Joseph enters, carrying a bag of groceries. Felicia sits at her sewing machine with Claryce, who is first to see Joseph.

CLARYCE

Joseph, come here.

(holding up jewelry)

I got these jewels at a 50 percent discount direct from the Tajima Company. Fifty percent! Now, if I sell them for $300, I automatically receive $100 worth to sell for my own profit . . . see?

FELICIA

I don't understand. What's in it for them?

CLARYCE

They aren't looking for large profits: they're interested in maximum turnover.

JOSEPH

(kissing his mother)

Aren't we all.

CLARYCE

The more people I get involved selling, the better it is.

JOSEPH

And you want mother to go in with you?

CLARYCE

Exactly! But, she is very difficult.

JOSEPH

Mother, it's very simple. Claryce, your good friend here, wants you to help her make a little money. She sells you jewelry at a discount—

(to Claryce)

—40 percent?—and you both try to pawn off everything on your friends.

CLARYCE

Come on, Joseph, I've already brought three people into the group! I'm area manager. I could get more discounts and win a free trip!

JOSEPH

Mother, help your friend leave town, please.

Joseph takes the groceries into the kitchen. He starts to unpack them, then stops to get pills from the cabinet. He pours a glass of water and swallows the pills.

FELICIA

(off-screen)

Are the jewels real?

Joseph has bought a new set of coffee cups. He starts to wash and dry them. We hear Claryce leave. The apartment door slams shut. Felicia enters the kitchen. She is serious and stern.

FELICIA

(in Creole)

I left some food for you. You want to eat?

JOSEPH

(in Creole)

Later.

FELICIA

(in Creole)

Will you go with me tomorrow?

JOSEPH

(in Creole)

What about tomorrow?

FELICIA
(in Creole)
Your father. You know I'm not used to talking
with those white people, the doctors, the nurses. I
need you there.

JOSEPH
(in Creole)
Don't worry. It's just a formality. Everything
will be just fine.

Joseph kisses his mother.

INT. HATCO—NIGHT

Sarah's colleague, the woman, is shutting the gates when Joseph enters.
She doesn't bother resisting this time and admits him.

WOMAN
(shouting)
Sarah! The fruitcake's here!

Sarah enters shortly.

JOSEPH
Hey, don't you know it's closing time!

SARAH
I have to finish these or Jean will get mad at
me.

JOSEPH

Why don't you tell him to get mad at me?
(seeing her angry look)
Okay, okay, I'll just wait here. I've nothing to do
anyway . . .

Jean enters.

JEAN

Honey, I left everything on my desk.

He notices Joseph.

JEAN

Joseph! How are you?! How is life?!

JOSEPH

Fine, thanks. You know how it is.

JEAN

Ah, well then.
(to Sarah)
I have to go out immediately.
(beat)
You must be tired. You can leave those papers
until tomorrow.

SARAH

Jean, you know I can't. The inspector is coming
tomorrow and everything's got to be ready.

JEAN

As you like.

Jean goes to his office, gets his jacket.

JEAN

Will I see you later?

Sarah points to the papers on her desk and shrugs.

JEAN

Well, okay. I'll call you later.
(to Joseph)
You should come in more often. We should talk. Sarah tells me you write. I need someone to write copy for me. If you're interested ... Well, think about it.
(to both)
See you.

He goes to the door, turns one last time and exits.

EXT. BROOKLYN STREET/HATCO—NIGHT

It is getting dark. People pass by. Most stores have closed, and the street is quiet. HATCO's main lights are out, except for Sarah's office window.

INT. HATCO—OFFICES—CONTINUOUS

We hear a typewriter. An empty room. Sarah sits at her desk finishing a letter. Taking the finished letter out of the machine, she turns to Joseph. He has fallen asleep in the chair, his head against the wall. Her expres-

sion softens watching him sleep. He wakens and they smile at each other. Joseph shakes himself, surprised he fell asleep.

SARAH
(in Creole)

It's late.

JOSEPH

And I wanted to keep you company.

SARAH

I could have been kidnapped and you wouldn't have heard a thing.

JOSEPH

Are you finished?

SARAH

Almost . . .

(beat)

I'll do the rest early tomorrow. I am tired.

Joseph comes to her and touches her cheek. She looks at him. The phone rings.

SARAH

You scared me . . . Yes . . . I'm just leaving . . . Everything's ready . . . Well, almost . . . No! . . . We'll see . . . See you in the morning . . . He's gone . . . Okay, you too . . .

There's a moment's silence after she hangs up.

JOSEPH

What's the matter?

SARAH

Nothing.

JOSEPH

Come on . . .

SARAH

It's nothing, nothing important.

JOSEPH

Is he jealous?

Sarah laughs loudly.

SARAH

Jealous? Jean? He's too sure of himself.

JOSEPH

Then why did you lie about me?

SARAH

I don't like to complicate things, okay? It's no
one's business, not even yours.

EXT. BROOKLYN STREET—NIGHT

*Sarah leads Joseph past a preacher haranguing a crowd with tales of
the evil tentacles of the octopus called Drugs.*

SARAH

Did you find that guy? The one that came in
the other day?

JOSEPH

Forget it. I made a mistake.

SARAH

You acted like he was the devil himself. Did he
grab you with his "evil tentacles"?

Silence.

SARAH

(teasing)
Don't want to talk about it, eh? It's someone
from Haiti, isn't it? Who?

JOSEPH

Drop it.

SARAH

Tell me, tell me, please, please, please.

*Silence. Joseph looks very dark and serious. His expression sours
Sarah's fun.*

SARAH

Be a sourpuss, see what I care . . . But now you
have to feed me or I'll make a scandal, right here.

INT. RESTAURANT—NIGHT

Sarah and Joseph eat while telling each other jokes in Creole. The room is small, dark, and smoky.

INT. CAJUSTE APARTMENT—NIGHT, LATER

Joseph and Sarah enter laughing, but realize they have to be quiet. Joseph tiptoes into the kitchen and gets two beers from the fridge.

INT. APARTMENT—LIVING ROOM—NIGHT

The string of lights over the Williamsburg Bridge can be seen from the window. Sarah stands at the edge looking down at the streets. Joseph sits on the floor with his back against the couch. Sarah joins him and they are quiet for a moment. Joseph looks at her tenderly and with curiosity.

JOSEPH

Do you really love him?

SARAH

Who? Jean?

JOSEPH

Yes, your "fiancé." Do you love him?

SARAH

It's a question of definitions. It depends.

JOSEPH

On what?

SARAH

I enjoy his company. He's intelligent, ambitious,
even charming sometimes . . .

JOSEPH

You used to be more romantic.

SARAH

So, there's no contradiction.

JOSEPH

(lightly)

The right man!

SARAH

(seriously)

He is someone I need right now.

JOSEPH

So, you've become an opportunist?

SARAH

What business is it of yours?

Joseph turns away from her and drinks his beer. Sarah turns him around.

SARAH

(angry)

To answer your question: *yes*, I love him. That's
what you wanted to hear!

JOSEPH

I didn't want to hear anything.

SARAH
(a shouting whisper)
I love him! I love him! I love him!

Joseph grabs Sarah and kisses her full on the lips. It's a deep, passionate kiss that Sarah returns.

Sounds of the streets at night float up to the room. Joseph moves his hands up Sarah's back, caressing the back of her head, pulling her deeper into the kiss. She runs her fingers down the buttons of his shirt, unfastening them one by one. Joseph pulls it off when she's finished. Sarah removes her blouse.

Outside the window, the D train rattles across the Manhattan Bridge. An ambulance whines down Flatbush. TV sets cast a bluish glow against the walls of apartments across the street.

INT. FACTORY—DAY

Joseph and Jeff are feeding beams to the saw. Joseph is clearly tired and dazed. He is looking beyond the blade of the saw into a memory. He loses his grip on the beam. Jeff shouts. A large chunk of wood flies up, knocking Jeff to the floor. A foreman rushes over and shuts down the machine. The foreman looks in anger at the confused Joseph.

EXT/INT. JOLICOEUR'S CAB—DAY

Jolicoeur's cab races off the Williamsburg Bridge back into Brooklyn. Joseph sits in the passenger seat next to Jolicoeur.

JOLICOEUR

Justin's right, if they had any balls, they'd be down there organizing rebels and fighting ... A few men and bang! bang! bang!

JOSEPH

Justin's idea of a gang bang.
(beat)
And you?

JOLICOEUR

I'm too old. But ten years ago! ... With Colonel Pluviôse in Florida ... Intensive training for two months. Man, you should have seen it, a proper little army.

JOSEPH

Yes, but could they win the Super Bowl?

JOLICOEUR

Don't laugh. It could have worked. It's just that half the men failed to show up the day we were supposed to attack.

JOSEPH

And the rest were captured by the American Coast Guard.

JOLICOEUR

We all have our off days ...
(beat)
How much longer are we gonna look for this guy?

They have driven into a square with no principles of urban planning: the bus kiosk is arbitrarily placed in the middle of the street, there is a wooden hut with a law offices sign on it next to an Oriental bazaar, and, despite the presence of some fruit and vegetable stands, there is no sign of any new or active business. The square is rusted and old. A clock strikes five.

JOLICOEUR
(pissed)

You're not gonna find him in this mess.

Joseph bangs the dashboard in anger. He hits it so hard that he knocks over a plastic St. Christopher statue, breaking it. Jolicoeur looks furious.

JOLICOEUR

Listen, I have other things to do. This is useless.

JOSEPH

Pull over.

JOLICOEUR

Hey, I thought the fun was just starting!

JOSEPH

Over there's fine.

The cab pulls over and Joseph gets out. He comes around to the driver's window.

JOSEPH

Look, thanks a lot. I think I'll do the rest of this
alone.

JOLICOEUR
Man, you are a fool . . . Just don't kill anybody.

The cab pulls away leaving Joseph alone in the crowd. The trains thunder overhead on the elevated tracks. We follow Joseph down the street. He stops now and then to ask a question, but gets nowhere. Joseph looks around and around, turning in circles in the middle of nowhere.

INT. FACTORY—DAY

Joseph pulls on his work gloves and switches on the motor for the saw. The great saw grinds into speed. Jeff enters and is watching Joseph, who has become transfixed by the saw. Joseph's face registers fear and confusion. Jeff puts his hand on Joseph's shoulder and Joseph jumps.

JEFF
Joseph, what is it?

Joseph comes out of it and does not seem to recognize where he is. He recognizes Jeff and smiles.

JEFF
What's wrong, man?

JOSEPH
You're on your own.

Joseph removes his gloves and hands them to Jeff. He walks out.

EXT. WILLIAMSBURG—NIGHT

The square is quiet and empty. A few bus drivers are playing softball on the square. An elevated subway train passes. The bank clock shows 10:00 p.m. Joseph sits at a café drinking coffee.

INT. CAJUSTE APARTMENT—MORNING

The TV hums. Pastor, in pajamas, watches the morning news. Joseph enters with a coffee and sits on the window ledge looking out. Hyppolite enters looking upset. He steps directly between Pastor and the TV, fascinated by the moving pictures. Pastor at first tries to peer around Hyppolite, but it's no good.

> **PASTOR**
> Hyppolite! Please!
> > *(beat)*
> Hyppolite!

> **JOSEPH**
> Leave the guy alone, you fuck!

> **PASTOR**
> *(angrily to Joseph)*
> Your mother has been looking for you. Where were you?

Joseph leaves the room and goes to his bedroom. Sarah catches him in the hallway. She is getting ready for work. She pulls him into her room and pushes him down to sit on her bed.

> **SARAH**
> Don't you think you've gone too far?

Joseph looks completely confused.

> SARAH

You completely forgot and she's been talking about it for the past month! Now it's too late: she had to go down there and make the decision on her own.

> JOSEPH

Shit.

> SARAH

You only had yourself to think about . . . until now.

> JOSEPH

I quit work yesterday.

> SARAH

Oh that's just perfect! Well done!
(beat)
Now what are you going to do?

He comes over to her and tries to kiss her neck. We hear a car horn. Sarah breaks free.

> SARAH
> *(coldly)*

I have to go. We can talk later. Maybe Jean could . . .

> JOSEPH

Fuck Jean! Fuck him! Talk to *me*!

He tries to kiss her but she struggles free.

SARAH
This really isn't the time for that!

He pins her against the wall.

JOSEPH
Then we'll make the time.

The car horn sounds again.

SARAH
How long're you going to carry on this little
game? I'm tired of it. Let me go!

JOSEPH
Playing "Little Miss Innocent"? Sarah . . .

*He bears down on her, kissing her. The door opens and Felicia enters.
Joseph and Sarah break apart.*

FELICIA
(to Sarah calmly)
Jean is waiting for you.

Sarah exits. Felicia with all her might hits Joseph across the face.

FELICIA
That's for your father.

Joseph rubs the wound. Then she hits him again even harder. It staggers him.

FELICIA
And that's from me!

INT. DREAM—EVENING

An empty room, 9 x 12 feet. Damp floor, shiny walls. The sound of water dripping.

                                                              CUT TO:

INT. HSCC—DAY

Hegel admits Joseph into the sitting room. Children are learning Creole.

HEGEL
Joseph, I'll be right with you. It's a bad time.

Hegel exits. Joseph sits with the children. Soon they incorporate him into the lesson. The clock on the wall advances one hour. The children leave. Hegel has not yet returned. Joseph wipes the blackboard clean and leaves.

INT. HAITIAN CORNER—DAY

Joseph sits alone inside, looking out the window, while everyone else avoids the heat by sitting outside. Cesar is behind the counter.

CESAR

Of course there's no guarantee . . . Can't you get more work together? If this guy wants to meet you, it's because he likes your work. They don't like wasting time, these guys.

Silence.

CESAR

What's the matter?

Joseph starts laughing.

JOSEPH

These poems are just me masturbating.

CESAR

Sex sells, Joseph.

JOSEPH

Do you know how to get cards?

CESAR

Green cards?

JOSEPH

Business cards. Friends of mine and I used to write hundreds of them. We had it all worked out. We found a small dark workshop that belonged to an old man we nicknamed "Gutenberg." He let us in nights. We copied the names of lawyers, doctors, and engineers from the phone book. Then we printed up cards for them and sent them free sam-

ples. If they liked what they saw, we asked for orders. Imagine! At a time when everyone was trying to lay low, forgotten.

CESAR

That reminds me . . . I have forgotten something!

*Cesar rushes upstairs and returns with a red notebook. He hands it
to Joseph, who treats it like a holy book. He weighs it to be sure it is real.*

JOSEPH

Where did you find this?

CESAR

I have my sources. Private collection.

Joseph tries to give it back, but Cesar refuses.

CESAR

Keep it. It's time to remember.

Joseph studies the book.

JOSEPH

Seven years in prison.

The book is that time. Joseph tosses it on the counter.

JOSEPH

The past is the past. Burn it!

Joseph exits.

INT. CLARYCE'S APARTMENT—DAY

The apartment is full of trinkets, photos, embroidered cushions, and antique furniture so that the room appears small. The bed is separated from the rest of the room by a Chinese screen.

JOSEPH
You sure have a lot of stuff!

Claryce enters dressed in a form-fitting summer dress and carrying a tray with brandy and coffee. She sets it down on the coffee table before Joseph.

CLARYCE
Yes. I adore collecting things.

Joseph takes his brandy and almost finishes it in one swallow. Claryce watches him as she sips her coffee.

CLARYCE
Would you prefer rum?

JOSEPH
No. This is fine.

CLARYCE
It's from back home.

JOSEPH
This?!

CLARYCE
No. The rum.

Silence. Joseph points to a photo on the mantelpiece.

JOSEPH

Is that your husband?

CLARYCE

It's a very old photo. It was all I could carry. A long time afterward, the president spoke on the radio: "There are no political prisoners left." I knew what he meant. He was a good man. We weren't married that long.

JOSEPH

And Cesar?

CLARYCE

We help each other, take care of each other.
(beat)
Joseph? Do you like me? Why do you run away from me?

JOSEPH

I'm not running away from you.

Claryce stands and walks to the screen.

CLARYCE

Joseph . . . ?

She unbuttons the back of her dress and lets it slide to the floor. She stands naked. Joseph comes to her and takes her in his arms. He kisses her neck and shoulders and slides down to kiss her breasts, her belly. She pulls him back onto the bed. They remove his clothes quickly and roll on

*the bed. In the heat, they are quickly covered in sweat. She talks to him
lovingly but her talk stops when Joseph suddenly lies rigid and quiet.*

JOSEPH
I'm sorry. This shouldn't be happening.

*He collects his clothes and gets dressed. She slips on a blue kimono and
follows him into the room. She takes her brandy glass and downs it in
one drink.*

CLARYCE
Joseph, you forgot this.

She hands him an envelope.

CLARYCE
For your mother.

JOSEPH
(taking it)
I'm sorry.

CLARYCE
(turning from him)
Sorry?

The door opens and shuts. When Claryce turns back, he's gone.

EXT. HATCO—LATE DAY

Joseph watches the building entrance from across the street. Sarah and Jean appear, say goodbye with a kiss, then walk separate ways. Joseph follows Sarah.

INT. CAJUSTE APARTMENT—LATER

Sarah is holding up an evening dress for size. Felicia is at her sewing machine. Joseph enters and goes straight into the kitchen. Felicia stops work and follows him. Joseph hands her the envelope from Claryce. Silence.

JOSEPH
When are you taking him?

FELICIA
Tomorrow.

Joseph exits. Felicia counts the money.

INT. CAJUSTE APARTMENT—PARENTS'
BEDROOM—CONTINUOUS

Joseph enters. His father is sitting on the edge of the bed, dressed in his Sunday best for no real reason. Hyppolite stares at a candle burning on the night table. Next to him on the bed are his newspaper clippings and photographs. Joseph picks up one or two, looks them over, then puts them back. Silence. Joseph sits on the windowsill across from his father.

JOSEPH
Father . . . ? Look at me . . . I know . . . I feel responsible too . . . I know. I've let you down. You

can't wipe the slate clean. I thought I could start
from fresh, forget everything. But I can't. Do you
understand? I was afraid. I am afraid. Like you.
You refuse to speak, but I know you hear me. I
know you understand me. You must understand
me!

(beat)

You see . . .

(laughs)

. . . our journey together continues.

Joseph sits next to his father and looks again through some of the photos.

JOSEPH

Marching with the national flag . . . I never
walked so much in my life. I didn't complain. Remember? I didn't complain about my feet. Remember what you said to me? You scared me with
that strong voice: The people have taken to the
street and you have sore feet! . . . That made me
forget my sore feet.

*We see a photo of a demonstration. We see other photos. Hyppolite gets
up, goes to Joseph, takes the album from him.*

JOSEPH

If only I could do as much for you today . . . I won't run
away, run away. I shall come to get you—we'll talk. The
old, long stories . . . the one about Kompe Paul and the
gold. The one about Mathilde with her twin boys . . .

They stand face to face. Hyppolite raises his head, stares at Joseph. He moves his lips imperceptibly, as if going to reply. Joseph breaks down and hugs his father with all his might.

JOSEPH

Oh, father!

The album falls.

INT. HSCC—OFFICES—EVENING

Hegel is talking with Wilson about a series of photographs.

HEGEL

Use this on the front page. Put these in the back.

WILSON

So, we'll drop the carnival article.

HEGEL

Just run it in two weeks.

Joseph enters and walks straight up to Hegel.

JOSEPH
(urgently)

I must speak with you, now.

Joseph goes directly into Hegel's office. Hegel excuses himself from the others and joins Joseph.

JOSEPH

Do you have anything?

HEGEL

What?

JOSEPH

What did you find out?

HEGEL

(loses his temper)

He's starting again. Your fucking stories . . . Are you crazy, Joseph? Haven't you anything better to do? This isn't Haiti! How many times do you have to hear that? You've been here two years, at least; it's time you get a grip on yourself. Let go of the past! I ask you to work with me, you say no. I read your goddamn poetry on the air, and you come back with stories about dead torturers. I haven't let you down for one second, but you are fucking with me. I'm your friend. I'm on your side. We are all on your side. Stop treating us like enemies. Join the living.

JOSEPH

You mean you don't give a damn.

HEGEL

Have it your way. But I'm out, as of now.

Hegel exits, walking downstairs and out onto the street. Joseph fol-
lows.

JOSEPH

I have to know. I have to be sure. The prison.
The smell of lying in my own urine. If I don't find
him, it's like leaving me there forever.

HEGEL
(turning on Joseph)
Fuck you, man! Don't play this game with me.
The door to your cell is open. You are free to walk.
The choice is yours.
(beat)
Now let me go. Some of us have to work for a
living.

Hegel leans hard on his cane as he crosses the street. Joseph watches him get in a beige station wagon and leave. The station wagon!

EXT. HSCC—NIGHT

Rain makes the streets shine.

INT. HSCC—CONTINUOUS

Brunel forces the lock to the office door with a crowbar. Joseph follows Brunel inside.

BRUNEL
What are you looking for?

Joseph goes straight to the file cabinet in Hegel's office and starts methodically to search it.

JOSEPH

I'll know it when I see it.

Brunel keeps watch. Joseph's search, though, is taking time, and Brunel is getting very nervous.

BRUNEL

Hurry up, man!

Joseph turns from the file cabinet in frustration and starts to rifle the bookshelves. He suddenly stops. He stands slowly, holding an old photograph. It's a school photograph. Boys lined up in rows at the end of the year. Ten of the faces are crossed with an "X."

JOSEPH

Got it!

Brunel watches him fold the picture and put it in his pocket. Brunel gets the idea and looks around for something he can take. He grabs a tape recorder. Joseph is suddenly upon him, slamming him up against the wall.

BRUNEL

You got yours! Can't I get something out of this?!

JOSEPH

It's not what we came for.

He shoves Brunel in the direction of the door.

EXT. HAITIAN CORNER—LATER

Joseph, alone, peers inside. It is closed and empty. He rings one of the buzzers and waits. A window opens on the second floor. Claryce peers out. Claryce comes down to let Joseph in.

                    CLARYCE
          Do you know what time it is?

                    JOSEPH
          I can't go home tonight. Please, I need a place
     to stay.

                    CLARYCE
          I'm not your mother.

                    JOSEPH
          Please . . . let me in.

                    CLARYCE
          Don't think this means you can come and go
     whenever you want.
                         (beat)
          Well . . . ?

Joseph follows her inside. The door is locked.

INT. CAJUSTE APARTMENT—LATE MORNING

Joseph returns at a time he hopes no one's home. He enters quietly and looks around. It appears empty, then he hears a sound from the bathroom. Hegel steps out.

JOSEPH

You've come to arrest me.

HEGEL

You've made a big mistake, son.

JOSEPH

I don't think so.

HEGEL

You have. And it's serious. Everyone's against you.

JOSEPH

So, I found it, didn't I?

HEGEL

You can try explaining that to the others. But they won't believe you.

JOSEPH

You lied to me.

HEGEL

Did I?

JOSEPH

It was you with Sylvain.

HEGEL

I couldn't let you in on what was happening. Too much depended on it. Ten years of hard work. The lives of comrades.

JOSEPH
(incredulous)

What?

HEGEL

Give me the photograph. Let me show you something.
(beat)
It's useless to you until you know what it means. Do you know what it means?

Joseph, intrigued, hands it over. Hegel points to faces.

HEGEL

Sylvain gave us a list of names. Some of them had to be eliminated. We were able to warn them. They were the lucky ones. They're alive.

JOSEPH

Why? Why would he?

HEGEL

He needed asylum. He killed a man in a bar. The son of a foreign diplomat. The government tied to cover it up, but they couldn't. They let him down and sent him into permanent exile.

                    JOSEPH
          I want to see him.

EXT. BROOKLYN STREET—DAY

Joseph and Hegel sitting in Wilson's car in front of the house, still in discussion.

                    JOSEPH
          So, you've all given him asylum.

                    HEGEL
          Be serious.

                    JOSEPH
          I am.

                    HEGEL
          It was a fair exchange: ten lives for one.

                    JOSEPH
          Sylvain, the national hero!

                    HEGEL
          That's not the point, Joseph. I understand your
          anger.
                    (beat)
          He got in touch with us. Maybe as a means of
          vengeance . . .

                    JOSEPH
          Incredible. Now what?

                    HEGEL
          Now?
                    (beat)
          Now nothing. Don't forget that you were the
          one to stir up the whole thing—which I hope you
          will keep to yourself. This would be a good oppor-
          tunity for a lot of people here to sabotage the work
          we are doing.

Pause.

                    JOSEPH
          I want to see him.

                    HEGEL
          What do you want from him?

                    JOSEPH
          That's my business.

                    HEGEL
          I don't want to be an accomplice to a petty case
          of vengeance.

                    JOSEPH
          Accomplice? Who is an accomplice here? Don't
          turn the roles around! He may have fooled you,

maybe even used you—to infiltrate—who knows.
He gave you some names to gain your confidence,
to fool you, and look how well it has worked.

HEGEL

Nonsense, Joseph!

JOSEPH

The only one seeing clearly around here is Sylvain. And all he wants is for you to protect him
with your silence. You make me sick! All your little
compromises, your understandings . . . That's lux-
ury, man! Fuck it.

*Joseph gets out of the car and slams the door. He comes back to Hegel,
leaning in the window.*

JOSEPH

Just because you now live in New York, all you
do is talk about democracy. What democracy? You
forget where you come from? We never had time
for that kind of game. Surviving was the name or
get killed . . . like our whole generation.

HEGEL

Joseph Cajuste, the great judge. But you are so
modest. Of course you plan to change everything
yourself. Our little efforts are too plain, too boring.
You want something more dramatic. Isn't that
right?

Silence.

HEGEL

Get in the car.

Joseph looks back at Hegel.

EXT. BROOKLYN STREETS—DAY

The station wagon dodges through traffic and turns onto the Williamsburg Bridge. Leaving the bridge, the car turns right, into a side street. The square is behind them. A few yards further on, the car stops.

HEGEL

This is where we get out.

Joseph obeys, uncertain. Hegel leads him across the street to an old-fashioned Jewish restaurant. Through the window, Joseph sees scattered guests sitting at the few tables. When Hegel tries to pull Joseph inside. Joseph resists.

HEGEL

What's the matter? You wanted to see Sylvain, didn't you?

Joseph doesn't answer, but follows Hegel quietly.

INT. BROOKLYN RESTAURANT—DAY

They sit in a corner, Joseph with his back to the street. He sweats. It is stiflingly hot. Behind the cash register, at the end of the counter, a small man is counting bills. No one takes any notice of him.

HEGEL

What are you waiting for? It's just a few steps.
Have you lost your courage?

*The small man at the cash register raises his head and looks at Hegel
and Joseph. Joseph's hands tremble. He hides them under the table.*

HEGEL

There you are, Joseph. Make him pay. No
golden exile for a man like that.
(beat)
And why stop there? There are so many in-
significant . . .
(relishing the word)
. . . collaborators.

JOSEPH

. . . Where . . . where is he?

HEGEL

Get started. You are going to be busy.

JOSEPH

It's not what I want.

HEGEL

True. You sometimes get sent to jail here for
murdering people. But you must admit that's a
small price to pay for such a simple and elegant
solution. But it'll set a good example. Go on!
(beat)
He is in the kitchen.

                          JOSEPH
               You don't understand.

*At that moment, the kitchen door opens. Joseph starts, but it is only
the waiter, who has come over, begrudgingly, to take their order. The
waiter takes out a crumpled piece of cardboard from his dirty jacket
pocket and throws it on the table, then leaves. The kitchen door swings
open again, and we see a shadow figure in the back. Joseph is overcome
and exits. We follow Hegel out the door. Hegel finds Joseph doubled over,
throwing up.*

INT. BLUE CASTLE BALLROOM—NIGHT

*Joseph is ordering a drink, rum-soda, at the bar. A large crowd is
dancing to the lively cadence of the orchestra. Extravagant clothes and
opulence surrounds Joseph, but he is obviously drunk and doesn't notice.
Joseph turns as the master of ceremonies announces.*

                          EMCEE
               Dear friends, the Magnum TX Band! Let's
               hear it!
                          (applause)
               Yeah, Magnum TX . . . and now, the tombola,
               organized by the Cambria Circle Masonic Lodge.
                          (turning to a plump girl)
               Please, draw the first numbers.

Joseph orders another drink.

                          EMCEE
               First prize: a Byron Toaster; "Byron is what we
               want." Thank you . . . Now, the winning number.

(accepting the paper)
Come closer, Miss Incredible! She's so shy!

The voice of the emcee continues over as Brunel enters and sits next to Joseph.

BRUNEL

Hey brother, what's happening? Let's have a
drink. Drinks arrive.

JOSEPH

But, here's to our grand reconciliation.
(drinking)
Did you bring your brother a present?

Brunel taps his pocket, then leads Joseph into the bathroom and into a stall. He locks the door behind them. He pulls out the package and Joseph starts to unwrap it.

BRUNEL

Not here, man!

Joseph pulls out a gun.

JOSEPH

Why not? I like it.

Joseph puts it in his pocket, smiles, then leads Brunel back into the noisy bar.

BRUNEL

Listen, keep cool, all right? Don't get cut.

Joseph finishes his drink in one swallow and heads toward the door. Brunel orders another. But sidestepping through the crowd, Joseph sees Sarah. He walks up behind her.

JOSEPH
May I have this dance?

They step out onto the floor and start to dance. Moving more slowly than the rest, it is clear that they are in their own world. Joseph's embrace becomes more provocative. Brunel watches from the bar. Jean watches from the crowd. We begin to see all the regulars from the Haitian Corner dancing. Even Felicia is present. Joseph starts to kiss Sarah's neck. But when he tries to kiss her on the mouth, she gently frees herself from his grip. He stands suddenly rock-still in the center of the dancers. She backs away from him and joins Jean. The room around Joseph spins.

INT. CAJUSTE APARTMENT—DAY

Joseph sits on the floor with the parts of the gun spread out before him on newspaper. He is cleaning it. Sarah and Felicia are arguing in the kitchen.

SARAH
(over)
Who cares what other people think? It's my life! We're not in the village!

FELICIA
(over)
What will Jean think?

Joseph reassembles the pistol. He wipes the grease from his hands.

FELICIA
(over)
If it weren't for the rest of you, I'd go back tomorrow.

Joseph loads the pistol. He wipes the exterior dry.

FELICIA
(over)
What have I got to stay for anyway? There's
nothing here for me. They've taken everything
worth having. I am old.
(beat)
But don't worry: I'll see you married first!

*Joseph is rubbing the gun across his forehead. He puts the muzzle in
his mouth and holds it there for a moment. His finger is taut, ready to
pull the trigger. He stops.*

INT. APARTMENT—JOSEPH'S BEDROOM—NIGHT

*The sounds of children playing float up from the street. The room is
dark. Joseph lies on the bed, eyes wide open. Sarah enters.*

JOSEPH
. . . Yes?

SARAH
May I turn the light on?

JOSEPH
Leave it off.

Sarah closes the door and steps into the shadows. Joseph sits up.

SARAH

We must talk.

Silence.

SARAH

Have we really reached this stage? We are back where we started. We are in the square at the fountain. I throw water at you. We fight. Mother is yelling.

JOSEPH

I don't remember.

Silence.

SARAH

I want to get out of here. If marrying Jean is the only way to do that, then I will marry him.
(beat)
I can't be torn in two. My love for you . . . I've made up my mind. That's what I have to tell you. I came in here . . . You aren't listening!
(beat)
I didn't come to argue with you. I wanted to say that nothing will ever change with us.

Sarah takes his hand and places it between hers. She kisses his hand. He takes it back.

JOSEPH

Leave me alone, please.

SARAH

I want something from you first. You forget all the nights I spent at your bedside after we got you back. You were delirious. Now you have let everyone down: mother, father . . . me. There was a time when I would have given up everything, *everything*, for you.

(beat)

I was a little girl in love. You were never my brother, you were always my man. I gave myself to you. Isn't that enough?! Must you ruin everything?!

Joseph stands to leave.

SARAH

Joseph!

JOSEPH

What do you want?

SARAH

Don't you know?

He opens the door . . .

SARAH

Joseph!

. . . and leaves.

CUT TO:

INT. DREAM PLACE—NIGHT

The empty room. Walls covered in brown chalk. Joseph, thin, skeletal, shivers in the shadows.

VOICE
(loud, stern)

Stand up straight!

A hand wraps a Coke bottle in a cloth and strikes Joseph with it. A uniformed shoulder. The cloth turns red. Joseph screams as loud as he can.

CUT TO:

INT. SUBWAY—NIGHT

Joseph looks out the window at the shining lights. The train pulls into the station. Joseph exits. He is preoccupied. He bumps into a lady on the platform. She yells at him, but he ignores it.

EXT./INT. BROOKLYN RESTAURANT—SHORT
TIME LATER

It is the restaurant where Sylvain Theodore works. Joseph enters. A waiter greets him at the door.

WAITER
Sir, we close in fifteen minutes.

Joseph walks past him concentrating on the room.

JOSEPH
I just want a coffee.

Joseph takes a seat at a table and the waiter is heard shouting an order for coffee. Joseph does not see Sylvain and grows nervous, impatient. The coffee arrives, but he doesn't drink it. He pays and leaves.

INT. RESTAURANT—KITCHEN—CONTINUOUS

Joseph arrives at the back of the restaurant. Standing near the garbage cans, he watches Sylvain through the half-open door. Sylvain is finishing work. He is arranging huge saucepans, cleaning a tray, wiping down the stove. The kitchen is large compared with the restaurant itself. It is like a kitchen for a large hotel. The ovens are arranged in the center of the room, under one large hood. Bright fluorescent lighting is reflected in the many pots, pans, and other aluminum objects. We get the sense that the kitchen reflects the glory of a past era. Sylvain senses that someone is watching him and turns toward the door. Joseph just manages to hide behind a wall. He holds his breath. Sylvain sees nothing and returns to work. Joseph, with his back to the wall, is sweating profusely. He seems on the verge of panic. He takes a deep breath. He turns to the door again. This time he opens it, softly, trying not to make noise. He enters. Sylvain turns in surprise and is stunned for a moment. He doesn't

*understand what is happening. For a split second there is an expression
of panic in his eyes. But perhaps we are mistaken.*

SYLVAIN
(calmly)
Who are you?

Joseph does not answer. He steps forward. Sylvain steps back.

SYLVAIN
What do you want?
(beat)
You are not supposed to come in here.

Joseph takes another step forward.

SYLVAIN
You can't talk? What do you want? Do you
want some soup?

*Sylvain goes to an urn, takes a bowl, and ladles some soup into it. He
extends the offer to Joseph. Joseph won't take it.*

SYLVAIN
You don't look hungry to me.

JOSEPH
I don't want any soup.

Sylvain puts down the soup bowl.

SYLVAIN
From Haiti? You are from Haiti. I can see that

you are from Haiti.

JOSEPH
Yes, Colonel, I am.

SYLVAIN
(smiling)
Colonel? What are you saying? What do you
mean? I am no colonel.

Silence.

SYLVAIN
(angry)
I don't know what you are talking about! Get
out!

*Sylvain starts to approach Joseph, but Joseph draws the gun. It is clear
he is not used to it yet. Still, Sylvain backs off.*

SYLVAIN
This must be a mistake! There must be an explanation!

*Suddenly, the swinging doors to the dining room burst open and the
owner enters. He sees Joseph, a stranger.*

OWNER
(to Sylvain)
What's going on here? Who is this, Baptiste?
You know you can't let anybody back here.

SYLVAIN
(feigning embarrassment)
It's okay, it's nothing, just a friend. I'll take care
of it.

*Sylvain steps over to the light switches and turns off one bank. The
room is considerably darker.*

SYLVAIN
Really, everything's okay. Go on home. I'll use
the back door.

OWNER
Okay. That's your problem. See you tomorrow.

*The owner exits. The sound of footsteps fading. A door shuts. Heavy
shutters are pulled down. Then, silence.*

JOSEPH
Baptiste? Is that what you call yourself these days?

Joseph flips the safety off.

SYLVAIN
Listen, Cajuste, don't do anything stupid.

JOSEPH
Oh, you're starting to remember!

SYLVAIN
I have to protect myself, don't I? Things aren't
that easy.

JOSEPH

It won't do you any good.

SYLVAIN

What do you mean? You don't want to make
me responsible for everything that happened?! . . .
You'd have done the same thing in my position.
Listen, you're young . . . You've your whole life in
front of you. Be reasonable.
(beat)
Kill me and you will end up back in prison. A
silly circle, don't you think?

*Sylvain starts to approach Joseph. A shot rings out. Sylvain falls back
onto the vegetable boxes behind him. Joseph, dripping with sweat and
trembling, holds the gun with both hands at arm's length in front of
him, pointing directly at Sylvain. Sylvain looks at Joseph with frightened eyes. He has been scratched by the first shot.*

SYLVAIN

Cajuste, listen, calm down. Look, I didn't
choose my role.
(gesturing to the surroundings)
You think this is my idea of paradise, of reward?
. . . After all I did for those people, I'm not worth
two cents here!
(beat)
They're the guilty ones!

*Joseph fires a second shot. It ricochets a few inches from Sylvain's head,
pierces an oilcan, causing oil to spout. Sylvain laughs nervously.*

SYLVAIN

It's all a mistake, isn't it, Cajuste? You're not
going to do it anyway . . .
(to himself)
I knew those bastards wouldn't leave me alone.

JOSEPH

Shut up!

*Joseph fires a third shot. Sylvain's cries of fear and rage. Cornered,
Sylvain turns back and forth like a caged tiger, knocking over trays and
pans. Joseph takes aim again, but he is trembling badly. Sylvain drops
to his knees.*

SYLVAIN

Don't do it! No, don't do it! Please . . . no . . . I'm
sorry, I'm sorry . . .

Sylvain crawls on all fours trying to escape and to hide under the tables.

SYLVAIN
(whimpering)
. . . sorry, sorry, sorry . . .

*Sylvain can no longer move and he closes his eyes waiting to be shot.
Joseph reloads the gun, but it takes some time. Then he starts to shoot
without hesitating. The first bullet misses Sylvain's head and hits a pan.
The others hit objects all around Sylvain, but not him. Joseph enjoys his
superiority. Sylvain is at his feet, crying. Joseph is no longer trembling.
He calmly takes aim, enjoying it. He hits a jar of candied fruits. The
liquid spills out over the table and drips to the floor. Joseph smiles. Sylvain releases a cry of rage.*

SYLVAIN
(crying, shouting)
Go on! Do it! Shoot! Get it over with,
please . . .

Sylvain begins weeping. Joseph raises the gun and aims at Sylvain. Joseph no longer smiles. He stays like this a long time. He looks around the room at the chaos, then at Sylvain, who thinks his last hour has come. Joseph lowers the gun very slowly and opens the chamber. He removes the only remaining bullet. Wiping the sweat from his brow, he steps closer to Sylvain. Sylvain is huddled on his knees, shivering, weeping. Joseph tosses the bullet to Sylvain. It bounces on the tile floor. Joseph exits.

EXT. RESTAURANT—BACK ENTRANCE—NIGHT

Joseph walks around to the street. He crosses the boulevard and goes to the bus stop. Bathed in bright light, he checks his watch. The bus should be along any minute. He waits.

END.

Lumumba: Death of a Prophet
(documentary; 1991)

When *Haitian Corner* was shown at the Berlin International Film Festival—this would have been in 1988 or '89—a Swiss producer offered me a story of a Swiss doctor in Africa, the usual descent-into-Hell, story of war and the clash of civilizations. I was curious and, frankly, relieved and happy that right then, at what you might call the beginning of my career, a producer who had seen my movie was offering me a new project. So I agreed to read the script. Eventually, I declined, but I maintained a good relationship with the producer, who later on became one of the producers for *Lumumba: Death of a Prophet.*

It is my belief that you can still make your mark as an artist, as a film director, with a project that falls into your lap. The challenge has to do with how you transform it. It doesn't have to be your own idea; you can also transform someone else's idea. And I thank God that this has always been my approach because otherwise I would still be waiting for, you know, the miracle that was going to take me to Hollywood Heaven. I would have waited forever. Instead, I have always worked, and part of my work was to take projects that happened my way and make them my own: to transform each one into something that had personal meaning for me. As an artist I don't always need to start with my vision, but I must always end with it. And you could say *Lumumba: Death of a Prophet* is the most dramatic example of this. It was

111

my second full-length feature and my first feature-length documentary.

My parents had worked for the UN in Congo and for the Congolese government for twenty-five years. My father was an agronomist and my mother worked for many years as the assistant to the mayor of Leopoldville (now Kinshasa). I'd gone to school there for three years, starting when I was eight, before we moved to New York. But my parents later moved back to Congo, and I returned often to visit them, even after they sent me off to boarding school in France.

When I started writing my letter of intent for the *Lumumba* feature film we were planning on making, I realized that I was in fact writing about a totally different story—the story of the Haitians who went to work in Congo, and of how a newly independent African country asked for help from the people of Haiti, a proud and militant country that for nearly two hundred years had been the only one in the world. The history of how the huge and rich Congo had looked to the small Haiti for help is in some ways an absurd story, the work of a Machiavellian mind. The Belgians had all just fled, and so they sought to bring in black doctors, teachers, engineers, and agronomists from Haiti to replace the European ones that had suddenly left. This endeavor could have failed miserably, but the Haitians were well received and integrated. These themes all belonged in the film, it seemed to me. This had happened at a time, the early sixties, when most African countries were just becoming independent. Up until then one was summoned to choose either the Russians or the Americans. The non-aligned movement of Nkrumah, Nasser, Ben Barkah, Gandhi, etc. was still a radical provocation, not the status quo. So this film became my first confrontation. With whom? With myself. By posing questions about images of black mythology, black politics, and black aesthetics, I was questioning my own place in the world—and it became my story as much as it was Lumumba's. I became the instrument with which to engage the audience.

The rest of the film was the story of an assassination, of the making of a martyr, of a man who was doing nothing more than asking for independence at a time when this was not permitted in this part of the world, in Africa, and so he was killed.

What I learned while making the film turned out to be a deeply painful experience for me. First of all, it took me a year and a half before I could begin to accept Lumumba as a sympathetic character. I couldn't warm up to him, and the reasons for my alienation eluded me. Then I realized that everything I had learned about Lumumba came from the same sources—journalists or politicians from the West who had covered the crisis in the Congo. For them, it was a fearful, traumatic, and arrogant confrontation and they had responded by investing their understanding of Lumumba with all the usual, often racist, clichés. I had been contaminated by those clichés. The underlying racism of the world's biggest newspapers, of the *New York Times*, of *Le Monde*, was naïve in a way. It represented how the world saw Africa, not in political terms, but in primitive, one-dimensional, tribalistic terms. Politics is understood to be complex when it is happening in New York or London, but not if it is happening someplace in Africa. This was, of course, a major obstacle.

So my perception of Lumumba began with him as this crazy, uneducated, ambitious, and corrupt leader. But after a while I saw him as an autodidact, someone who had not much to start with, who was totally isolated, and who could not manage the complexity of the task before him other than as a martyr. The only forceful imprint Lumumba could leave was to die for the cause of African independence.

An important outcome of this creative process was that it taught me the importance and challenge of shaping one's image. You must hold the key to your own image-making because if you don't, other people will. And this is the real problem of storytelling: who controls your image, who tells your story.

This is the problem today for those of us who do not rule the world. Cinema has already been molded by and for a Eurocentric point of view, albeit by wave after wave of immigrants. *Lumumba,* for me, is about those who do not have a history of being on the side of power, and who have to begin to take control. Lumumba failed in his attempt to do that, and was killed for even trying, but he succeeded in one sense, in the same way that, in American history, for example, John Brown did. John Brown failed in his mission to liberate slaves and was also put to death, yet the freeing of slaves came in the wake of his actions and it came in large part because he had made the case for emancipation so compellingly.

—RP

Lumumba:
Death of a Prophet
A film by Raoul Peck

Text, subtitles, and commentary translated from the French by
Catherine Temerson

<u>Main Crew</u>
DIRECTED BY Raoul Peck
WRITTEN BY Raoul Peck
PRODUCED BY Andreas Honegger and Raoul Peck
EXECUTIVE PRODUCER Dagmer Jacobsen
CINEMATOGRAPHY BY Matthias Kälin and Philippe Ros
FILM EDITING BY Aïlo Auguste-Judith, Eva Schlensag, and
    Raoul Peck
SOUND BY Eric Vaucher and Martin Witz

EXT. BRUSSELS—STREETS—DAWN

The Place des Martyrs in Brussels at dawn. A deserted, mysterious square, in a state of decay. The sound of a coming storm.

VOICE OVER (AUTHOR)

In Katanga
They say a giant
Fell in the night
And the water that falls from the heavens
The water that falls from foreheads
The water that falls from eyes
The water that flows and ripples
Into the tea-colored river
All the water weeps and moans
On this night
When death has the face of a giant

In Katanga
If they point and
Say to you mother
This is the place
Where the lost child lies
Don't believe a word mother
Don't believe it
It was a giant mother
Who fell in the night
On this night
In Katanga

ARCHIVAL FOOTAGE—CONGO

Patrice Lumumba, in a car, is acclaimed by the crowd. He greets people and smiles.

EXT. BRUSSELS—TRAM—DAY

Faces are seen through tram windows. People look into the camera. The Grand-Place in Brussels. A man leans on a cane, limping hurriedly through a downfall of wet snow. A Belgian flag. Rain. People pass by in the rain.

VOICE OVER (AUTHOR)
A prophet predicts the future. But the prophet has died and taken the future with him. No matter what he says. Today, his sons and daughters are weeping. Though they don't even realize it, and didn't even know him. His message has been lost. His name has remained.

Should the prophet be brought back to life? Should he be allowed to speak once again? One last time?

Or should we let the wet snow of the Grand-Place wash away the last traces of an absent memory?

. . . And leave it at that.

CREDITS:
Lumumba
"Death of a Prophet"
A film by Raoul Peck

ARCHIVAL PHOTOS AND FOOTAGE—CONGO

Photo of a school. Schoolchildren dressed in white. Super 8 footage: shots of a city, Leopoldville.

VOICE OVER (AUTHOR)

Haiti, 1960.

Leopoldville, capital of the former Belgian Congo.

It's the period of the Cold War.

The period of the damned.

That year sixteen African countries would be granted independence.

Africa is like a hot potato in the colonists' hands.

They drop it and blow on their hands.

Raoul Peck, as a young boy. Family photos: father, mother, and brothers. Photos of other Haitians in Congo: teachers, engineers, doctors . . .

VOICE OVER (AUTHOR)

In 1962, I went to join my father in Congo with the rest of my family. He was part of the first contingent of Haitian teachers, physicians, and engineers recruited for Congo. Someone had come up with the idea that French-speaking blacks were best suited to make up for the shortage of civil servants and professionals left by the Belgians' departure.

We were housed in one of those neighborhoods of abandoned villas in which the new Congolese middle class had also moved.

I was eight years old and becoming acquainted with a new world and a new language.

My father was an expert in agriculture; my mother the personal secretary to Leopoldville's first mayor. She kept this position for many years despite reshufflings, conspiracies, and coups d'état.

Photo of Mother.

VOICE OVER (AUTHOR)
Today the Congo has become Zaire, and Leopoldville, Kinshasa. And my mother is no longer here to see these images.

Super 8 footage: parents caught sharing a moment of tenderness.

ARCHIVAL FOOTAGE—BELGIUM

Black screen followed by a photograph of Leopold II at the Berlin Conference.

VOICE OVER (AUTHOR)
My mother told me:
"Once upon a time there was a king who dreamed of having a kingdom eighty times bigger than his own. He kicked up such a fuss at the Berlin Conference that his colleagues gave him the Congo: a heavy, indigestible cake that they hoped he would choke on. Seventy-five years later his great grandson King Baudouin must return this territory to its original owners."

INTERVIEW—PATRICE LUMUMBA

JOURNALIST
I'd like to ask you a few questions. First of all, how old are you?

LUMUMBA

I'm thirty-five.

JOURNALIST

Where were you born?

LUMUMBA

I was born in Katakokombe territory, in the province of Kasai.

A press conference at Patrice Lumumba's house. The drawing room is full of people. The faces look tense. Lumumba is speaking.

ARCHIVAL PHOTO—CONGO

Photo of people at a meeting.

VOICE OVER (AUTHOR)

One day my mother brought home a photo she found in a dusty drawer of her office at City Hall. Patrice Lumumba. This was the first time I heard the name. I've kept the photo up until today, though I don't really know why.

The scene intrigues me. What are these people doing together? Some appear bored; some are there by chance; others have no choice.

A peculiar Flemish picture entitled "The Press Conference."

A farewell scene perhaps, without the participants realizing it? Only the man in the middle seems to know what he's doing there. Like Christ, he is surrounded with people but alone. Perhaps no one listens to him anymore. Perhaps they are actors, placed in the scene as extras. A director has told them, "Look objective!"

INTERVIEW—LOUIS WILLEMS

Author, seen from the back, seated, getting ready to interview Louis Willems.

VOICE OVER
The director says, "Action"!

Title: Louis Willems. Belga Agency (1960)

VOICE OVER
. . . And the witnesses begin to speak.

WILLEMS
We have a proud tradition of freedom of information in Belgium. We don't have a minister of information. Ours is a very democratic country as far as public opinion is concerned.

INTERVIEW—JACQUES BRASSINNE

Title: Jacques Brassinne. Belgian Embassy. Leopoldville (1960)

BRASSINNE
As you know, all the big news agencies are Western-based, hence, biased, even if they don't realize it. Therefore there's no point in criticizing them for lack of objectivity. No, on the contrary, they try, as much as possible, to be objective, but you know, when I'm speaking to you, I'm not objective either.

INT. BRUSSELS—SUBWAY—DAY

Long shot: traveling forward along a subway concourse. Gare du Midi. A street with a traffic jam.

VOICE OVER (AUTHOR)

I wanted to find all the pieces of the puzzle.
I wanted to find traces of the prophet.
Why look here in Brussels and not elsewhere?
Why elsewhere?
I looked for the soul of the prophet. He who journeys with no return; he for whom rest is no longer possible.
Stopped in his tracks, lost. Far from home. Won't the Marshal of Zaire allow him to return either?
Others say (confidently) that the prophet is dead. But they have never been able to show his body. Too bad for them.

EXT. BRUSSELS—NIGHT

Streets. People waiting at a train station.

VOICE OVER (AUTHOR)

The prophet prowls around this city.
He returns to tickle the feet of the guilty. Serves them right. They are forever linked to his fate.
They say Tolenga's son is dead. But the people who say this have never been able to show his body.

INTERVIEW—PIERRE DE VOS

Title: Pierre de Vos. Special correspondent (1960).

DE VOS

First of all, I don't believe in objectivity. Secondly, even if these journalists had their own view of Lumumba and his behavior, even if he had won them over, they couldn't very well come out and say it, particularly in Belgium, because they worked for newspapers that supported Belgium's presence in Africa. Therefore it was out of the question for the head of a newspaper . . . because the press is free, but journalists aren't. Therefore it was out of the question for journalists to support someone who wanted to oust the Belgians.

ARCHIVAL FOOTAGE

Remains of a riot. Carbonized cars. Europeans running around a Volkswagen, pursued by a Congolese soldier. Riot (1959).

ARCHIVAL PHOTOS

Photos of Kasa-Vubu, Lumumba, etc.

VOICE OVER (AUTHOR)

My mother told me:
"The Belgians' rule for governing is simple: treat the Negroes well, but keep them dumb. But the dummies got fed up and became Nationalists. The colonials here can't cope."
The first riots break out. Two faces emerge from

the unrest: Joseph Kasa-Vubu, a moderate who would become the candidate of the middle class. And Patrice Lumumba, of the Congolese National Movement (MNC), a united nontribal party.

Lumumba being taken to the Jadotville prison.

VOICE OVER (AUTHOR)

January 20, 1960, negotiations for independence begin in Brussels without Lumumba, in prison for inciting civil disobedience.

The Congolese delegates make a show of solidarity and demand his release.

ARCHIVAL FOOTAGE—BRUSSELS

Lumumba in Brussels, stepping off the plane.

VOICE OVER (AUTHOR)

The colonial government releases Lumumba. He arrives at Brussels airport, his wrists bandaged. Amongst those who embrace him at the bottom of the steps are the future accomplices in his assassination.

INTERVIEW—JEAN VAN LIERDE

Photo of Jean Van Lierde.

VOICE OVER (AUTHOR)

Jean Van Lierde, pacifist, friend of Patrice Lumumba.

VAN LIERDE

Lumumba won the elections. This upset the Belgians. The palace wasn't happy and none of the Belgian politicians were happy. They said a way had to be found for Patrice Lumumba not to be the winner, for many Belgians saw him as a shady individual, a Communist, someone who would cause trouble. And the tension was particularly enormous because people realized that since he had won the elections it was impossible for the future political government not to take him into account . . .

ARCHIVAL FOOTAGE—CONGO

King Baudouin's speech:

VOICE OVER (AUTHOR)

June 30, 1960. Independence Day. The king speaks at length about the colonialists, and about Leopold II. He says that these pioneers of African emancipation should be remembered. He says it is best not to change anything if there is no certainty of doing better.

KING BAUDOUIN

The independence of Congo represents the crowning of the work conceived by the genius of King Leopold II, a work undertaken by him with tenacious courage and continued by Belgium with perseverance. It marks a decisive hour in the destiny, not just of Congo, but—I can state this unhesitatingly—of all of Africa.

Photos of the Congolese Parliament. Kasa-Vubu speaking.

VOICE OVER (AUTHOR)

The king has spoken. He has said what he wanted to say. Then the president says what he wanted to say and thanks the king. Meanwhile, on the other side of the platform, someone is putting the finishing touches on a speech that was not scheduled for the ceremony. He would say what was supposed to be left unsaid.

Lumumba's speech before the Congolese Parliament:

LUMUMBA

. . . Victorious fighters for independence, today victorious . . . All of you, my friends, who have fought tirelessly at our sides, I ask you to make this June 30, 1960, an illustrious date that you will keep indelibly engraved in your hearts, a date whose significance you will proudly teach to your children, so that they will in turn pass on to their children and grandchildren the glorious story of our struggle for liberty.

INTERVEW—FRANÇOIS VANDERSTRAETEN

Title: François Vanderstraeten. Major in the Force Publique (1960)

VANDERSTRAETEN

. . . Actually, the first sign that something was wrong was at around noon when I was listening to Minister Lumumba's speech in Kinshasa. At that point I said to myself, there is something here that doesn't quite correspond to what we had hoped.

Black screen.

VOICE OVER (AUTHOR)

The pictures have been lost. The voice remains.

VOICE OVER (LUMUMBA)

We have known ironies, insults, blows that we endured morning, noon, and night, because we were Negroes. Who will forget that a black man was addressed informally, certainly not because he was a friend, but because the honor of being addressed formally was reserved for whites alone?

Silent pictures of the audience.

INTERVIEW—JACQUES BRASSINNE

BRASSINNE

I think, in fact I can assert, that the king was in a bad mood after this speech and wanted to leave immediately and return to Belgium. But for reasons of state he stayed and attended the scheduled dinner where Lumumba made a speech that was much more polite toward Belgium. But by then I think the damage was already done.

ARCHIVAL FOOTAGE—KING AND AUDIENCE

The king and the audience. Reactions.

VOICE OVER (LUMUMBA)

We who have suffered in our body from colonial oppression, we tell you, all that is henceforth ended.

INTERVIEW—HENNEQUIAUX

Title: A Belgian officer

HENNEQUIAUX

In my opinion, he was an overexcited fellow who was incapable of discriminating between what is important, less important, and not important at all . . .

INTERVIEW—JULIANA LUMUMBA

Title: Juliana Lumumba. Journalist. (1990).

VOICE OVER (AUTHOR)

Juliana Lumumba, Patrice Lumumba's daughter.

JULIANA LUMUMBA

At that time, the rallying cry for true nationalists who loved their country, and for all politicians, was independence, economic freedom, economic independence, and all that. He really believed in it, and people realized these weren't just election slogans to win votes, but here was a man who would be unwilling to compromise on the independence of his country and on his principles. I think that's why there was this whole coalition against him—not just the press but also the church, which was very hostile, very strongly opposed to Patrice Lumumba. And even other politicians who had issued the same rallying cry, and said the same things, weren't attacked in the same way.

ARCHIVAL PHOTOGRAPHS

Photos of Lumumba at a gala dinner.

VOICE OVER (AUTHOR)

You're abandoned at the wheel of a race car going 200 kilometers an hour, though they know you barely know how to walk. You're told, go ahead, it's your turn. A rough apprenticeship.

Just before the festivities, Lumumba confided to a friend, "At long last I'll be able to rest."

It's amazing how wrong a prophet can be.

MONTAGE OF PHOTOGRAPHS AND FOOTAGE— BRUSSELS

Montage of pictures to the music of "Independence cha-cha." A Belgian soldier mounting guard, the Belgian Museum of the Colonies, stuffed animals, Tintin and Milou on a Brussels rooftop.

VOICE OVER (AUTHOR)

Sometimes you think you see the link between things, sometimes it escapes you. What is there to say about a thirty-year-old murder?

There are memories it is best to get rid of. For the executioner and for the victim as well.

And then the assassin is not often the one you think.

"There are many ways of killing."

INTERVIEW—ANICET KASHAMURA

Photos of Anicet Kashamura.

VOICE OVER (AUTHOR)

Anicet Kashamura. Information Minister in the Lumumba government. (1960).

KASHAMURA

What happened was we didn't know we were being given independence, on the one hand, and on the other . . . Let's put it this way: they gave us independence with their right hand and took it back with their left. This was common practice. All the colonialists did this, more or less. Even France. Independence works that way. The former colonizing country tries to get the country back or bring about a restoration. Unfortunately in our case, it succeeded.

ARCHIVAL PHOTOS

Photos of officers, then a rebel's face and a car burning.

VOICE OVER (AUTHOR)

Just two days after the celebrations of independence, the soldiers are unhappy. No promotions and still the same Belgian officers. They revolt.

Photos of Europeans insulting Lumumba.

VOICE OVER (AUTHOR)

The Europeans start panicking. The exodus of civil servants and professionals cripples the administration.

INTERVIEW—JEAN KESTERGAT

Title: Jean Kestergat. Special correspondent. (1960)

KESTERGAT

Well, I was a bit surprised, because up until then, we had always assumed that the Force Publique would remain intact after June 30, which was the best guarantee of what was called the Belgian wager—in other words, setting up a Congolese government, a Congolese parliament, with an administration that would remain overwhelmingly Belgian. Seeing this begin to collapse was rather frightening.

ARCHIVAL PHOTOS

Photos of Belgian soldiers lying in wait.

VOICE OVER (AUTHOR)

Despite the legitimate Congolese government's opposition, Belgian troops are sent in.

INTERVIEW—JEAN VAN LIERDE

VAN LIERDE

It was dreadful. Patrice didn't want the Belgians to leave. It was the men in the Force Publique, who had been taught to crush their brothers, who rebelled. Against the Congolese government, against the Belgians, and against the colonialists who were still in the country. But, it's true, this image will remain. Because the outrageous thing is that, at the time, the press said, "It's his fault that there's this rebellion, that they're trying to rape women, etc. . . . It's because of his speeches and the MNC's politics." Whereas it was really because of the Force Publique that all this happened. The press distorted the facts terribly at the time.

ARCHIVAL PHOTOS

Journalists perched on a sheet metal roof. Lumumba's outdoor press conference.

VOICE OVER (AUTHOR)

The country breaks apart. With help from the Belgians, Moise Tshombe proclaims the independence of Katanga, the Congo's richest province.

Lumumba at a press conference.

VOICE OVER (AUTHOR)

Lumumba, having no money, no executives, no administration, no army, calls on the United Nations. They will come, and he will regret it.

INTERVIEW—PIERRE DE VOS

VOICE OVER (AUTHOR)

Pierre De Vos. 1991. Director of information, Belgian television.

DE VOS

As I was saying, there was a political desert around Patrice Lumumba. Unquestionably, as the Belgians always said, this independence came very quickly—too quickly, the Belgians said. I don't think there was any point in waiting any longer. The country had to become independent and June 30, 1960, was fine. But Belgium had done nothing to prepare Congo for its independence. There was only a handful of people with university degrees. The country needed someone to govern it, since they wanted to eliminate Lumumba, and Kasa-Vubu was incapable of controlling the country. So whom did the West choose? The head of the army. It's the same script everywhere. There was no one else. All in all, I don't think it was a bad choice. Mobutu can be blamed for many things, but he did restore the country's unity, he put an end to the massacres, that's not bad after all . . .

ARCHIVAL FOOTAGE—INTERVIEW—JOSEPH DESIRE MOBUTU

Title: Joseph Désiré Mobutu. 1960: Colonel / 1991: President/Marshal

Interview by a Belgian journalist:

JOURNALIST

Colonel, who are you?

MOBUTU

I'm almost 30 years old . . . I first went to school here in Leopoldville, and then to the school of the Christian brotherhood in Coquilhatville. After finishing school I was drafted into the Force Publique as a corporal for a term of seven years. I spent two years at the accountancy and typing school in Luluabourg. Then I was assigned to the headquarters of the Force Publique here in Leopoldville for four years. When I was demobilized, I was hired as a journalist at *L'Avenir de Léopoldville* and eventually appointed editor in chief of the African news desk.

Family photo of Mobutu at home.

VOICE OVER (AUTHOR)

A family, like any other family.
No, you cannot read ambition on their faces.
"Don't bite the hand that feeds you." He will take the hand and all the rest. And then one day, he will appoint himself marshal.

INTERVIEW—SERGE MICHEL

MICHEL

We tried for a while . . . There were so many journalists. And there were some journalists who weren't really journalists. For example, the Chinese walked in ranks, a small camera slung around the neck, on a string, they weren't journalists of course.

Title: Serge Michel. Press Attaché. (1960)

VOICE OVER (AUTHOR)
Serge Michel. Algerian FNL militant. Patrice Lumumba's Press Attaché.

MICHEL
All kinds of fantasies went into these people's work, if you can call it work. A lot of them wrote in a bar. Before long, I started going to the Memling Bar looking for journalists. When Monsieur Latour arrived, somewhat late, he asked me what I thought he should read to catch up. I said, I recommend Maurice Nadeau's *History of Surrealism* published by Le Seuil. He noted it down scrupulously, I don't know if he read it . . .

Black screen, followed by cars on a highway.

VOICE OVER (AUTHOR)
Black holes. Images in my head. Images that are banned but harmless. Perhaps the marshal of Zaire would allow us to shoot in his country, but his intelligence agency is irritated and restless.

Are these black holes more scathing than the images they are meant to hide?

EXT./INT. BRUSSELS—DAY

Wasteland in an industrial neighborhood in Brussels. A crowded departure hall of a train station. Brussels Central station. On a large television screen, an advertisement for the film Wild at Heart.

VOICE OVER (AUTHOR)
There are images and those who create them.
Some journalists wrote:
Lumumba the careerist dictator,
The First Negro of a so-called State,
Mr. Uranium,
The Elvis Presley of African politics,
The demented Prime Minister.
They wrote:
The ambitious manipulator,
The politician of the bush,
The Negro with the goatee,
Lumumba the goblin,
The apprentice dictator,
Half-charlatan, half-missionary.
The power of images, as someone said.

Abandoned industrial neighborhood in Brussels.

VOICE OVER (AUTHOR)
Thirty wasted years. One day we'll have to start
all over again from scratch.

INTERVIEW—PATRICE LUMUMBA

Continuation of the previous interview with Patrice Lumumba:

LUMUMBA
My parents were Catholic and married in

church. We are four children, all boys. We were all raised in the Catholic doctrine. But the primary school I went to was Protestant.

ARCHIVAL PHOTOS

Photos of the Belgian colonization. The natural resources, the "savages," "civilization."

VOICE OVER (AUTHOR)
My mother told me:
"In King Nzinga's kingdom, there were huge forests and yes, there were slaves, but also ivory, diamonds, and various metals that we didn't yet know were 'precious' . . .
"In King Nzinga's kingdom, the 'savages' thought they were happy. Several centuries later, some missionaries came to tell them they were not. Then the colonialists arrived . . ."

The building of the railroad.

VOICE OVER (AUTHOR)
My mother told me:
"They say that in the Belgian Congo, the Matadi-Leopoldville railroad cost the lives of an entire province. One Negro for every crosstie, one white man for every kilometer. Initially, at a senior level they decided to give compensation of one hundred francs to the wife of each native who died on the construction site.
"This plan had to be abandoned. To save money? Not even. Payments required keeping

accounts and accounts would make it possible to
add up the number of dead at the end of the
year. It was too horrifying."

ARCHIVAL PHOTOS

Photos of President Kasa-Vubu, Lumumba, and Baudouin.

VOICE OVER (AUTHOR)

My mother told me:

"Lumumba managed to stay in power for only
two months. But what kind of power? America in-
terfered once again, instead of the Belgians. America under the guise of the UN, the United Nations.
The others followed suit, as usual."

INTERVIEW—SERGE MICHEL

MICHEL

The UN had a particularly guilty conscience in
that there was actually an incredible misunderstanding. It was Lumumba, with Kasa-Vubu's ac-
cord, who had requested UN assistance. Not just
peacekeeping forces; above all, technical assistance
and general assistance, to help the country get off
the ground. Yet it was done as if Congo—the
Congolese government—was under the supervi-
sion of the United Nations secretary-general.
Which was intolerable. The entire tragedy
stemmed from that.

ARCHIVAL FOOTAGE

A few pictures: The liberation of Auschwitz. The former executioners lower their heads.

Music: Congolese military parade music.

A low-angle shot of marching soldiers. Mobutu, in full marshal uniform, getting ready to deliver a speech.

INT. BRUSSELS—AIRPORT—NIGHT

Brussels Airport at Zaventem. An Air Zaire airplane takes off.

VOICE OVER (AUTHOR)

It is 11:00 p.m. at the Brussels Airport. The last flight of the day is to Africa. So we roam about aimlessly looking for brothers. We would like to leave too. The television producer had warned me: "We need shots of Zaire. That's what the audience is interested in."

No one cares about the rest. His frankness does him credit. Very well. But how can we get to Zaire? Before we'd even applied for a visa, we received a telex from Kinshasa: "We are interested in your project, we would like to meet you . . ." The sender's number: Zaire secret service. So we decided to miss our plane.

ARCHIVAL FOOTAGE

An airplane. Just landed. Lumumba steps off the plane, his hands tied behind his back.

Black screen.

JOURNALIST
Monsieur Lumumba, are you a Communist?

INTERVIEW—LOUIS WILLEMS

WILLEMS

. . . I wouldn't say he was a staunch Communist. I've always believed that a Congolese, a Bantu, an African, can't be a Communist, because he's social, extremely social. The family is all-important. The clan. They're Communists before the fact, you could say. The country, the clan, the family. You know, if my brother dies, I take his wife as my wife, not in a sexist spirit like ours, but because I have to help her and the children. That's what the clan is all about. So it's Communism to the letter. It's Christianity too, you could say, to the letter . . . in spirit. So perhaps he was a Marxist, perhaps . . . I don't know . . .

ARCHIVAL FOOTAGE—INTERVIEW—CONGOLESE JOURNALIST

A young Congolese journalist (1960)

CONGOLESE JOURNALIST
Lumumba is a Communist, he can't deny it.

ARCHIVAL PHOTOS

Photo of François Lumumba and his father.

VOICE OVER (AUTHOR)

On that tragic day, despite his toothache, François Lumumba made the photographers wait and posed in his father's place . . . for a photo that would never be used.

Grim photos of the Belgian colonization (hard labor, hands cut off, etc. . . .)

VOICE OVER (AUTHOR)

My mother told me:

"The conquest of Congo on the ground would be a bloodier business than the Berlin Conference. They created an army, 'la Force Publique': black soldiers, white officers. The Congolese who could not pay their mandatory taxes were sentenced to hard labor. Those who resisted were killed. The luckier ones had their hands cut off."

ARCHIVAL FOOTAGE—CONGO

Mobutu's speech, in a solemn, peremptory tone of voice.

MOBUTU

A general amnesty is extended to all Zaireans living in exile who, in word or deed, have endangered the national security . . .

ARCHIVAL PHOTO—CONGO

A group of pioneers with their Congolese workers, posing for a photo. White faces, black faces.

VOICE OVER (AUTHOR)

Looking at these photos, I wonder what these faces hide? What dreams? What secrets?

What do these men have in common?

This one beats his wife. So does this one.

This one is a believing Christian, but an inveterate gambler.

This one loves music, but prefers to get drunk on palm wine.

This one dreams of sailing far away, to the country of the white men he admires.

This one would like to become a great chef. Or at least a soldier.

Though this man still doesn't know how to read, he is paying a lot of money for his eldest son to study at the University of Louvain.

And then the others. They too have their dreams, their illusions, their destinies. All united by chance on this yellowed photograph. United by chance due to a king's ambition. Brussels again.

EXT. BRUSSELS—STREETS—DAY

A man waiting for the tram. Another man sitting in a bus. Other faces in the bus. A woman passing by.

VOICE OVER (AUTHOR)

His name might be Ramon, like a friend of mine … And Marie-Claire, who still hasn't showed up … That's Lionel. He would have liked to be a classical guitarist … somewhere in the Pacific.

VOICE OVER (AUTHOR)
Ah, here's Marie-Claire!

ARCHIVAL FOOTAGE—MOBUTU SPEECH

MOBUTU
This being said, what happens if you return from exile or are released from jail and start again the next day? I'll catch you and send you right back to jail.

INTERVIEW—PATRICE LUMUMBA

LUMUMBA
I've always been against injustice. I was thoroughly educated in the true Christian doctrine, you might say. And I had feelings. My mother and father told me one shouldn't be mean, one should be kind to people and not hit back when someone hits you … So I never understood why in school they told us one should be kind and show Christian charity, and that there should be brotherhood among men. How can one reconcile what the Europeans taught us in school, the principles of civilization and ethics, with the acts the Europeans committed against the black population? In observing these things on a daily basis, in comparing the principles we were taught and the acts committed by those teaching us, I kept coming to a contradiction. That's when I started to become more and more aware of things. I began to study

revolutions throughout human history—particularly the French revolution, the roots of revolutions, why people rebelled . . . they fought for their freedom. I came to understand that in all revolutions, there was a deep goal—the struggle against injustice, against oppression.

ARCHIVAL FOOTAGE—INTERVIEW—VAN DER MEERSCH

Title: A minister.

VAN DER MEERSCH
Lumumba was what the British call "unreliable." In other words, someone who can't be counted on, who can't be trusted to take a definite path in future . . . you see what I mean? He was an intelligent man with a quick mind. An orator, with a considerable influence over crowds. But he was passionate and his kind of intelligence lacked level-headedness, judgment, and moderation. Seeing through a man like that and determining his long-term convictions was an impossible task. There was a risk, unquestionably!

ARCHIVAL FOOTAGE AND PHOTOS

Small poster for the French magazine L'Express. *A photo of Lumumba with the caption, "Death . . . of the devil."*

Shots of family, friends, children, filmed in Super 8 by the author's father.

VOICE OVER (AUTHOR)

Gradually I am able to decipher my memories of Congo.

We came to help our brothers of color, we were told. But we were separated by two hundred years of different destinies. We were black but we were white. We were different. We were "moundele." With my friends, I took advantage of the ambivalences opportunistically. I was Congolese when it was convenient and "moundele" when it exempted me from a chore in the group.

My father is trying out his new camera. He has managed to find a group of fools as guinea pigs.

Among them, a future psychoanalyst, a truck driver, a lawyer, two businessmen, a filmmaker, and a male nurse.

ARCHIVAL PHOTOS

Photo of Lumumba.

VOICE OVER (AUTHOR)

My mother told me:
"Lumumba is illegally dismissed by the man who had become president thanks to him."

ARCHIVAL FOOTAGE

Kasa-Vubu announces Lumumba's removal from office to the press.

KASA-VUBU

On September 5, 1960, in accordance with Article 22 of the constitution, we dismissed the prime minister, Monsieur Patrice Lumumba, and several other ministers.

ARCHIVAL PHOTOS

Mobutu before the press after his first putsch.

VOICE OVER (AUTHOR)

Lumumba in turn dismisses President Kasa-Vubu. But it is too late. He no longer has the support of the army. The American embassy has just paid the soldiers' wages with brand new bills.

ARCHIVAL FOOTAGE—INTERVIEW—MOBUTU

Mobutu makes the following statements to a journalist concerning the conflict between Kasa-Vubu and Lumumba.

MOBUTU

I'm making my own peaceful revolution, which is the same as the army's, and, as you know, I've met with Mr. Kasa-Vubu and Lumumba to find out the position of each.

JOURNALIST

Do you believe in an imminent reconciliation?

MOBUTU

I'm strongly in favor of reconciliation. If need be, the army will impose it.

ARCHIVAL PHOTOS

VOICE OVER (AUTHOR)

The irony of history. History has no irony.
It settles its scores.
In spite of his friends' objections, Lumumba
kept Mobutu close to him.
"Don't bite the hand that feeds you."
He took the hand and all the rest.

INTERVIEW—SERGE MICHEL

MICHEL

Mobutu was with us until the end! He spent
his days with us. He ate with us! . . . He ate with
us, but he drank mostly. What I mean is, he was
completely integrated in our family life, the life of
our small group.

INTERVIEWER

Who was in this small group?

MICHEL

I'm not going to mention names, since they
wouldn't mean much now. But there were political
personalities who were very representative of
Congo and they were with us all the time. Let me
give you an idea of how unbelievably people be-
haved. One evening, Mobutu was late for dinner
and so was I. We had a long table, he sat at one
end and I at the other, and he grumbled. He had
already had a lot to drink. He grumbled and tried
to attack me. He tried to attack me by asking what

I had done in the army. The joke was in poor taste. So, I told him I hadn't been in the army. Lumumba was sitting on a couch with two or three other people, and a pile of papers, working. It was close to midnight. Mobutu got up to leave. He said, "Okay, Patrice, I'm going." And Patrice said, "Yes, go to bed," irritated. Then a few minutes after leaving he returned and said, "I'm taking some champagne, I need it, I have a reason to celebrate." So Lumumba said, "You're annoying us, you know where the champagne is, go to the kitchen, help yourself." He took a magnum of champagne and left. Three quarters of an hour later he returned with some armed soldiers—he was completely plastered—and said, "In the name of the people, you're under arrest. I arrest you all." So Lumumba stood up, grabbed him by the shoulders, turned him around, and said, "Go to bed." And he went to bed . . . So this was the first bungled coup d'état. Just so you get the idea of how unusual it was.

EXT. TERVUREN FOREST— RAILROAD—DAY

Tracking shot along the railroad tracks crossing the Tervuren forest. The forest landscape rushing by, snow on the ground. The leaves on the trees are red.

VOICE OVER (AUTHOR)
Why do these images keep recurring in my mind? What have they to do with Patrice Lumumba with a few million dead, with the uranium from Congo, with and old greedy king?

Is the holocaust the only unit of measurement for the human race?

Imagine there is no heaven or hell, imagine there is no explanation for all this.

And what if there had been no uranium in Katanga to build the Hiroshima bomb?

There is life and then there is death. Afterward, there is nothing.

One day he understood that the dead were not all alike.

Nothing new, you will say.

Thanks to the Red Cross, one million Biafrans were exchanged for five French missionaries. One Israeli soldier for three thousand Palestinians. A merciless arithmetic.

Since then, he has understood quite a few things.

He has understood that a man was as capable of killing one person as one thousand or six million.

And he has finally understood that it wasn't necessarily a matter of skin color.

INTERVIEW—JACQUES BRASSINNE

Title: Jacques Brassinne. Cabinet Director of the Liberal Reform Party. (1991)

BRASSINNE

During the month of December a strong feeling crystallized at all levels that if we wanted to see an effective government in Leopoldville, it was essential to neutralize Lumumba, neutralize in quotes. Now, for me, "neutralize" means placing him under house arrest, for some it means expatriating him, for others it means physically liquidating him. I don't believe the latter was done at the time. Political crime wasn't a Congolese practice, it was unheard of in those days. I'm not saying this wouldn't change later on. But at that time, I don't think anyone decided to liquidate the former prime minister. We all wanted him to leave. We all wanted him to present no further threat to the people in power . . . the Nbinza group, President Kasa-Vubu. A solution had to be found.

ARCHIVAL FOOTAGE—CONGO

Photos of Lumumba in his villa.

VOICE OVER (AUTHOR)

Everything caves in around Lumumba. Under house arrest in his villa, on November 27, 1960, he decides to leave the capital clandestinely, to join his supporters in the north of the country. Mobutu will send his soldiers after him.

INT. BRUSSELS—CONCERT HALL—NIGHT

Applause. A concert of classical music in a prestigious hall.

EXT. BRUSSELS—STREETS UNDER SNOW—DAY

Spectators in the Grand Place. A happy family; a man with a skeptical expression under an umbrella; a man with a camera, filming; a lady in a fur coat; a lady with a dog; a young mixed couple laughing to the camera . . .

VOICE OVER (AUTHOR)

There was no economic imperative for the Holocaust.

This made things clearer.

The old civilized Europe killed its own elite with meticulous care.

For each death the grief is the same.

EXT. BRUSSELS—STREETS—DAY

Music: from Don Giovanni.

Military cadets exiting the military school.

VOICE OVER (AUTHOR)

They didn't train engineers, lawyers, or physicians. But there was a Congolese bishop in Leopoldville.

INTERVIEW—PIERRE DE VOS

DE VOS

The king's trip in 1955 may have prompted the first departure. Because after that, there were lots of Congolese who visited Belgium. Now they were able to go to Belgium, whereas they couldn't before; it had been strictly forbidden. Before the war, if a Congolese came to Belgium he had to remain there. It was out of question for him to return to Congo because he would tell the population what Europe was like.

EXT. BRUSSELS—CEMETERY—DAY

Tracking shot of graves in Tervuren.

VOICE OVER (AUTHOR)

Good evening my brothers, Zao, Sambo, Mpeia, Ekia, Pemba, and Kitoukwa, who lie here forgotten. I say "honor" to you, you say "respect" to me! You never found your way back to your homeland either.

ARCHIVAL PHOTOS

Photos of the World's Fair in Brussels. A black family is exposed. Their faces.

VOICE OVER (AUTHOR)

They made you come here for the World's Fair of 1897 to display the benefits of the colony. Hard luck, from traveling around this cold country in a loincloth, you died of a common cold.

EXT. BELGIUM—CEMETERY—DAY

The Tervuren church. African graves.

VOICE OVER (AUTHOR)

In spite of the parish's reluctance, the vicar of Tervuren lent you a piece of ground to bury your remains. That's already something. You keep the prophet company. I say "honor" to you, you say "respect" to me, my brothers! But one day we will have to come and get you.

Start of traditional music.

ARCHIVAL FOOTAGE—FAMILY

Traditional music continues.

In Super 8, vacation pictures of the Peck family in Europe (Belgium, Italy, Spain, Greece, France).

VOICE OVER (AUTHOR)
In 1877, one hundred years to the day after Stanley's discovery of Congo, my family and I discovered Europe. But we took sweaters with us.

In Ostend or in the port of Piraeus, we are the blacks, the tourists.

We cannot get rid of that feeling of surprising the actors behind the curtains.

Three little girls on a boat. A bullfight in Spain. Death of the bull.

VOICE OVER (AUTHOR)
One day, unwisely, my father let me hold his camera.

My first shots.

Today, my daughter, who is looking at them with me, asks me how I felt at the time, watching the bull being killed.

I didn't dare tell her that my main concern was keeping the camera in focus.

ARCHIVAL PHOTOS—CONGO

*Pictures of Raoul Peck's mother at work with various politicians:
Paul-Henri Spaak, Aga Khan, etc. . . .*

VOICE OVER (AUTHOR)

My mother told me:

"Big upheaval. Since the marshal's second putsch, in 1965, my boss is a military governor. One day, he asked me to type the following order: ropes, black cloth, and wood.

"I understood that it was time for me to leave this office, where I had seen such a turnover of people."

Black screen.

VOICE OVER (AUTHOR)

. . . The black cloth was for making hoods, the ropes were for hanging Bamba, Kimba, Mahamba, and Anany, accused of conspiracy by the marshal. The wood was for their coffins.

EXT. BRUSSELS—DAY

Two faces, a white woman and a black man, waiting. A shot of a highway.

VOICE OVER (AUTHOR)

I asked my friend Césarine if she remembered the Pentecost hangings.

There are no pictures of these hangings.

But the pictures exist in our nightmares.

That evening, many wept in the people's city.

They shed tears of shame, tears of helplessness.

Montage: Empty Brussels street. Concentration camp: Auschwitz. Nazi prisoners. Tram, passing.

INTERVIEW—JULIANA LUMUMBA

JULIANA LUMUMBA

I think he knew it to some extent, because according to what I know from my mother, from people who were very close to him, not only did he feel misunderstood by his friends and fellow—countrymen, I think that in the end he knew he was going to die. Because he talked about it often. He kept saying to my mother, "I know I'm going to leave my children behind," and "I won't be here to bring them up." He often said, "I'll be deserting my children," and "I'm going to die." That was near the end. He knew it.

ARCHIVAL FOOTAGE—MOVIETONE NEWSREEL

Lumumba's arrest. Lumumba and his companions step off the plane. They are brutally beaten and thrown into a truck. Original audio of dramatic commentary throughout the scene by the British Movietone newscaster.

NEWSCASTER

They caught him on his way to Stanleyville and flew him back. Patrice Lumumba, securely roped. With him were men who served in his cabinet when he was prime minister. They were bundled into a heavily guarded truck and driven off toward a place called Binza. Lumumba had been under house arrest in Leopoldville, protected by UN troops, when he escaped. His capture was quite a triumph for Colonel Mobutu, who saw his enemy being brought back. Lumumba's bonds were tightened. They were taking no chances. His wife and child watched his humiliation. The whole affair serves of course to underline once again the conditions prevailing in Congo. It's not enough to arrest a man, he must apparently be beaten up as well, and put on trial later, no doubt. As for Mobutu's troops, they yelled and danced with joy. They had won a great victory. They finally captured Lumumba, after trying to lay their hands on him for months.

Black screen.

INT. BRUSSELS—CENTRAL STATION—DAY

The main stairway in the Brussels Central station (a shot that recalls the Odessa steps). A stream of travelers. A wide street seen from above at nightfall. A stream of cars.

VOICE OVER (AUTHOR)
This footage costs $3,000 a minute at the British Movietone News archives in London.
You get used to it. Everything passes. The images remain. A Congolese earns $150 a year.
The wounds of memory are expensive.

ARCHIVAL FOOTAGE—CONGO

Lumumba, conference. Lumumba, imprisoned in a truck.

VOICE OVER (AUTHOR)

Lumumba writes from prison:

"We are living in dreadful conditions that are against the law. The food we are given is bad and insufficient and often I go for three or four days with just one banana ... The clothes I have been wearing for thirty-five days have never been washed. I am not allowed to wear shoes ... I am writing to you secretly on bad paper ..."

ARCHIVAL FOOTAGE

Mobutu before the press.

VOICE OVER (AUTHOR)

December 6, 1960, Colonel Mobutu's statement:

"Lumumba has three servants at his disposal. He sleeps in a good bed and the national army is spending one thousand francs a day on him and his companions."

A piece of paper pushed into Lumumba's mouth.

INTERVIEW—SERGE MICHEL

Two photos of a youthful-looking Serge Michel in 1960, preparing Lumumba's press conference.

VOICE OVER (AUTHOR)

Serge Michel. 1991. Retired anarchist.

MICHEL

He was a mystic. A mystic of freedom ... A certain facet of his personality made me think of an eighteenth-century revolutionary, from the age of the Enlightenment, the age of the victory of freedom over slavery, of truth over falsehood, etc. . . . The victory of the word over evil . . . an ordinary man, but then he was a layman. A true layman.

INTERVIEW—KESTERGAT

KESTERGAT

Listen, I'll tell you quite frankly, I think it's a myth, but not a Congolese myth. A myth outside the country, mostly. I think the Congolese . . . There still exists a Lumumba Party in the Congo and it has supporters, but the Lumumba's charisma is gone. Africans like the living. I don't think the myth is very effective there. No, in fact I'm sure it isn't. Myths built around dead heroes work in Latin America, they work everywhere, but up until now in Africa . . . I don't know . . . Can you think of an example?

EXT. BRUSSELS—STREETS—NIGHT

The large, life-size Christmas nativity on Grand-Place. Close-ups of the Virgin Mary and the Three Magi Kings.

VOICE OVER (AUTHOR)

The prophet prowls around the Grand-Place. He returns to tickle the feet of the guilty.

Music: Christmas music.

VOICE OVER (AUTHOR)

Did I tell you about the prophet's death? Hush!

Three children crossing the square.

VOICE OVER (AUTHOR)

Let them cross. This story isn't for them.

INT. BRUSSELS—RECEPTION—NIGHT

A very formal reception. Wealthy people. A noble assembly. Sequence shot: guests waiting and drinking in different rooms, ending at the deserted bar.

VOICE OVER (AUTHOR)

The prophet doesn't want to be forgotten. He seeks a bit of warmth and pesters everyone. He would gladly have returned to his country, but the marshal's pardon isn't worth its weight in lead.

It took two sessions to make the bodies disappear.

They say two white men were seen in the savanna.

They say they drove all night.

They say that in the public works van there was a metal saw, two butcher knives, twenty-five liters of sulfuric acid, gasoline, a large empty barrel . . . and whiskey.

The prophet is prowling around this city.

A humiliated prophet.

A prophet without a grave.

How can he find peace?

Why the devil didn't he wait? Why didn't he let the situation deteriorate, then return as his country's savior?

The captain and his brother work all night.

They dig up the bodies, they cut, they saw, they burn.

They work all night.

They get drunk on whiskey.

The acid makes most of the remains disappear.

ARCHIVAL PHOTOS—BRUSSELS

Pictures of Brussels, devoid of people.

VOICE OVER (AUTHOR)

In the presence of a few Belgian advisors, Kasa-Vubu, Mobutu, and several others decide to deliver Lumumba and his companions to their worse Katangese enemies, Tshombe, Munongo, and the others.

Tshombe (with no sound) then Brussels again.

VOICE OVER (AUTHOR)

Coded message from a Belgian adviser to his colleague in Katanga: "Request the Jew's consent to receive Satan."

Brussels. Drawing of Villa Brouwez / Forest.

VOICE OVER (AUTHOR)

January 17, 1961. Lumumba and his companions are transferred to Katanga. In this villa in the suburbs of Elizabethville, they are beaten, humiliated, and tortured.

That evening, there would be a long list of visitors: Katangese ministers, Belgian advisers, officers. They all have come to sneer at their enemy.

At 10:00 p.m. a long convoy takes Okito, Mpolo, and Lumumba deep into the savanna.

They say they didn't want to pray.

They say they died with dignity.

They say that only Okito trembled slightly before facing the firing squad.

It was probably because of the cold.

They say that today the trees in the savanna are still filled with bullets.

EXT. BRUSSELS—HIGHWAY—NIGHT

A car races by. The author asleep in the moving car.

VOICE OVER (AUTHOR)

In Katanga
They say a giant
Fell in the night
And the water that falls from the heavens
The water that falls from foreheads
The water that falls from eyes
The water that flows and ripples
Into the tea-colored river . . .

Repeated four times.

Author sleeping in a car.

VOICE OVER (AUTHOR)

On the long road home, they scattered what

was left: a few pieces of charred bone, belt buckles, teeth . . .

Other shots of bridges, geometric structures.

VOICE OVER (AUTHOR)
Why in heaven do the Belgian highways stay lit all night?

I know, my story isn't a nice story.

But it's Patrice's story . . .

They say Tolenga's son is dead.

But the people who say this have never been able to show his body.

END.

The Man by the Shore (1993)

The Man by the Shore was my first film shot entirely in Haiti. I felt it was important to me personally to come back home. Making that choice became itself part of my own history. That decision led me as well to the mood and style of the film. The time I was revisiting, the period before my eighth birthday, was a time of happiness comingled with fear. It was a time of happiness because I was part of a large extended family. I had many uncles, aunts, and cousins and we shared vacations and lots of laughter. At the same time, fear was all around us because it was the time of Duvalier's first repression, so my memories are also of roadblocks, arrests, and assassinations. My father himself was arrested three times. Luckily for him, and for us, each time he was arrested friends intervened on his behalf.

Here is an image that stays in my mind: I am in the back of my mother's car in my pajamas as she goes from house to house looking for my father. There was a curfew at the time, so driving around at night as she was doing was illegal. Having me with her seemed irrational, since she could have just left me at home and doing so would have been wiser surely. The memory is associated with terrific complexity; on one hand, there is the warmth and security of being with my mother and on the other hand, there is the sense of anxiety, of terror even, because of what is happening all around us. And indeed, it turned out that we did not find my father that night because he had been arrested, just as she feared.

What kept me writing *The Man by the Shore* was this mixture of happiness and fear. It is there in the characters and in the story of the little girl—the story of a rape, which is, at the same time, filled with tremendous warmth and beauty—and it is also there in the history of Haiti itself.

What I am trying to do in this movie is to build on real stories. I was already deep into the writing of the screenplay when a close friend of mine, a woman, confided to me part of her personal story. Her story helped strengthen my resolve, confirming for me the importance and accuracy of what I was working on. What I always do in my films is start from true stories I have heard or researched and try to live through them while writing the screenplay and then shoot the film.

We were supposed to shoot *The Man by the Shore* in Haiti in 1991, but then President Aristide was overthrown and we moved the location to the Dominican Republic. This was early in the first Clinton administration and only a few years before the genocide in Rwanda.

The Man by the Shore was my attempt to make known the stories that mattered to me. The acclaim the film received was very important. It taught me that you could tell complex stories that would mean something to people with very different experiences.

Some years later there was a retrospective of my films in Haiti, and I remember a young girl, no older than fourteen, who raised her hand after the showing of *The Man by the Shore* and asked me, "Can you tell me who were the Tonton Macoutes?" She didn't know. I realized then just how important it is to work hard to save our memories. *The Man by the Shore* was the only film that kept alive the terrible history of that time.

You have to own your own history. Growing up in Haiti, it means that otherwise you are left with *Miami Vice*, *Rambo*, or *The Serpent and the Rainbow*—if you are lucky. If you don't fill that space, others will fill it.

—RP

The Man by the Shore
A film by Raoul Peck
with the collaboration of André Grall

Screenplay translated from the French by Catherine Temerson

CAST AND CREW

<u>Main Cast</u>

SARAH	Jennifer Zubar
CAMILLE DESROUILLERE	Toto Bissainthe
GRACIEUX SOREL	Patrick Rameau
JANVIER	Jean-Michel Martial
AUNT ELIDE	Mireille Metellus
MIRABELLE	Magaly Berdy
JEANNE	Johanne Degand
SABINE	Douveline Saint-Louis
FRANÇOIS JANSSON	François Latour
GISÈLE JANSSON	Aïlo Auguste-Judith
ASSAD	Albert Delpy
MADAME JANVIER	Michèle Marcelin

<u>Main Crew</u>

DIRECTED BY Raoul Peck
WRITTEN BY Raoul Peck, with André Grall
PRODUCED BY Pascal Verroust
ORIGINAL MUSIC BY Amos Coulanges and Dominique Dejean
CINEMATOGRAPHY BY Armand Marco
FILM EDITING BY Jacques Comets
PRODUCTION DESIGN BY Gilles Aird
SET DECORATION BY Silvano Lora
COSTUME DESIGN BY Chantal Bourigot

CREDITS

Music: Kompa music, featuring saxophone player Webert Sicot.
Voice over: François Duvalier speech

EXT. MAIN STREET—DAY

VOICE OVER (WOMAN)
(singing a traditional song)
Twa fèy twa rasin o . . . Jete bliye . . . Ranmase
sonje o
[Three families, three roots . . . Throwing is forgetting . . . Picking up is remembering]

A high-angle shot of the main street of a small provincial town. Very few people can face the scorching noon sun. A porter, exhausted, is pulling a cart in the middle of the road. A black 1957 Ford, amid infrequent passersby. A long sequence shot.

The camera sweeps over the façade of a house: a wooden balustrade, a balcony, a partly shut double door with metal shutters, and then the shadowy light of a room that gives off a sensation of coolness. The sound of the shoemaker Sauveur's steady hammering punctuates a children's song sung by a frail voice, suggesting a child at play (Sarah). Sounds of drawers being opened and shut, of light footsteps on the oak floor, the rise and fall of a voice, sometimes close, sometimes far.

SARAH
(singing)
. . . The little girl sitting by the fireside . . . throws
ash . . . at her mother's ass . . . throws ash . . . at her
mother's ass . . .

(reciting)
A child without a family cries twice. A toad
that loses its temper loses its behind.

On a wall is a photo of a woman, Gisèle Jansson, Sarah's young beautiful mother, smiling cheerfully. Between the double door of the balcony on the right and the stairwell on the left is a large brass bed cluttered with linen sheets and piles of books. Sarah, the little girl, sits on it for a moment.

SARAH

(reciting)
. . . The devil scares the devil, the devil doesn't
eat the devil. All sea creatures eat men, but only
the shark has a bad reputation.

She looks about 8 years old. She is wearing a white lace dress, a size too small for her. In her hands is a doll with European features. She is brushing its hair clumsily, with wide sweeping motions.

A mahogany cupboard. Sarah, in front of a dressing table, replaces the hairbrush with a comb. A gleaming bandoneon [small accordion] on a chest, suitcases with exotic stickers (Paris, Le Havre, Nice, Puerto Rico . . .) bric-a-brac, an old canopy bed—all of this in an indescribable disorder. The little girl grasps the photo of an attractive 30-year-old man— her father, François Jansson—wearing an officer's uniform.

Sarah keeps on singing. She jumps feet first into an open trunk and starts pulling out a wedding dress, which she treats as an enormous mass of rags, and sends flying behind her with a laugh.

VOICE
(off-screen)
Sarah, Sarah, come downstairs. You know I
don't like you playing in the attic.

VOICE OVER (SARAH)
It was the early sixties. In those days, the attic
in my grandmother's house was still an attic. I was
8 years old and the world already opened out onto
a disaster.

Carrying her doll, Sarah forces open a boarded-up door and comes out on the second balcony, screen left.

Her face freezes. Muffled blows and a harrowing cry are heard. End of sequence.

EXT. ATTIC—SOUTH BALCONY (SARAH'S POV)—
DAY

In the distance, between two buildings, a glimpse of the sea . . . Moving in closer, the balcony also looks out on the barracks' courtyard. In the middle of the courtyard, an officer in military uniform (François Jansson) and three militiamen in dark blue outfits. A twisted black mass is huddled at their feet. The scene takes place at a distance so faces can't be clearly distinguished. One of the militiamen, Janvier, steps back to the left to take better aim before striking. We then make out the body of a man attached to a stick, his hands tied behind his back, in the position known as "the top." The blow comes down hard and muffled, and is immediately followed by another better aimed blow. The little girl on the balcony remains paralyzed, rooted to the spot by the violence of the scene.

JANVIER
(to the prisoner)
You going to shut your trap?

Gracieux Sorel, the man on the ground, begins to moan. Janvier, the militiaman, suddenly shoves his stick into the man's anus. The man cries out at the top of his lungs, in powerless rage, intense pain, and terror.

Janvier gets ready to strike again.

SARAH
(with all her might)
No!!!

The four men look up. François Jansson, the officer who has remained in the background, signals to the child to go inside.

MILITIAMAN
(to Jansson)
Make her shut up.

He draws his gun, but Jansson stops him and pushes him roughly away. His gun and cap fall on the dusty ground. A punch in the jaw. The officer is tackled.

INT. SHOP—DAY

Sarah is sobbing. Behind a store's long counter, a woman in her fifties is sitting on a stool. Short, slightly plump, with light skin complexion, she is consoling Sarah who has put her head on her knees. She is holding back her own tears.

GRANDMOTHER (CAMILLE DESROUILLERE)
(in a low voice, with repressed anger)
It's only a bad dream, my darling. Only a bad
dream.

*She is staring out at the deserted street, yet her lively blue eyes don't
seem to see it.*

The swollen face of a man lying on the ground.

Title: Two Years Later

INT. CHURCH—DAY

*Grandmother is walking up the side aisle in an empty church. She is
wearing a fine lace handkerchief over her hair and very little makeup.
A voice calls out to her from behind a pillar.*

ASSAD
Camille!

GRANDMOTHER
Assad!

ASSAD
Dearest Camille. You have no idea. This year
has really been the longest ever.

GRANDMOTHER
Here too, you know. It hasn't exactly been paradise . . . but I'm sure you've heard all about it.

ASSAD

Yes, I have. Are you managing?

GRANDMOTHER

Oh, you know me . . . We grit our teeth.

ASSAD
(taking her arm)

Come, we'll be more comfortable here.

They sit in a corner of the nave, positioning themselves so they don't appear to be together.

GRANDMOTHER

I've got my grandchildren to look after. I had to take them out of the convent where they had been staying for a year.

ASSAD

Oh no! Where are they now?

GRANDMOTHER

At home, in my attic.

ASSAD

In your attic?

GRANDMOTHER

Yes. What else could I do? At least they're safe there. But for how long? Did you see my daughter?

ASSAD

Yes. I was finally able to see her and her hus-

band in Venezuela. They were going to leave for
Cuba.

GRANDMOTHER

And what about the children?

ASSAD

It's very hard on them not to see them . . . especially Sarah . . .

GRANDMOTHER

You have to help me get them out of here. They have to leave the country.

ASSAD

Right now the situation is difficult. Why not wait a bit? Eventually they'll forget Jansson.

GRANDMOTHER

It will be too late for his daughters.
(in a louder voice)
. . . Thy will be done . . .
(whispering, to Assad)
Janvier has become the all-powerful boss here.

ASSAD

So I've been told. I saw his work at the entrance to the village. The corpses are still out there in the broad daylight.

Silence.

GRANDMOTHER

I need three passports.

ASSAD

(astonished)

Three passports! Where do you expect me to find three passports?

GRANDMOTHER

You're the businessman!

ASSAD

Camille, everyone's afraid nowadays. Even the most corrupt people! Before, you could get a birth certificate even for a dead man. Now . . .

Their conversation is interrupted by footsteps. They separate. An overdressed lady is walking up the central aisle and glancing around.

LADY

(whispering)

Ti Jo! Ti Jo! Where are you?

GRANDMOTHER

(whispering)

It's Madame Janvier. The bitch.

(out loud)

Oh Lord, protect us from evil and from the demons that tarnish Thy name and Thy church. May Thy will be done . . .

Madame Janvier gives a start, pulls herself together, hesitates, then gives up and leaves.

INT. MILITARY BARRACKS (FLASHBACK)—DAY

Captain François Jansson is sitting behind his desk. Janvier is sitting opposite him. Subtle power play between the two men.

FRANÇOIS JANSSON
That showdown with Mr. Sorel?

JANVIER
He's a schemer. We've been keeping an eye on him for quite some time. He's been insulting the government on all the city walls.

FRANÇOIS JANSSON
You've got proof?

JANVIER
Proof?

Janvier gets up and starts walking back and forth.

FRANÇOIS JANSSON
Power is already making you giddy?

JANVIER
This Sorel, your cousin—

FRANÇOIS JANSSON
My daughter's godfather.

JANVIER
—He isn't above the law!

FRANÇOIS JANSSON
Neither are you, so long as I'm around.

JANVIER
(coming up close to him and muttering cynically)
You're tempting the devil, Captain.

Janvier leaves the office. The captain remains alone, pensive.

VOICE OVER (SARAH)
I remember Papa's nice uniform. Was it on my
birthday? Sometimes I wish I could understand.
Mama was playing the piano, I think.

INT. PARENTS' BEDROOM (FLASHBACK)—
MORNING

*Sarah's mother, Gisèle Jansson, is sitting at her dressing table, remov-
ing her nail polish. She is wearing a bra and a cream-colored nylon pet-
ticoat. Her husband goes up to her and kisses her.*

FRANÇOIS JANSSON
I love you.

GISÈLE JANSSON
(pushing him)
Go away.

FRANÇOIS JANSSON
(suddenly exasperated)
He's been acting like a numbskull for so long,
it was bound to happen!

GISÈLE JANSSON

Aren't you ashamed? Talking like that about my
cousin? Your own daughter's godfather?

FRANÇOIS JANSSON

There was no way I could help him . . .

GISÈLE JANSSON

You could have at least tried!

FRANÇOIS JANSSON

Should I have acted like a *macoute* too?

GISÈLE JANSSON

Just done your duty. Not handed the poor man
over.

FRANÇOIS JANSSON

Easy to say now. I didn't hand him over as you
say. Repeating it won't make it true.

GISÈLE JANSSON

Anyway . . .

FRANÇOIS JANSSON
(resigned)
I did what I could. I thought I would still be
able to fix things up. Later . . .

*She takes a dress out of a wardrobe and puts it on while François
Jansson slips into his pants. He sits down on the bed. She comes up to
him and he zips up her dress.*

GISÈLE JANSSON

Coward!

He slaps her in the face.

INT. ATTIC—NIGHT

The glow of a candle being clumsily lit. While everyone is still asleep, Sarah is up. Holding the candle in her hand, she walks over to her father's uniform, which is hanging on the wall, and caresses it. She pulls out the accordion from under a box and starts fingering the keys.

EXT. MAIN STREET—NIGHT

Everything seems quiet and the city is asleep. Gracieux Sorel is crouching by the lawyer's office, opposite the shop. He is staring up at the balcony of the attic. Camille's house is the only house on the entire street with closed shutters. All the others are letting in the cool evening air.

INT. ATTIC—NIGHT

Sarah begins to rummage around, in a trunk, in drawers, then in the wardrobe, and finally finds her father's gun.

EXT. MAIN STREET—NIGHT

A jeep, with Janvier and two militiamen aboard, is slowly patrolling the main street. Gracieux is alarmed, for he thinks he sees a faint glimmer of light behind the shutters of the attic. Janvier's jeep drives slowly past the house without stopping. Gracieux, hiding in a corner, watches it go by. After driving another twenty meters, the jeep comes to a stop and backs up until it is in front of the house again.

EXT. MAIN STREET—NIGHT

Janvier doesn't get out of the jeep, but he stares at the dark corner where Gracieux is. The latter comes out of his hiding place and walks over to the jeep. He is smiling, but there is fear in his eyes.

EXT. MAIN STREET—NIGHT

> **GRACIEUX**
> *(holding out his hand)*
> A Lucky Strike, Direct?

Janvier stares at him for a moment without replying then takes a pack of cigarettes out of his pocket. He lights one without giving one to Gracieux, who is still holding out his hand.

> **JANVIER**
> *(inhaling the smoke)*
> I don't have any.

> **GRACIEUX**
> *(singing in a low voice)*
> My sweet grog, my cigarettes, you are providing
> them to me, love . . .

Before giving the order to start up the car, Janvier hands Gracieux the remainder of his cigarette.

JANVIER
(with a chilling smile)
Here, and make it last.

GRACIEUX
(taking the cigarette butt)
Thank you, General, sir!

The militiamen drive off. Gracieux throws away the cigarette butt. Standing in the middle of the street, motionless, he watches the taillights of the jeep disappear into the night.

INT. ATTIC—NIGHT

Holding her booty, Sarah continues her rounds of the attic where her grandmother and sisters are sleeping. She stops in front of each bed, recites a magic formula, and aims her gun at each of the sleeping girls, one after the other.

EXT. BEACH (FLASHBACK)—DAY

A beach glistening in the sunlight. François Jansson is teaching his daughter how to hold a firearm and take aim at a target. Sarah is happy and laughing. Her father takes aim.

INT. ATTIC—DAY

Sarah making the same gesture.

INT. BARRACKS—JANVIER'S OFFICE—LATE
AFTERNOON

*Janvier is sitting self-importantly behind his desk, under a portrait
of François Duvalier, his Excellency, the president for life.*

GRANDMOTHER
You owe me seventy-five gourdes and sixty
cents.

JANVIER
(startled)
What?

GRANDMOTHER
You owe me seventy-five gourdes and sixty
cents. We don't give credit.

JANVIER
Ah, ah, ah! Madame Desrouillere. I like your
sense of humor.
(pause)
But first let's talk about serious matters. I've received complaints about you.

GRANDMOTHER
Complaints?

JANVIER
Oh, nothing to worry too much about. But still
you should do something about it.

GRANDMOTHER

Your wife?

JANVIER

My wife? What's my wife got to do with it?

GRANDMOTHER

Just a thought.

JANVIER

They say you are urging drivers to go on strike.

GRANDMOTHER

I do what?

JANVIER

Subversion.

GRANDMOTHER

I was at the bus station this morning, that's true.
Is that forbidden?

*Janvier opens the door to his office. Two militiamen haul in Nazaire,
the bus driver Grandmother had contacted.*

GRANDMOTHER

I had merchandise to order in Port-au-Prince.

JANVIER

Merchandise, eh?

GRANDMOTHER

Yes.

JANVIER

I see.

(taking out the wad of bills)

Five hundred dollars' worth to be exact.

(beat)

This man claims you owed him money.

The driver's swollen face.

GRANDMOTHER

That's true. For an earlier trip. I forgot.

JANVIER

Oh, you forgot.

Janvier turns around and slaps the driver in the face. He goes back to his desk and sits down.

JANVIER

You see what "forgot" can do to you? My men
don't joke around.

Grandmother takes a few steps and gets closer to Janvier's desk.

GRANDMOTHER

Release this man. He didn't do anything.

JANVIER

I make the decisions around here.

INT. ATTIC—NIGHT

A little clay man tumbles to the floor. Sarah is stretched out on her bed in her nightgown. She takes her clay man and begins to pull it apart tenderly, humming in a low voice.

SARAH

...The little girl sitting by the fireside ... throws ash ... throws ash ... at her mother's ass ... throws ash ... at her mother's ass ...

Grandmother is sitting on the bed in a nightgown. She looks worried.

GRANDMOTHER

Where did you learn that song?

SARAH

It's the mister's song ...

GRANDMOTHER

You shouldn't repeat such rubbish. It's the devil's song. You love your mother, don't you?

SARAH

No, I don't.

GRANDMOTHER

What do you mean?

SARAH

She's forgotten all about us.

GRANDMOTHER

Sarah, don't start up again. You know your mother loves you and so does your father. If they

could, they would come back for you. You must
pray, my child. The Lord is great. May His will be
done.

The racket of the loudspeakers can be heard from outside.

Music: Gede zarenyen woy woy . . . [Dance of the spider].

GRANDMOTHER
Do you hear? And that's the devil's music.

Sarah's nightmare:

VOICE OVER (SARAH)
Bits of memories come back sometimes.

*Gracieux is standing in front of Normil's house looking up at the attic
and signaling with his hand.*

VOICE OVER (SARAH)
The chronology is all mixed up in my head. No,
it wasn't on my birthday. It happened in the little
square in front of the hardware store.

EXT. STREET (FLASHBACK)—DAY

*Janvier's car stops in front of a wall with the words "Macoutes as-
sassins" written on it. He gets out of the car and goes up to the wall.*

VOICE OVER (SARAH)
That day, Dad had taken me for a drive.

Janvier turns to an albino passerby.

JANVIER

What do you read up there?

ALBINO

I . . . I . . . don . . . don't know how to read.

JANVIER

You don't know how to read. Idiot.

The albino leaves. Janvier gets closer, touches the graffiti on the wall, and notices that the paint is wet. He turns around, surveys the area, and walks over to one of the shops.

INT. HARDWARE STORE (FLASHBACK)—DAY

Background music: Twa fèy twa rasin o . . . Jete bliye . . . Ranmase sonje o.
[Three families, three roots . . . Throwing is forgetting . . . Picking up is remembering]

On the front of the hardware store: "DEMECIUS SOREL, Paint and Cement." Some customers are chatting at the entrance to the store. Janvier stands squarely in front of one of them.

JANVIER

Show me your hand.

The man holds out his left hand.

JANVIER

Show me the other one.

All the others are frightened and do the same except Gracieux (Démécius) Sorel. Janvier goes inside the store. He comes out a few minutes later, stares at Gracieux, and seizes his right hand. Then he grabs him by the collar and the nape of the neck, drags him out into the middle of the street, and forces him to kneel down. He slaps him in the face and walks around him. He draws his gun.

JANVIER

You're going to tell me you're not to blame, right? Not to blame, right? Stop shaking. Are you scared?

François Jansson arrives on the scene in his car. He stops the car and gets out.

JANSSON

Janvier, what are you doing?

JANVIER

He's fishy. I've got a few questions for him.

JANSSON

This is *not* the procedure!

Sarah is sitting in the rear of the car watching the scene petrified.

Janvier sticks the barrel of his gun against Gracieux's cheek.

JANVIER

You want to take over?

Jansson gets closer to Gracieux.

JANSSON

Okay, Sorel, get up.

Jansson makes Gracieux sit in his car and drives off. The car comes to a stop a few streets away. Jansson turns to his daughter.

JANSSON

Get out.

GRACIEUX

François, come on, you're not going to hand me over to that guy, are you?

Sarah glances in turn at her father and godfather.

JANSSON

If I don't, it'll be worse. Stay calm and behave like a man.

GRACIEUX
(shouting)

François, you can't do this to me! François, you can't do this to me! François, you can't! François you can't!

Long silence. Gracieux, now calmer, is ready to face the facts.

JANSSON
(looking at his daughter)

Get out, I tell you!

Sarah gets out of the car.

EXT. STREET—DUSK

Grandmother is walking very fast. Then she stops and sits down inside an old yellow Volkswagen.

INT. CAR/STREET—DUSK

> GRANDMOTHER
> Nazaire's been arrested.

> ASSAD
> I know.

Long silence. Grandmother rubs her hands. She looks at the shadows growing longer in the street.

> ASSAD
> I've only stayed this long in this godforsaken country because of you. Do you know that?

> GRANDMOTHER
> I was always honest with you. I never promised you anything.

> ASSAD
> Yes, that pathetic Syrian who doesn't even know how to write, your family used to say . . .

GRANDMOTHER
(in a weary voice)
Would it have changed matters?

ASSAD
I give up. I'm going back to Lebanon. My old
bones can't take it anymore. This country is merciless.

GRANDMOTHER
You can't leave, Assad.

ASSAD
It's over. It's all over . . .

GRANDMOTHER
(angry)
So, you want to run away!?

ASSAD
(lowering his head)
I'm an old man now . . .

GRANDMOTHER
(pointing to her wrinkles)
And I'm an old woman! Where am I supposed
to run away? And what about the children? You
promised me, Assad! The men go away, the men
give up, but the children stay?!

*Assad puts his hand on Grandmother's arm, but she removes it vio-
lently. She opens the car door halfway.*

ASSAD

Camille . . .

Grandmother stands still, tears in her eyes.

ASSAD

I'll take the girls with me.

Grandmother shuts the door again, lowers her eyes, and looks at Assad.

ASSAD
(gently)

But you come with us too!

Grandmother gives a faint smile, then shakes her head slowly but firmly.

GRANDMOTHER

My grave is here.

ASSAD

I'm talking about life, and you about oblivion.
Are you going to confront Janvier?

GRANDMOTHER

Don't worry. I'll take care of Janvier. That brute
is interested in only one thing, like all of them:
money and power. One day for the hunter, one day
for the prey.

INT. KITCHEN—DAWN

Sarah, who has rushed to the window, turns to Aunt Elide, a young woman in her thirties.

SARAH
What does "amnesty" mean?

AUNT ELIDE
It means you might soon be able to go out and play outside with your friends.

SARAH
What friends?

AUNT ELIDE
Everyone has friends.

SARAH
Including me?

AUNT ELIDE
You'll have some.

VOICE
(off-screen)
For life! François for life! Papa Doc for life!

INT. SHOP—DAY

The shop is empty. Standing on a chair behind the cash register, Sarah is playing with the keys of the cash register.

SARAH

Zippers, two dozen, that comes to eighty gourdes. Neckties, seventeen, that comes to seventeen
dollars. Buttons, twenty-five, neckties, forty-five.

*Grandmother is having a lively conversation with the neighbor from
across the street. A little girl about Sarah's age goes by accompanied by
her mother. The girl stops in front of the door, letting her mother walk
on. She looks at Sarah. The two children smile at each other. An arm
reaches back and pulls the girl forward.*

*Sabine and Jeanne, Sarah's sisters, come down from the attic, stylishly
dressed for the first time in ages. They are about to go out.*

SARAH

Where are you going? Grandmother doesn't
want us to go out.

SABINE

You still didn't understand? Papa Doc has par-
doned everyone.

SARAH

You shouldn't go out!

JEANNE
(to Sabine)

Come, let's go. Pay no attention to her.

*They exit, cross the street, and join their grandmother, who is chatting
with the shoemaker. All three walk away together.*

Hatian Corner

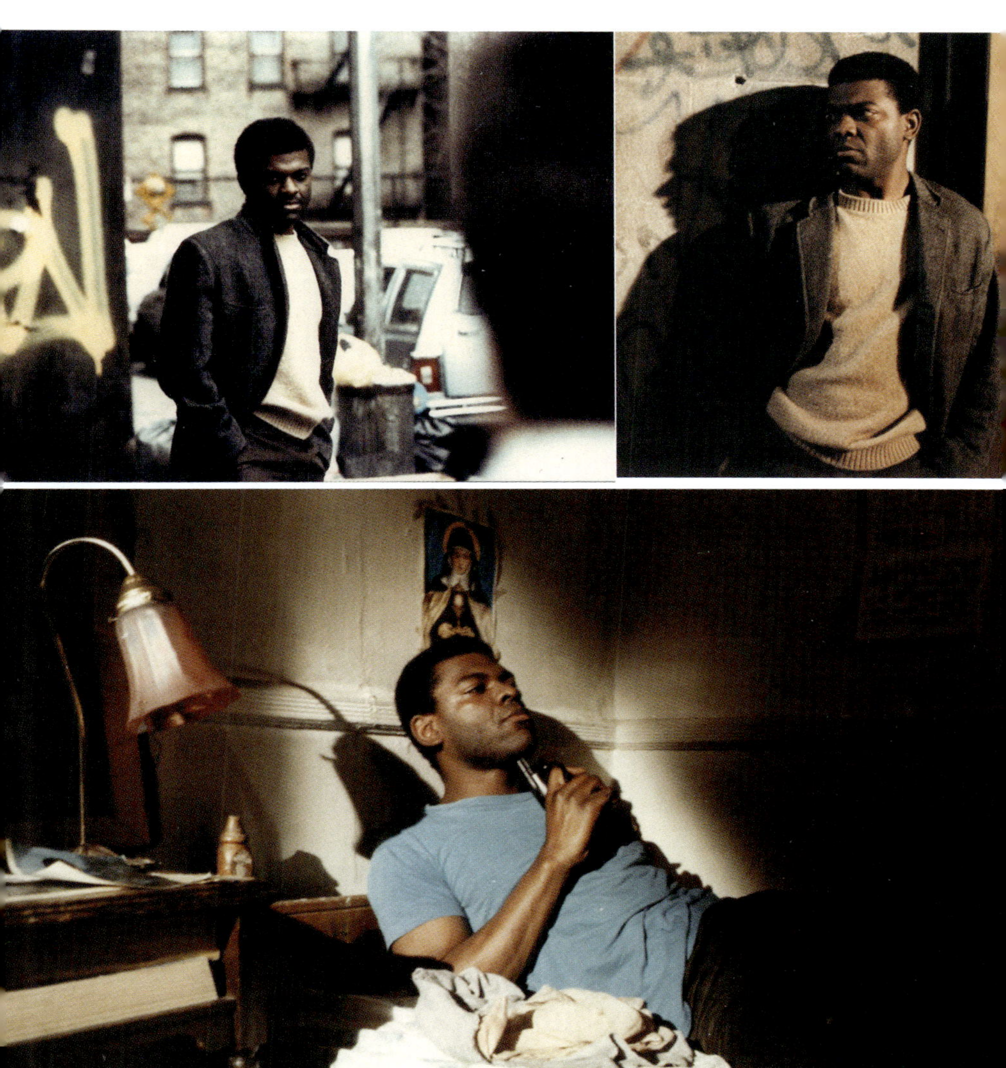

Patrick Rameau, as Joseph.

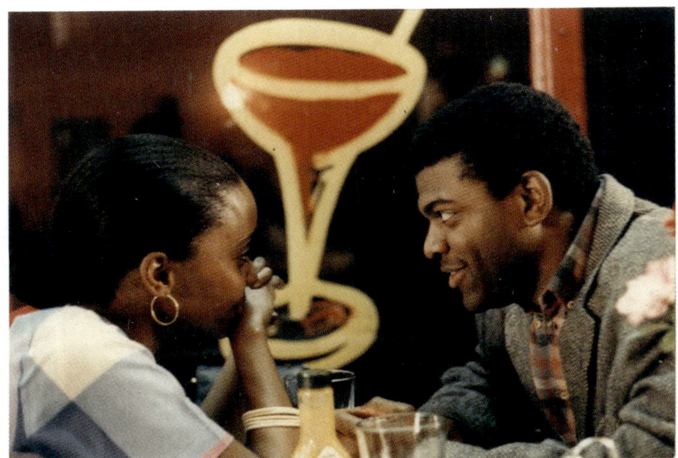

Left: Aïlo Auguste, as Sarah, and Patrick Rameau, as Joseph.

Below: Patrick Rameau, as Joseph.

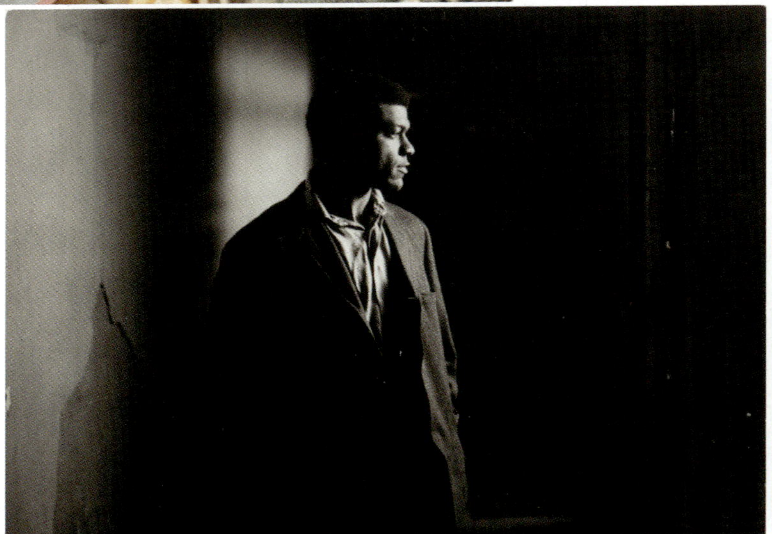

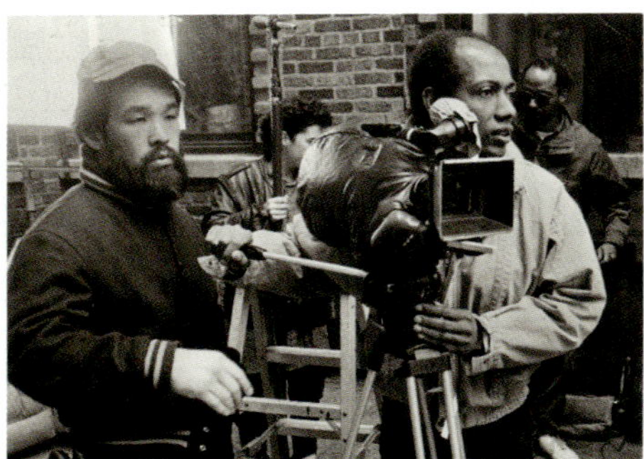

Cinematographer Michael Chin and Raoul Peck, on the set of *Haitian Corner*.

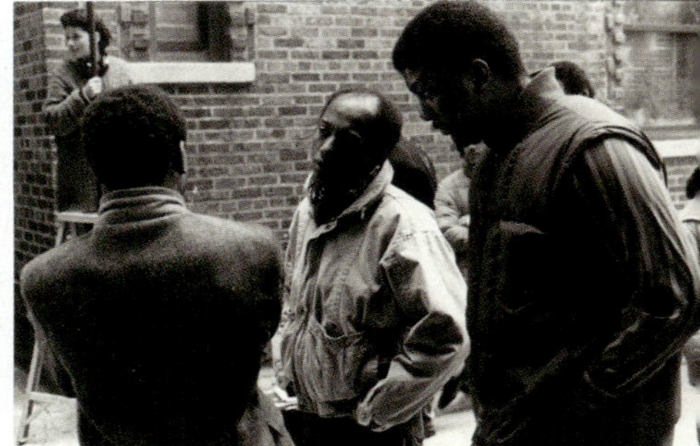

Raoul Peck talking to Patrick Rameau and George Wilson, as Hegel, on the set of *Haitian Corner*.

Lumumba: Death of a Prophet

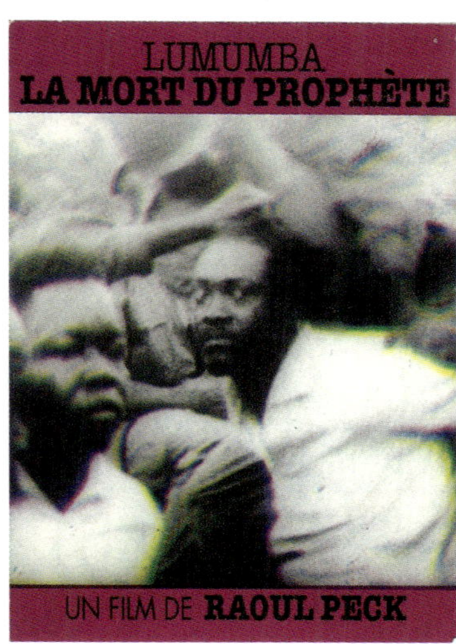

Poster for *Lumumba: Death of a Prophet.*

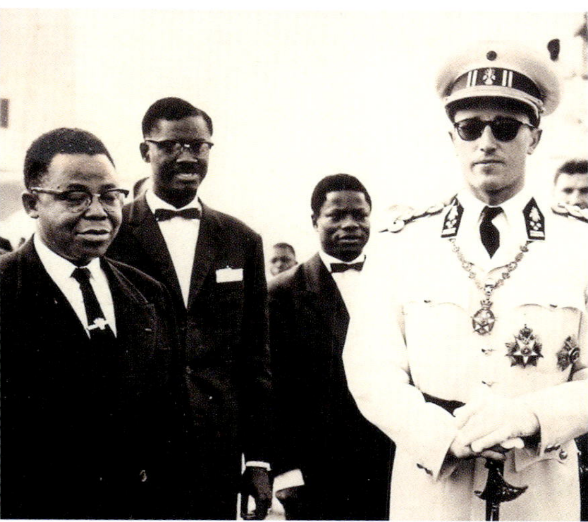

Left to right: President Kasa-Vubu, Patrice Lumumba, Justin Bomboko, King Baudouin I.

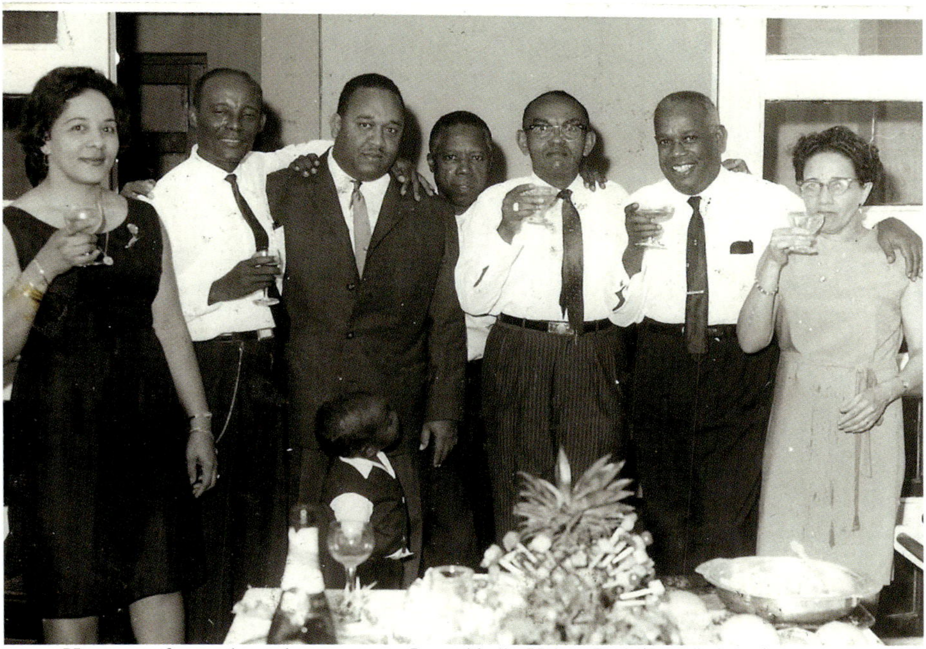

Haitian professionals at a home party in Leopoldville. Hebert Peck (Raoul's father), second from left.

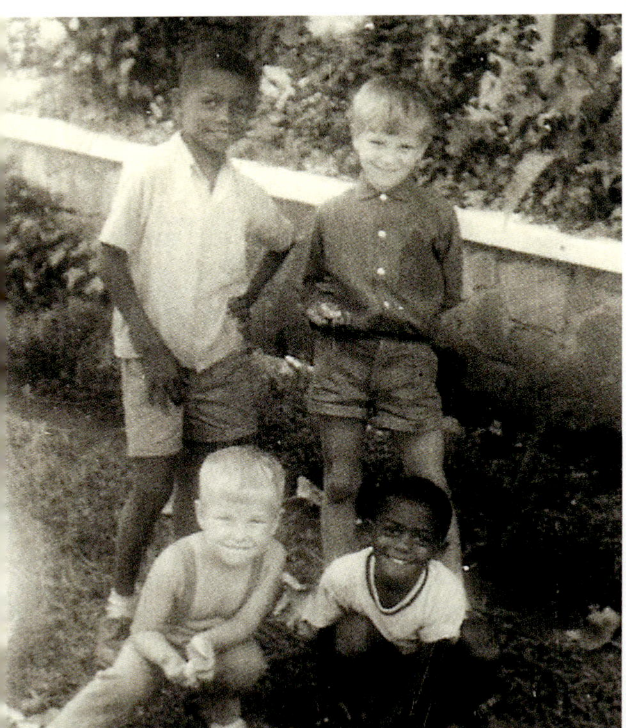

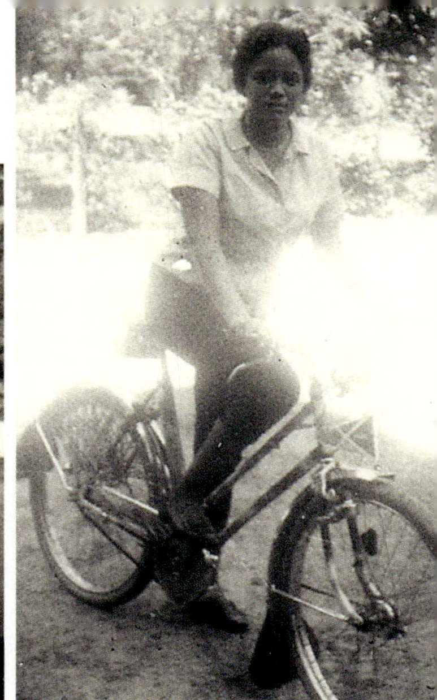

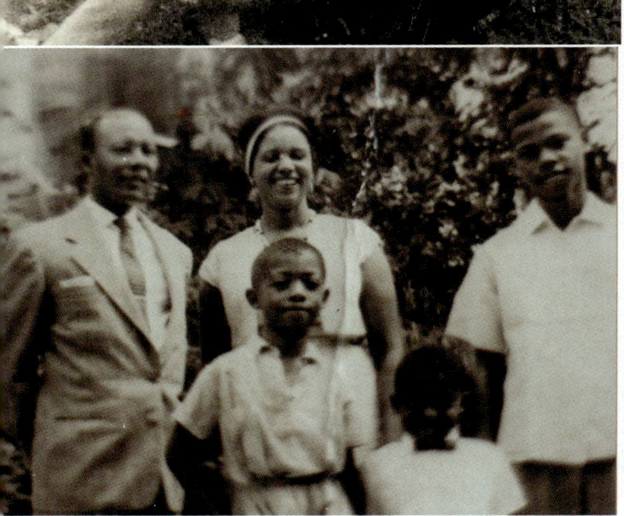

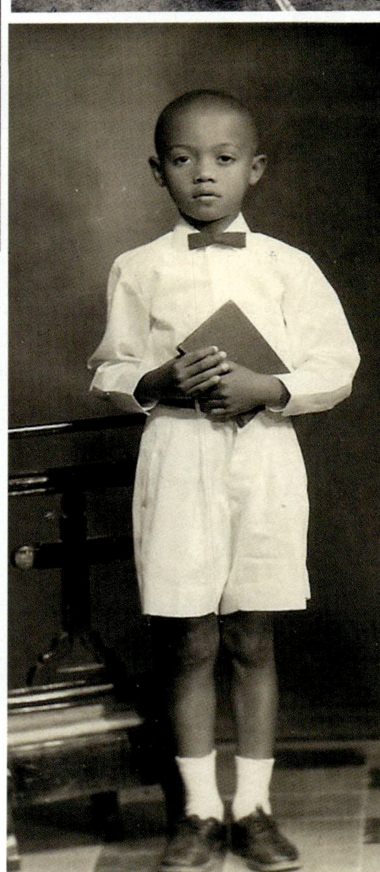

Clockwise from top left:
Peck brothers with Matelart brothers; Gisèle Peck (Raoul's mother) on a bicycle; Raoul's first communion; The Peck Family: Hébert, Gisèle, Raoul, Hébert Jr., Jean-Claude.

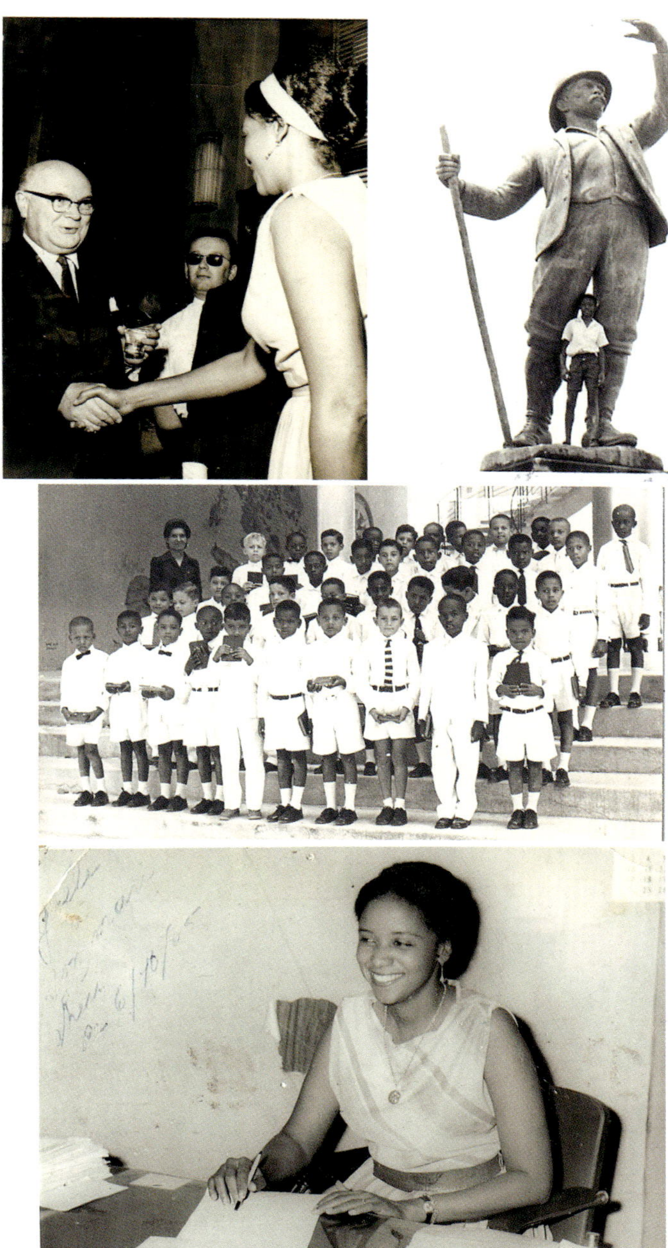

Top left: Gisèle Peck greets Belgian Prime Minister Paul-Henri Spaack at Leopoldville City Hall.

Top right: Raoul Peck at Statue of Stanley at Mont Galiema, Leopoldville.

Middle: Raoul Peck, class of 1960.

Bottom: Gisèle Peck at her office at Leopoldville City Hall.

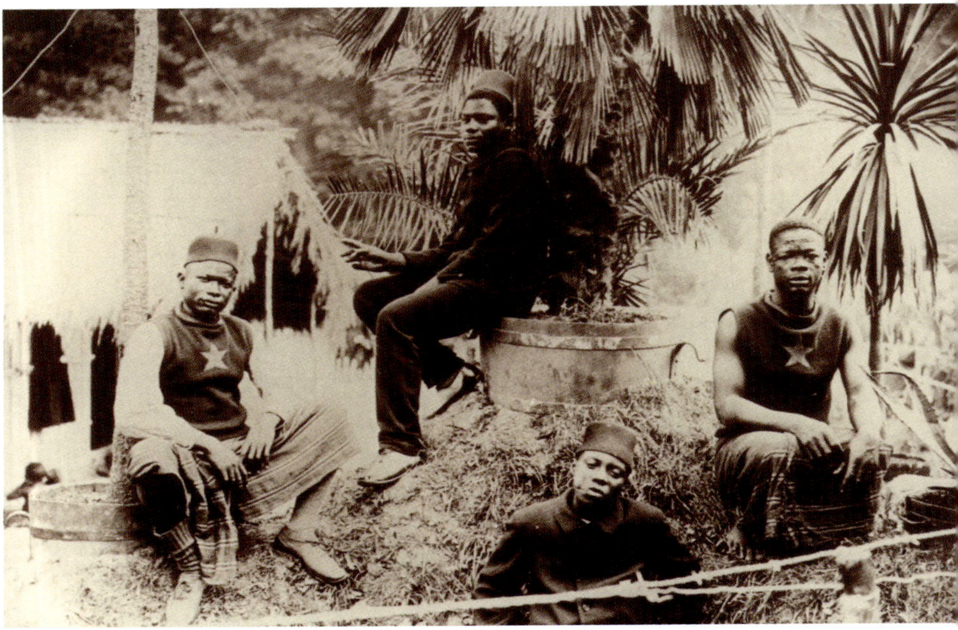

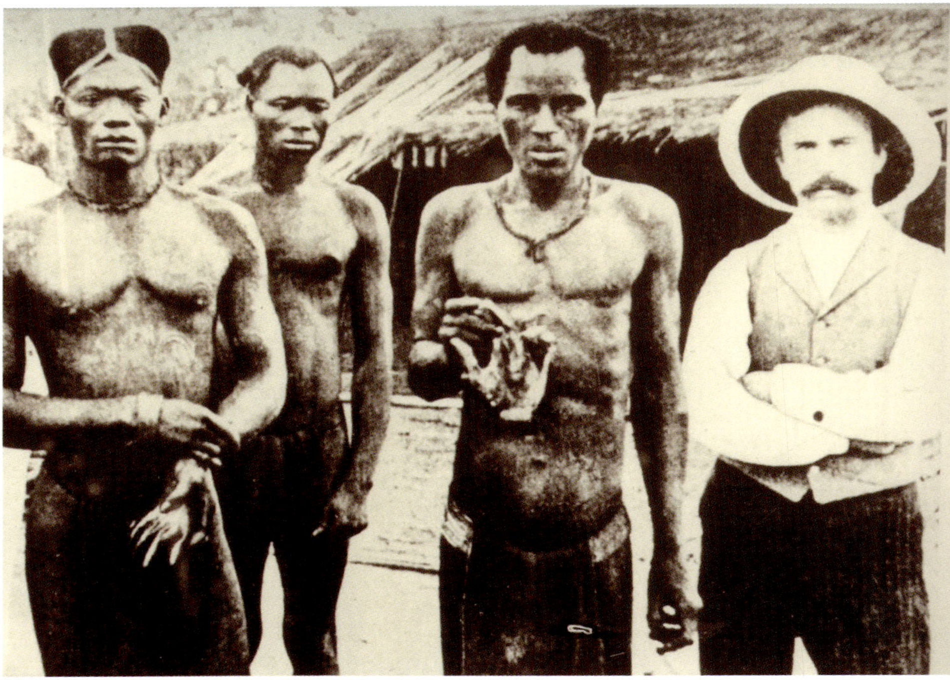

Top: Universal exposition in Belgium 1897, Exposed Congolese.

Bottom: British missionaries in the company of men holding hands cut off and Bolenge Lingomo, victims of ABIR militia in 1904.

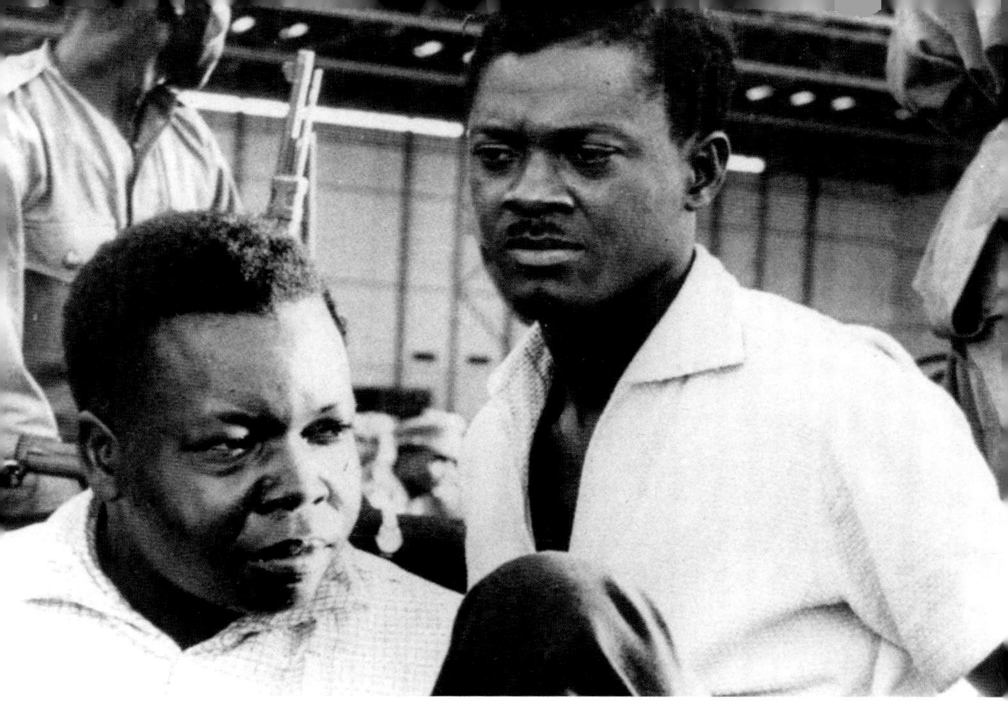

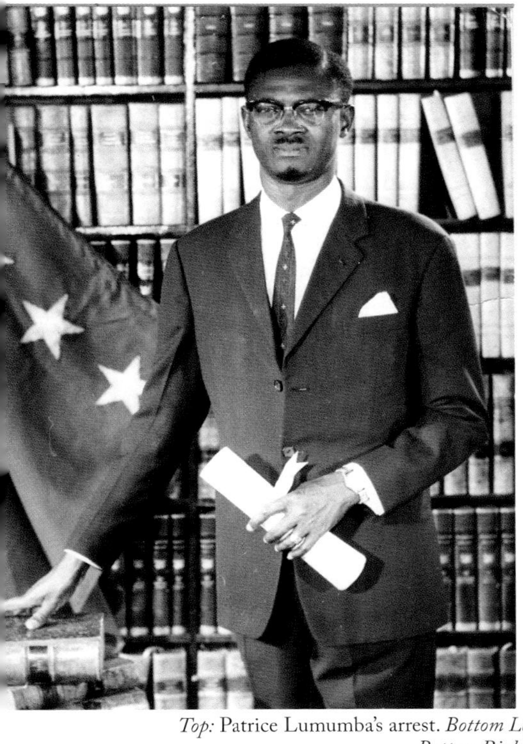

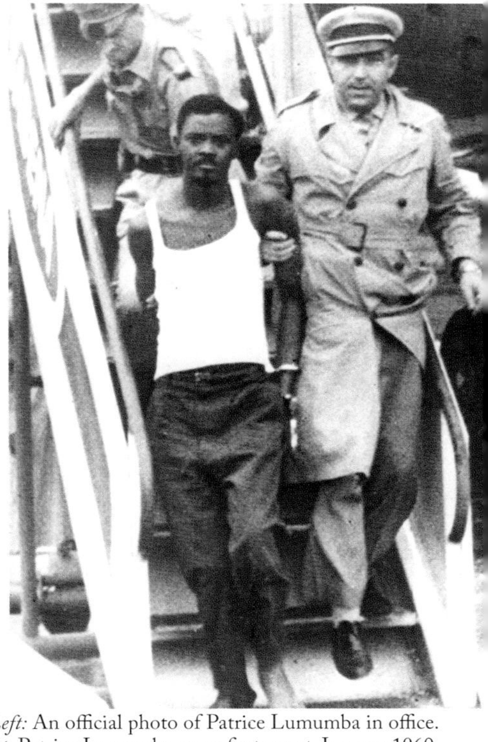

Top: Patrice Lumumba's arrest. *Bottom Left:* An official photo of Patrice Lumumba in office. *Bottom Right:* Patrice Lumumba upon first arrest, January 1960.

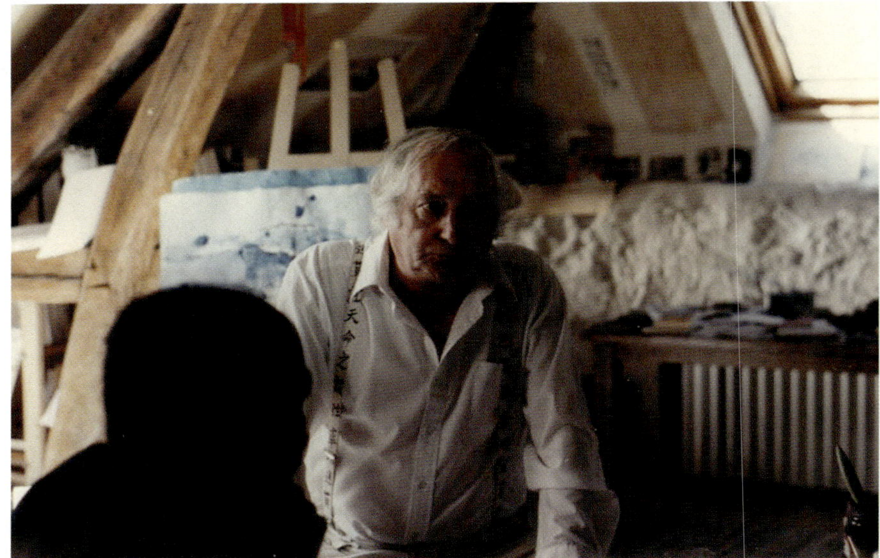

Serge Michel, Lumumba secretary and friend.

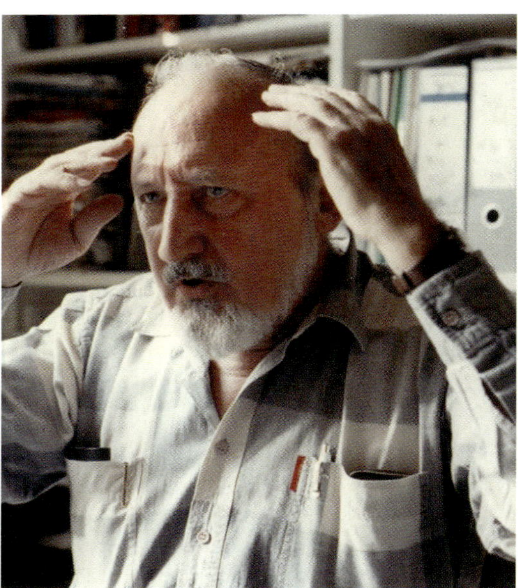

Jean Van Lierde, Lumumba's friend.

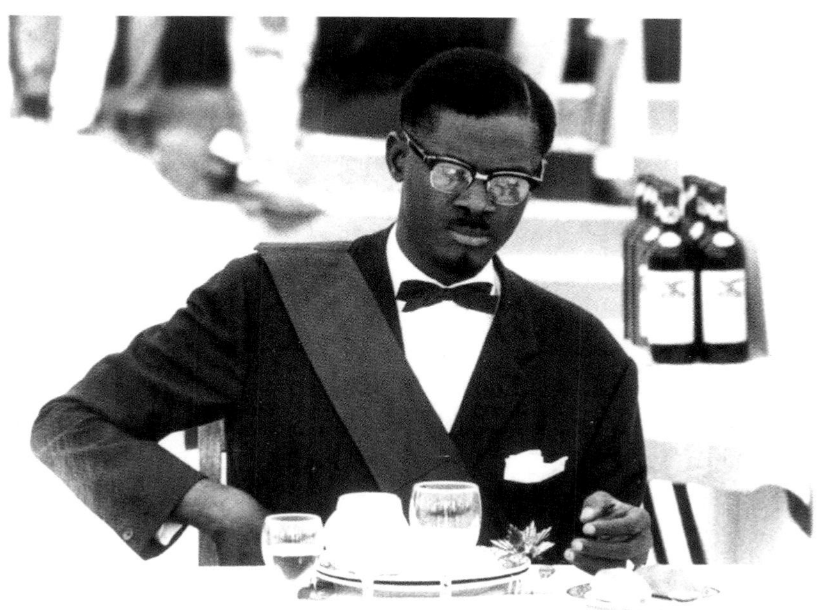

Patrice Lumumba at independence banquet. © *Robert Lebeck*

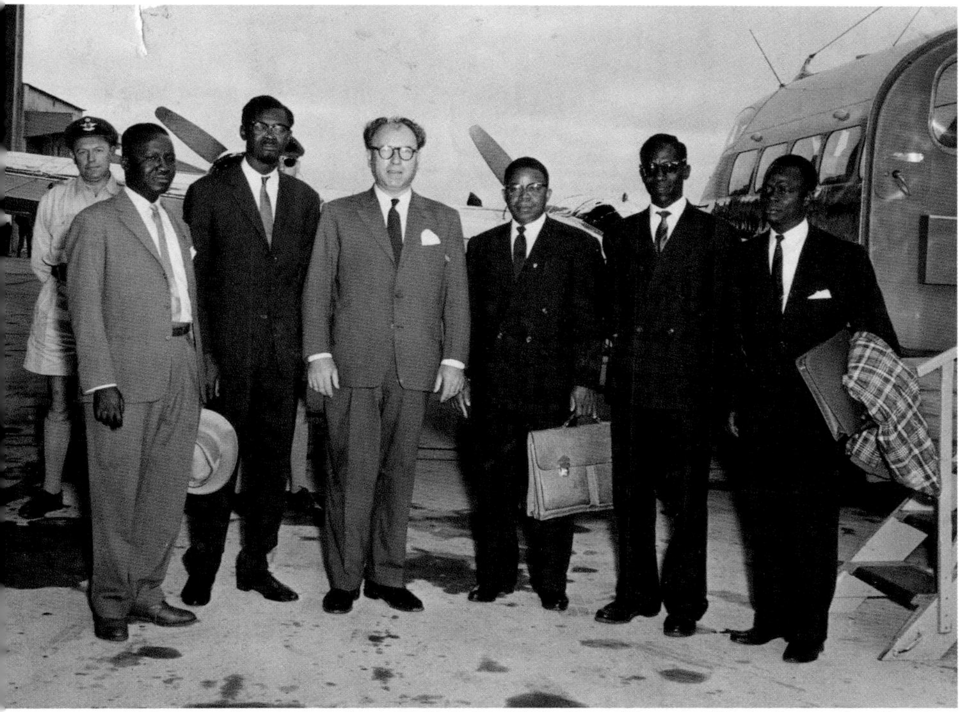

The general executive college, 1960. *Left to Right:* Remy Mwamba, Patrice Lumumba, Governor Henri Cornélis, Joseph Kasa-Vubu, Anicet Kashamura, Paul Boya. © *Henri Goldstein*

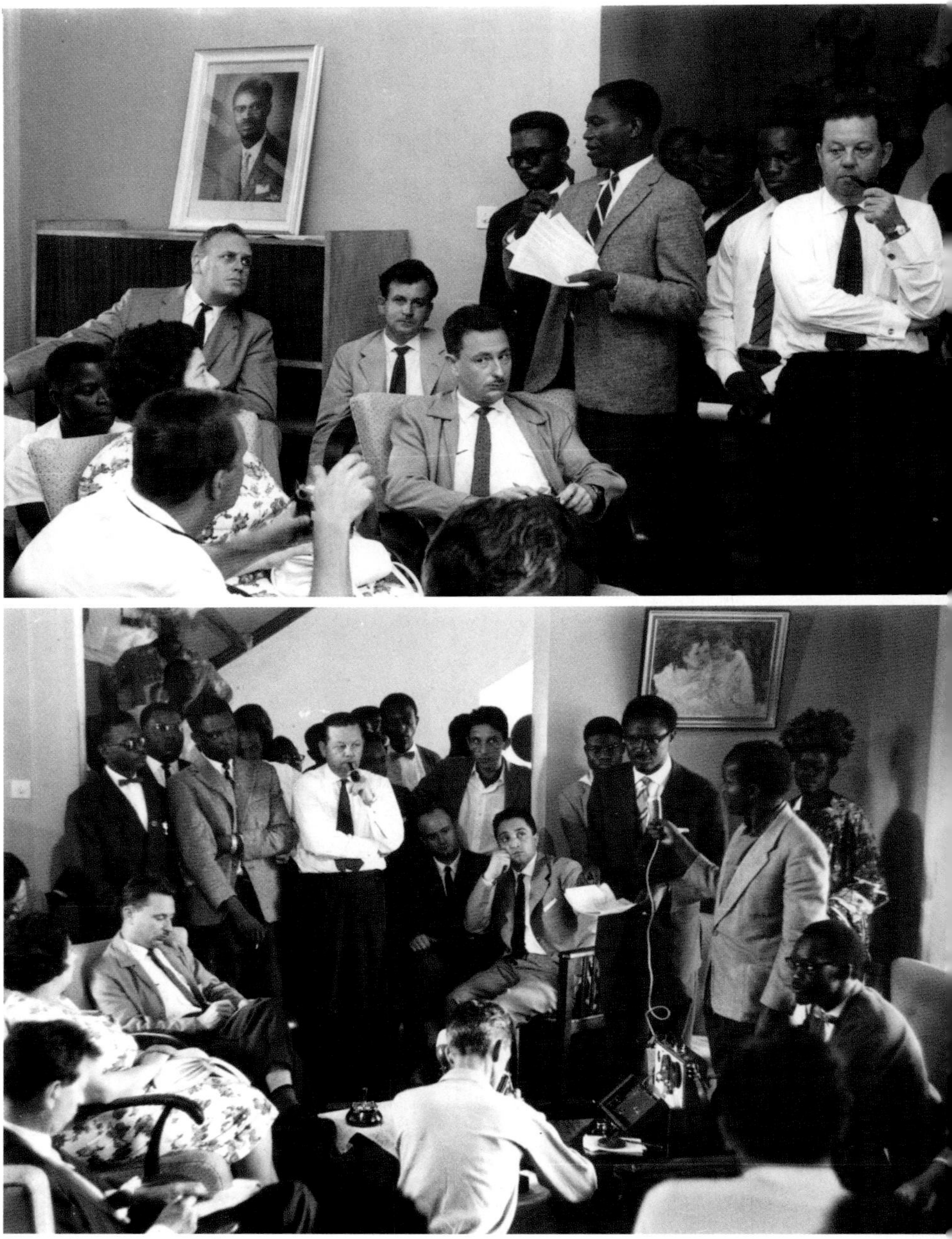

Lumumba at a press conference, 1960. © *George Bourdelon*

The Man by the Shore

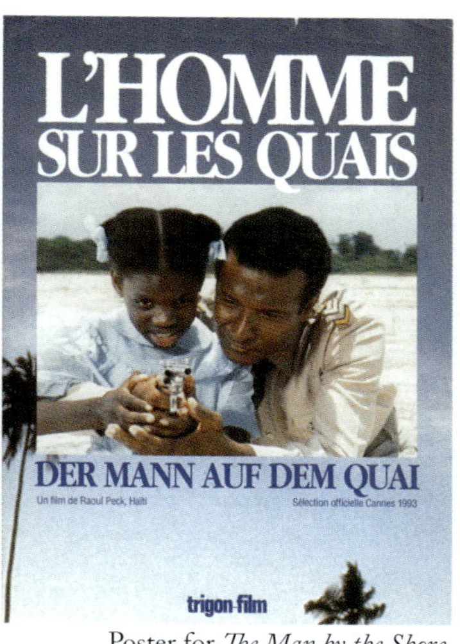

Poster for *The Man by the Shore.*

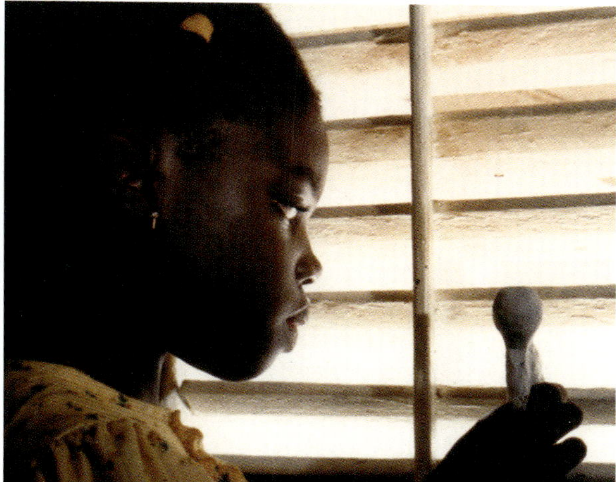

Jenifer Zubar, as Sarah.

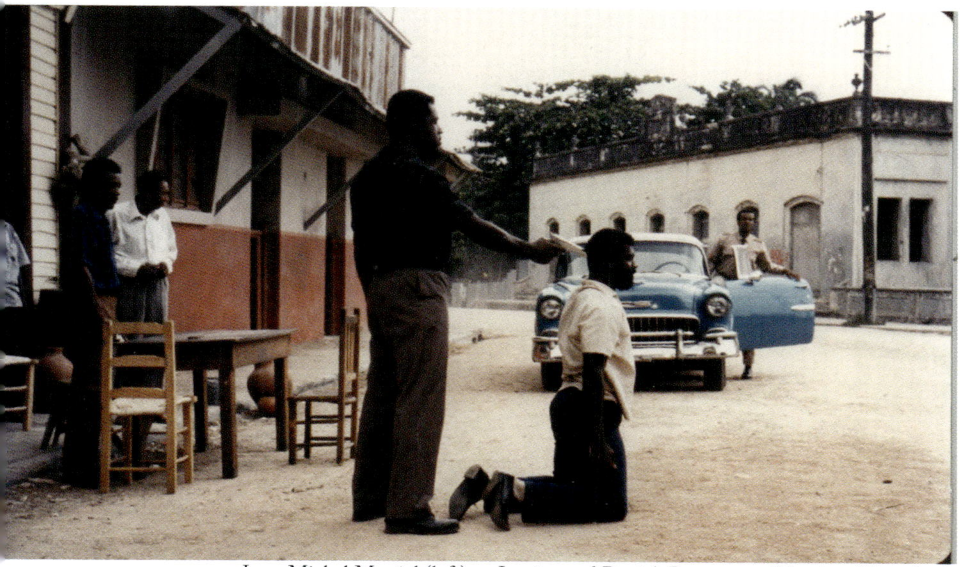

Jean-Michel Martial (left), as Janvier, and Patrick Rameau, as "Gracieux" (kneeling).

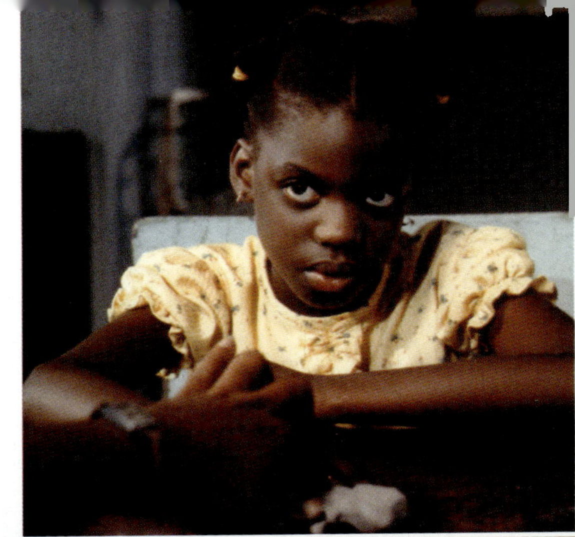

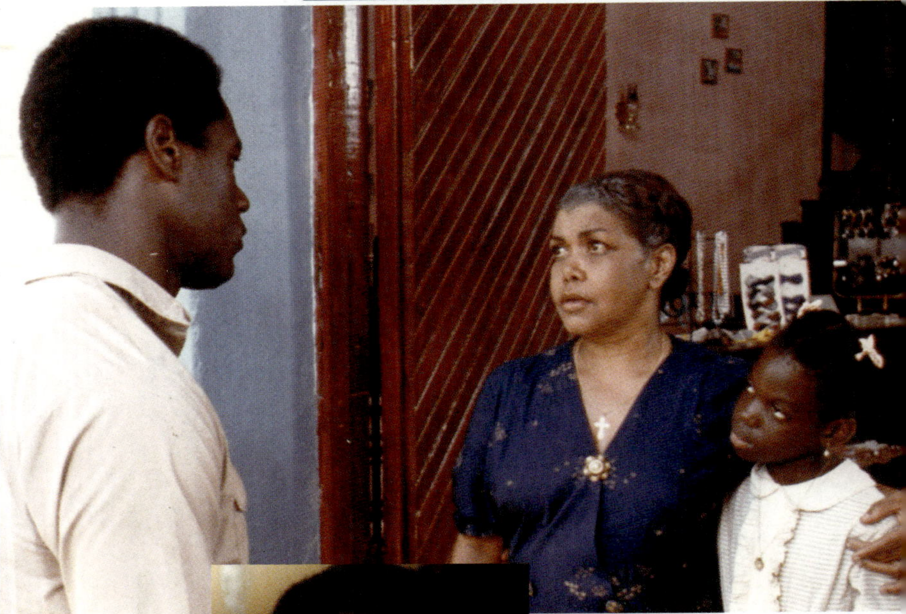

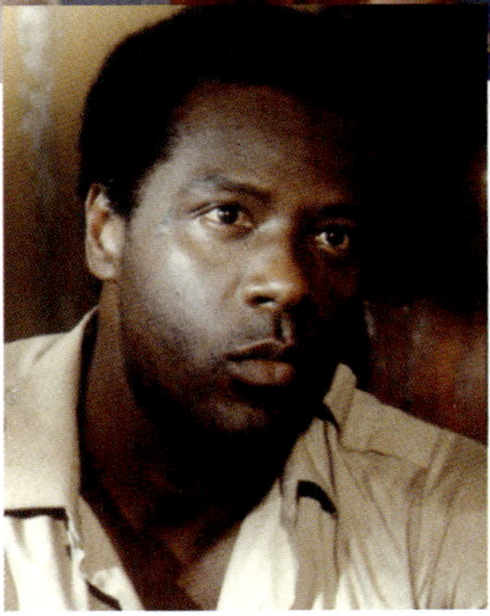

Top: Jennifer Zubar, as Sarah.

Middle: Jean Michel Martial, Toto Bissainthe, and Jennifer Zubar.

Bottom: Jean Michel Martial.

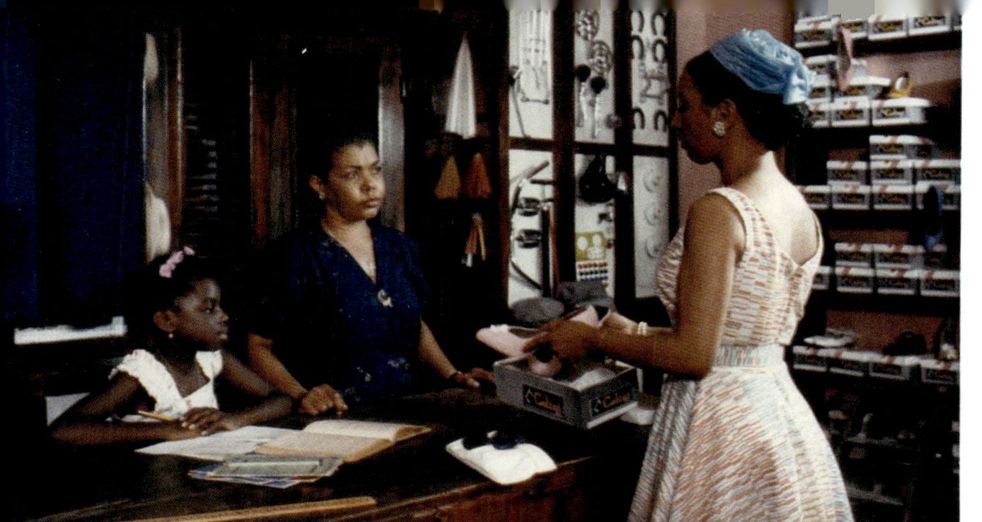

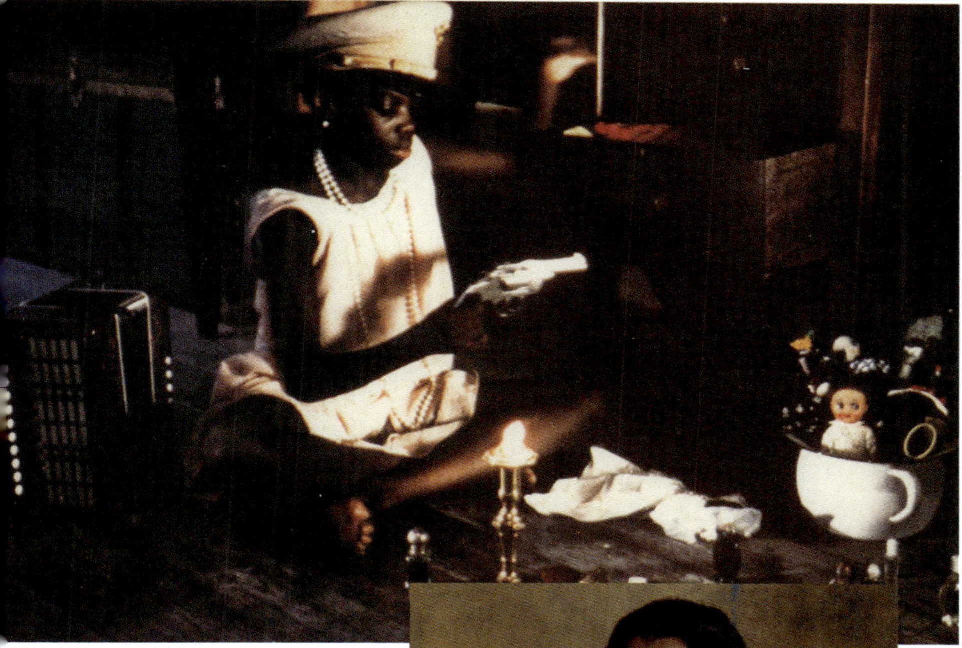

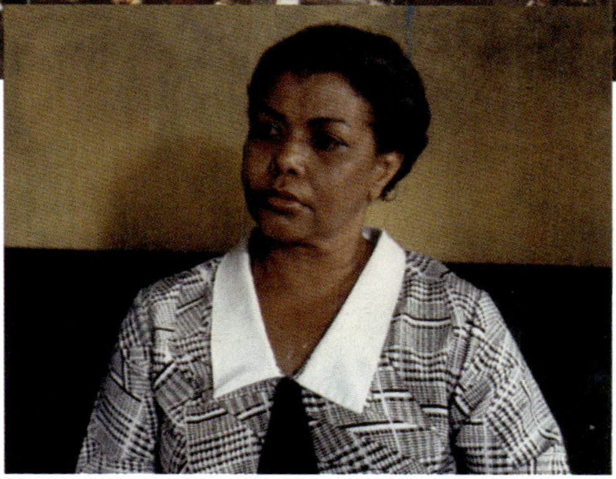

Top: Jennifer Zubar, Toto Bissainthe,
Michèle Voltaire.

Middle: Jennifer Zubar.

Bottom: Toto Bissainthe.

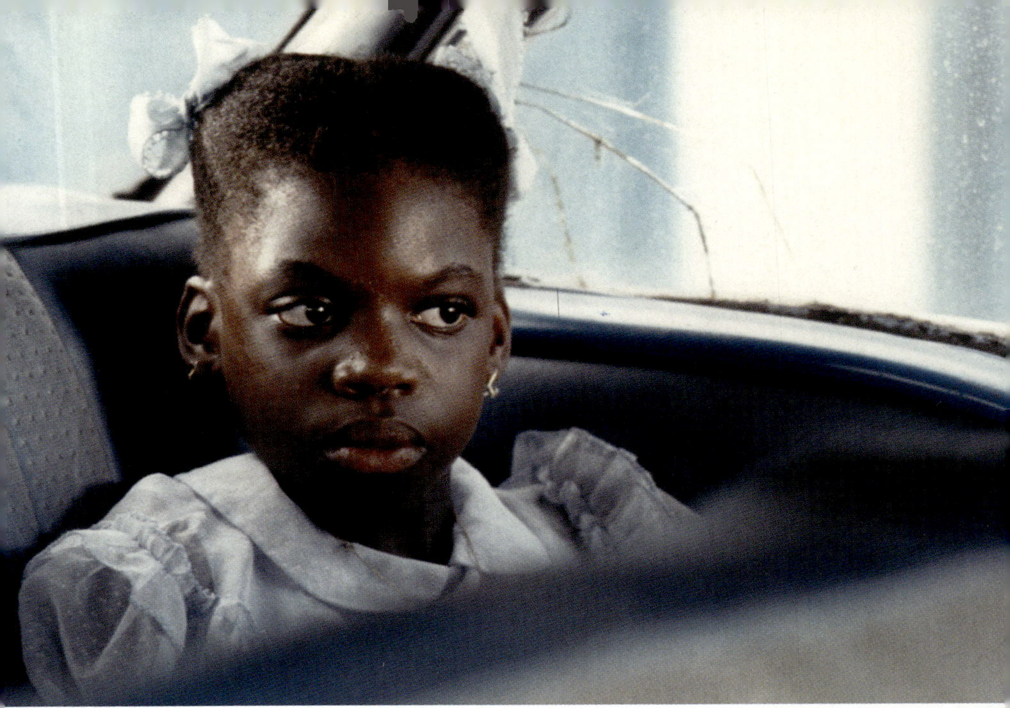

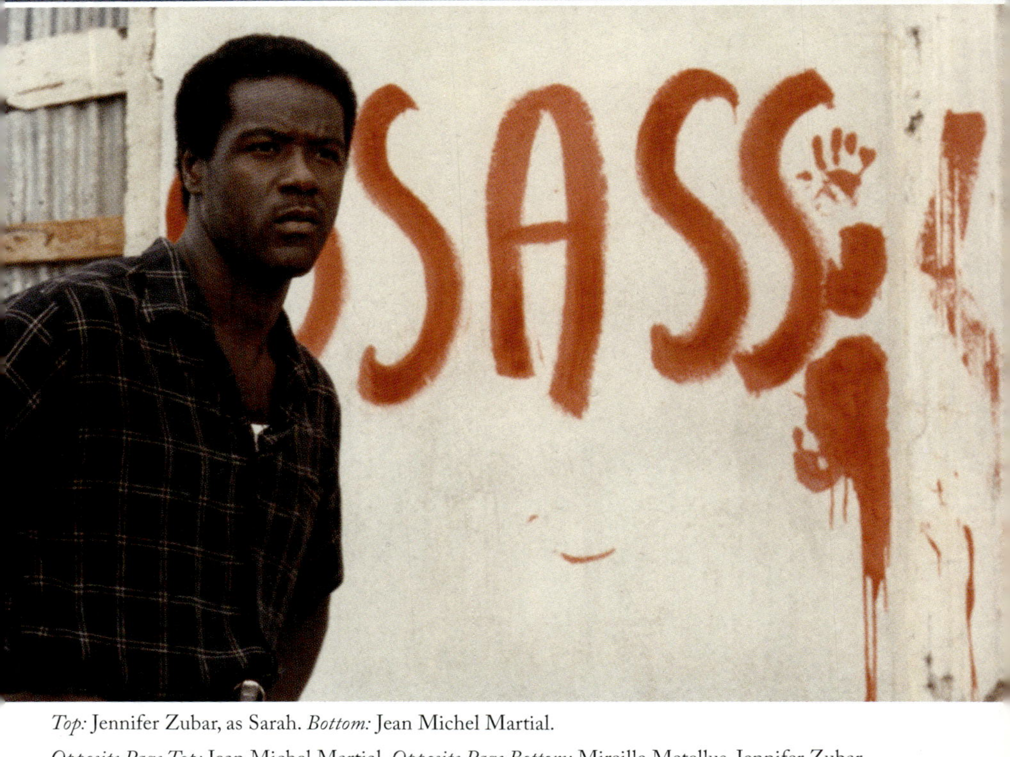

Top: Jennifer Zubar, as Sarah. *Bottom:* Jean Michel Martial.
Opposite Page Top: Jean Michel Martial. *Opposite Page Bottom:* Mireille Metellus, Jennifer Zubar.

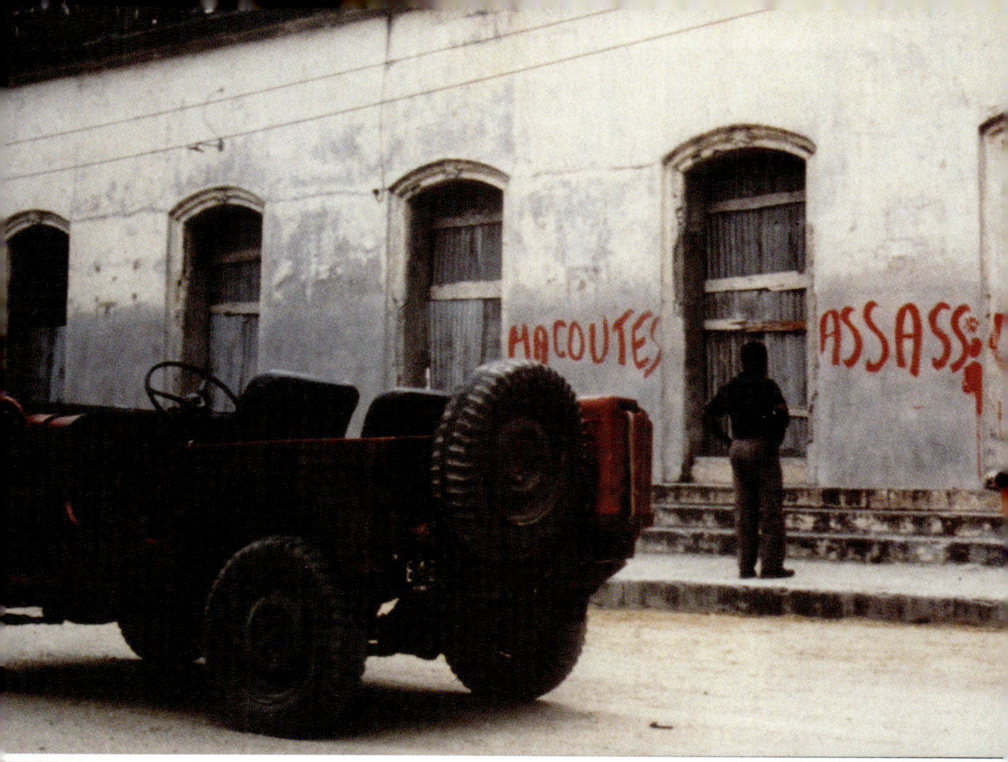

MACOUTES
ASSASS

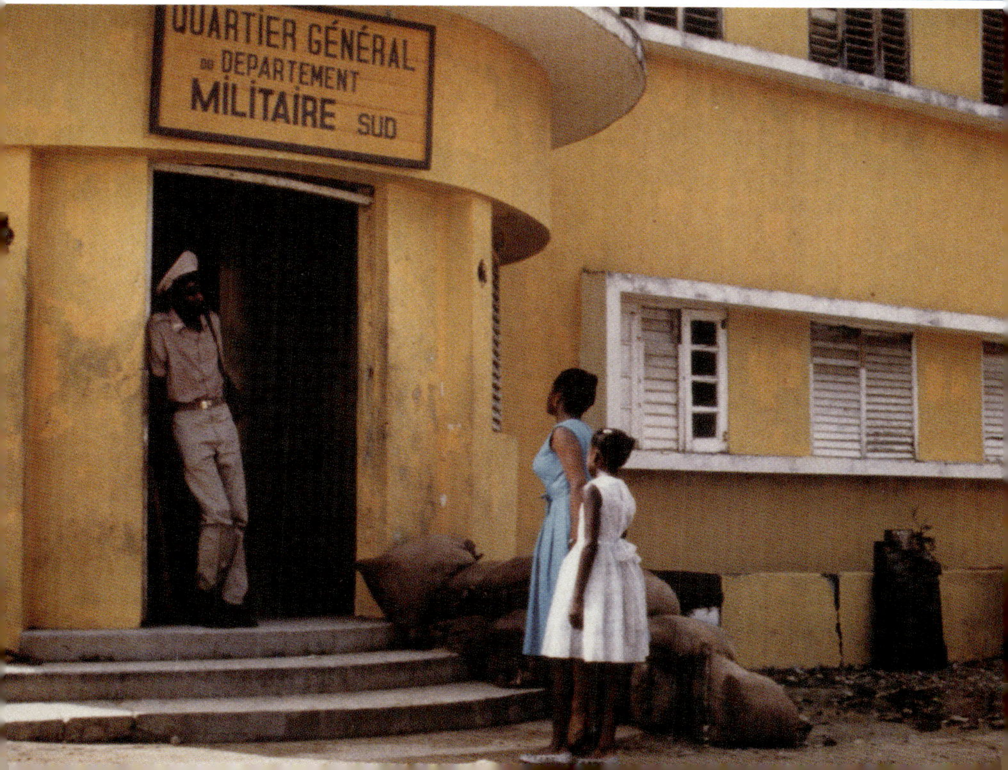

QUARTIER GÉNÉRAL
du DEPARTEMENT
MILITAIRE SUD

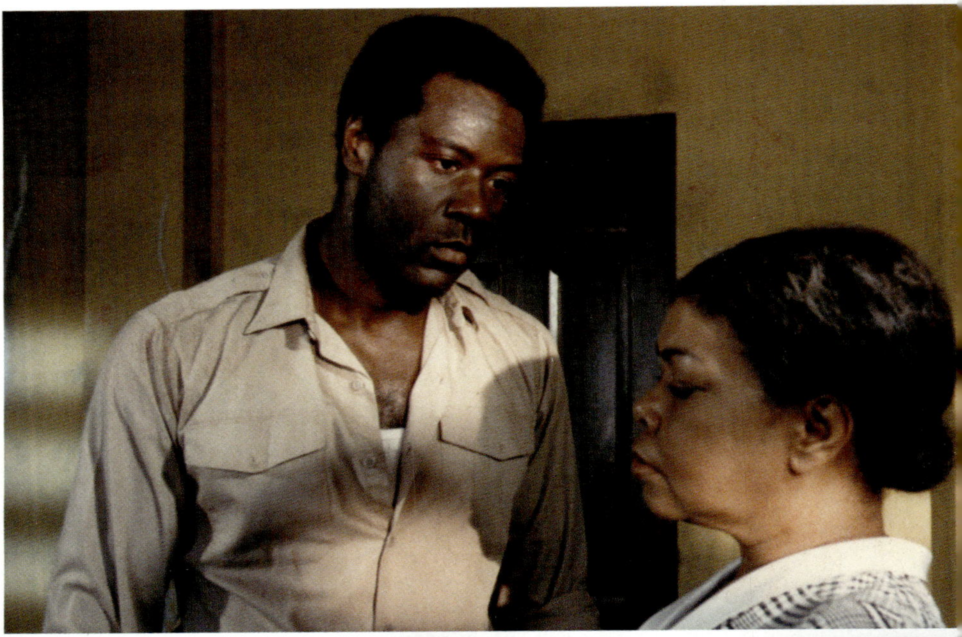

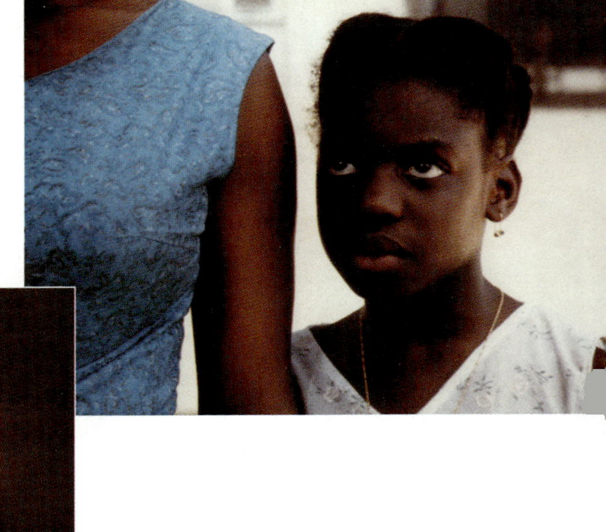

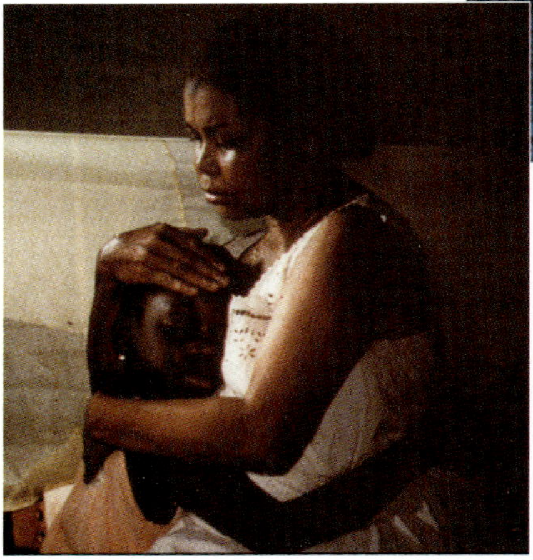

Top: Jean Michel Martial, Toto Bissainthe.
Middle: Jennifer Zubar, as Sarah.
Bottom: Jennifer Zubar, Toto Bissainthe.

Lumumba

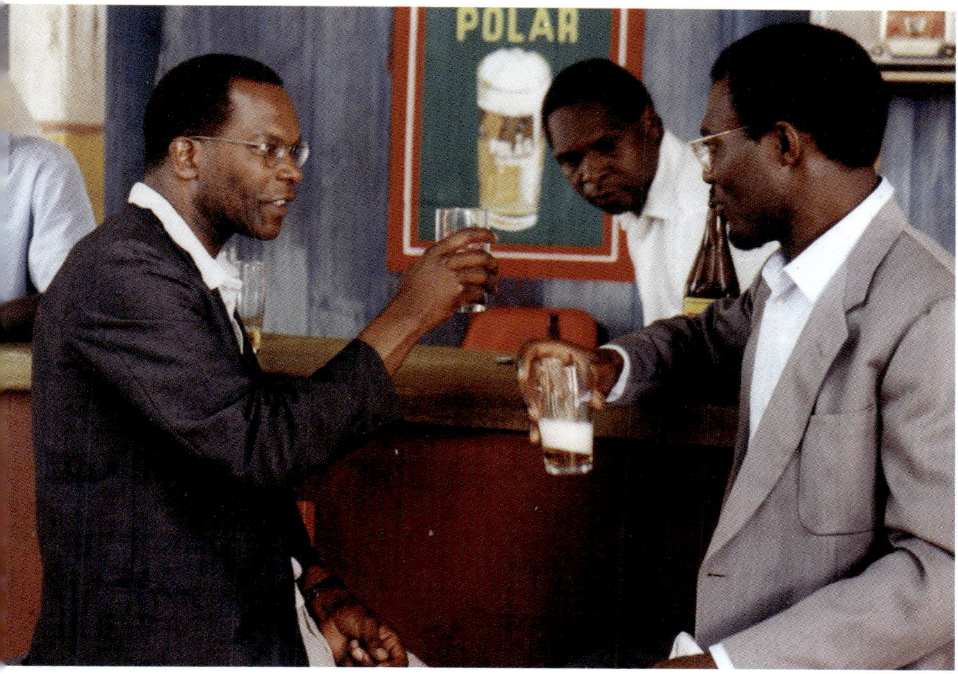

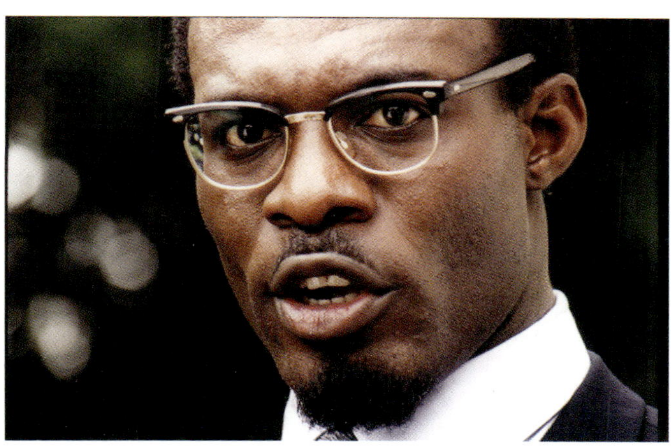

Alex Descas (left), as Joseph Désiré Mobutu, and Eriq Ebouaney (right), as Patrice Lumumba.

Eriq Ebouaney.

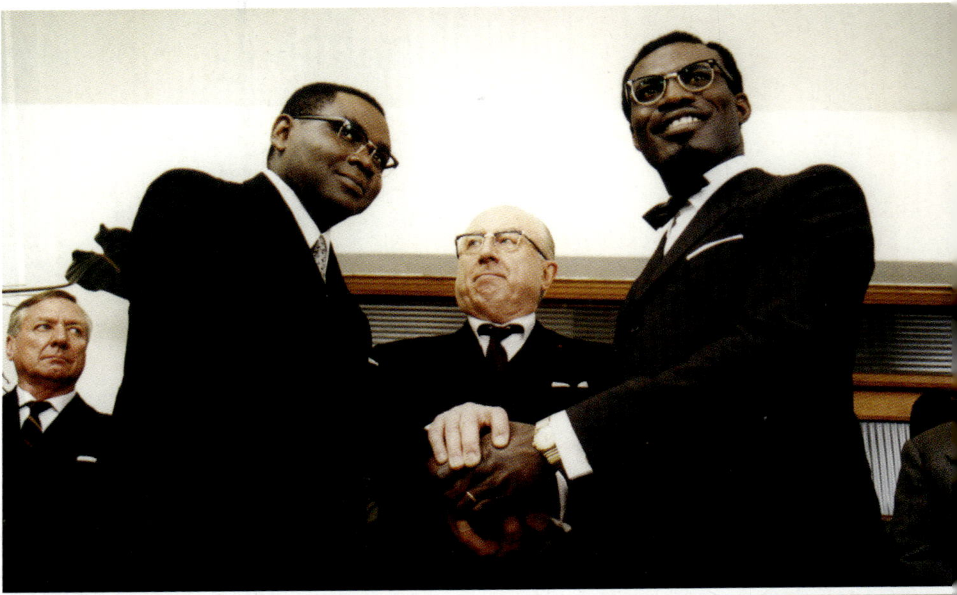

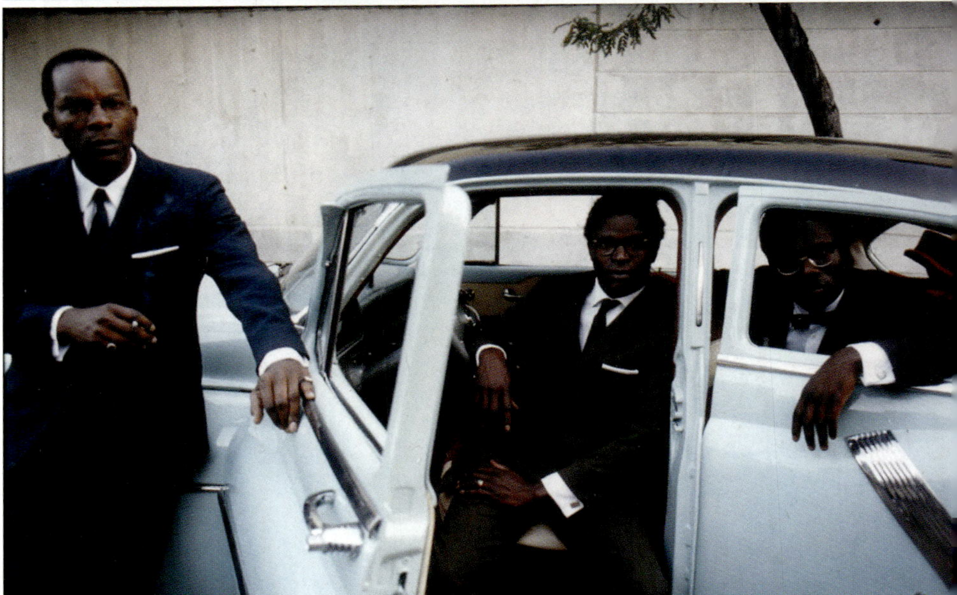

Top: Maka Kotto, as Kasa-Vubu; André Debaar, as Ganshof van der Meersch; Eriq Ebouaney.

Bottom: Alex Descas, Théopile Sowié, Eriq Ebouaney.

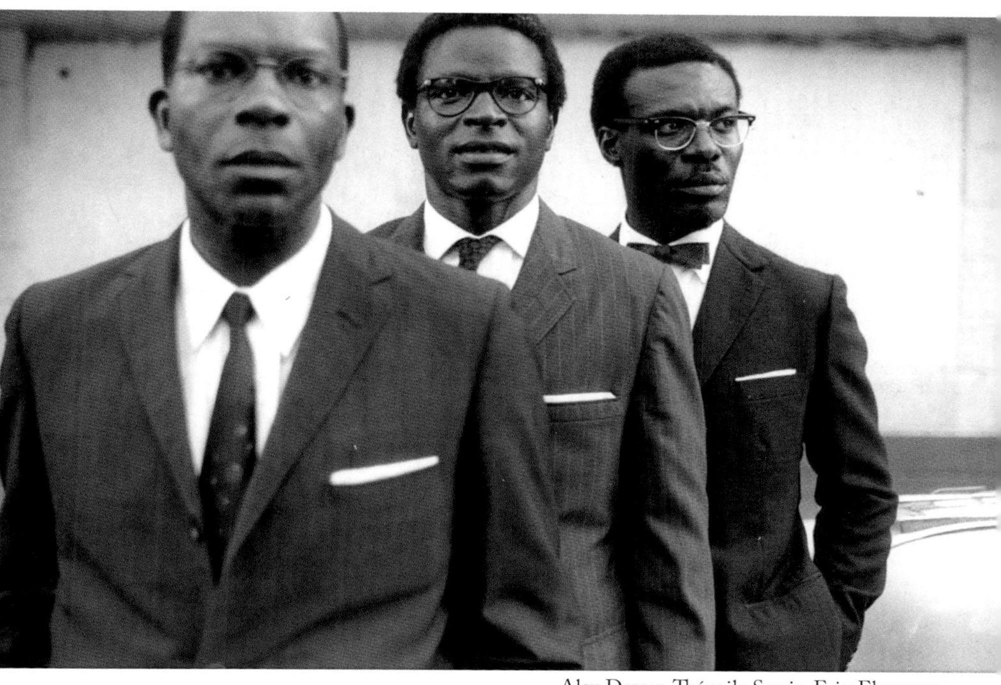

Alex Descas, Théopile Sowie, Eriq Ebouaney.

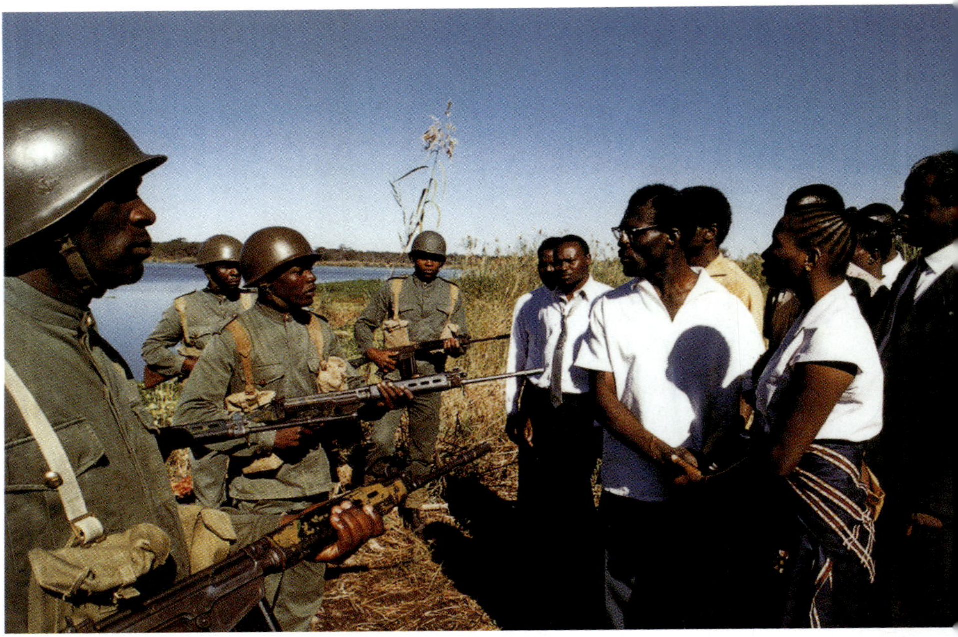

Lumumba's arrest.

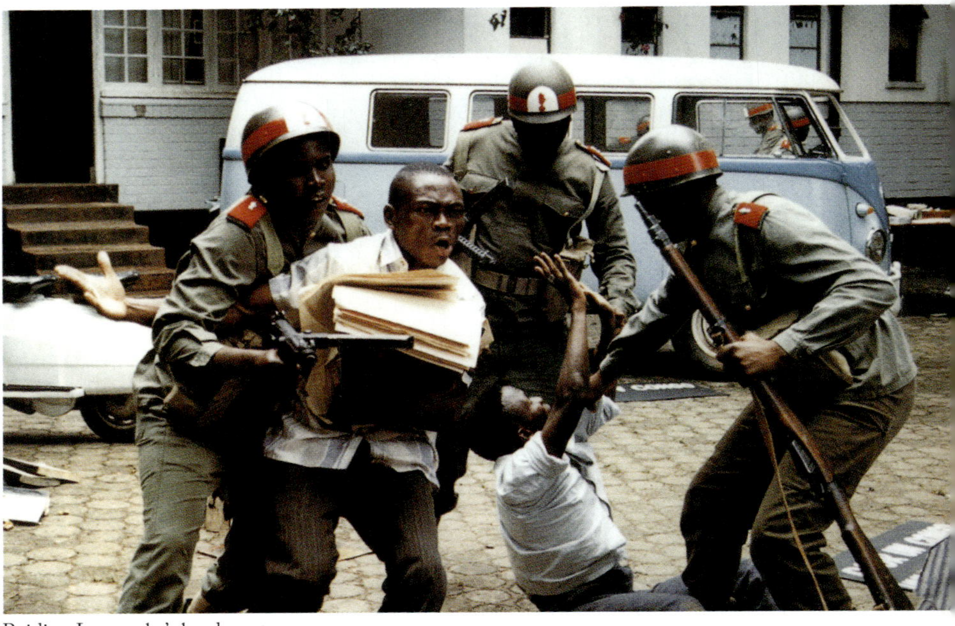

Raiding Lumumba's headquarters.

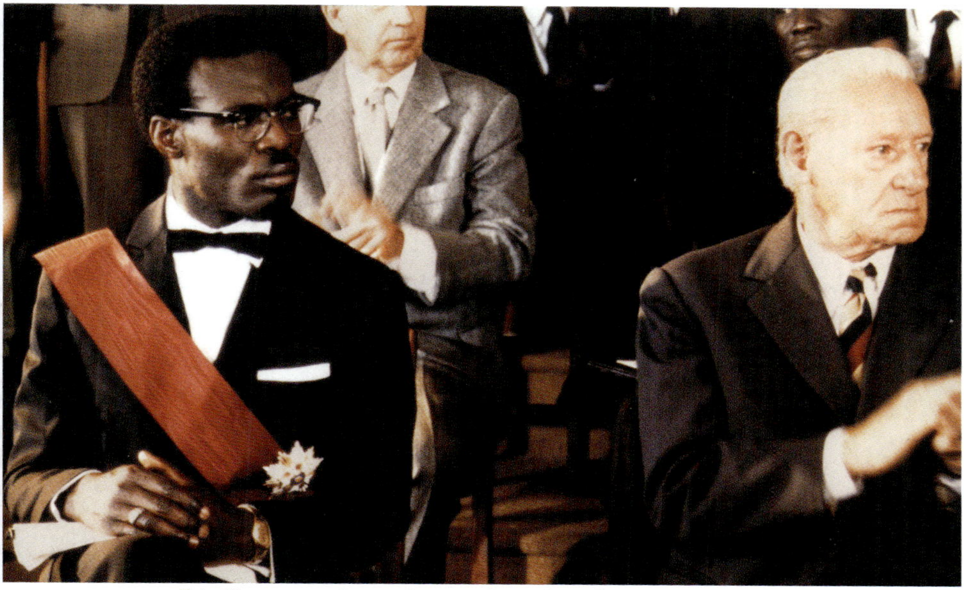

Eriq Ebouaney, as Lumumba, attending independence inauguration, June 1960. © *Robert Lebeck*

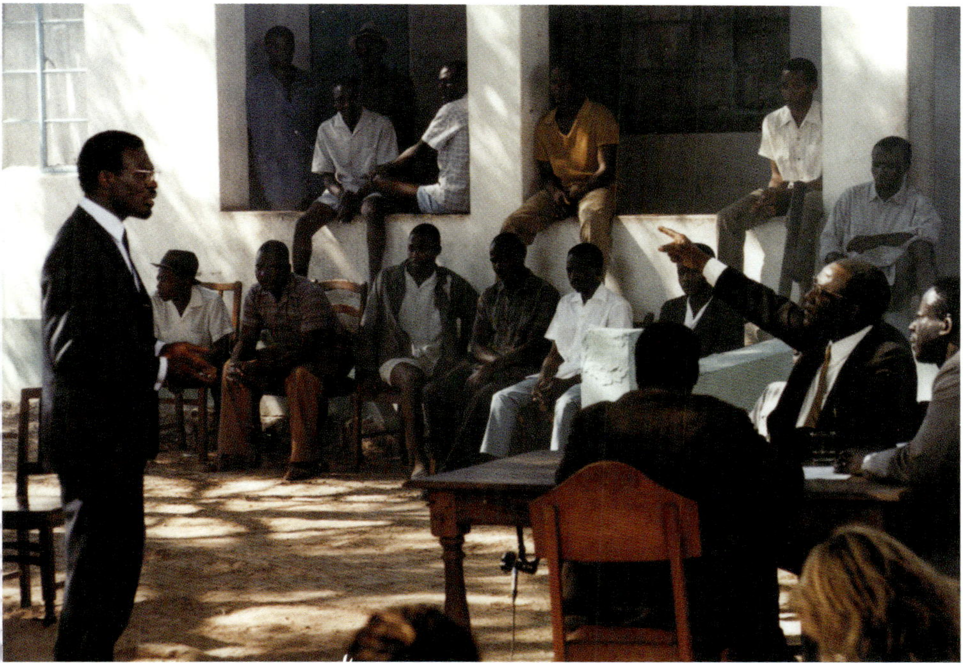

Eriq Ebouaney, as Lumumba, speaking at political meeting.

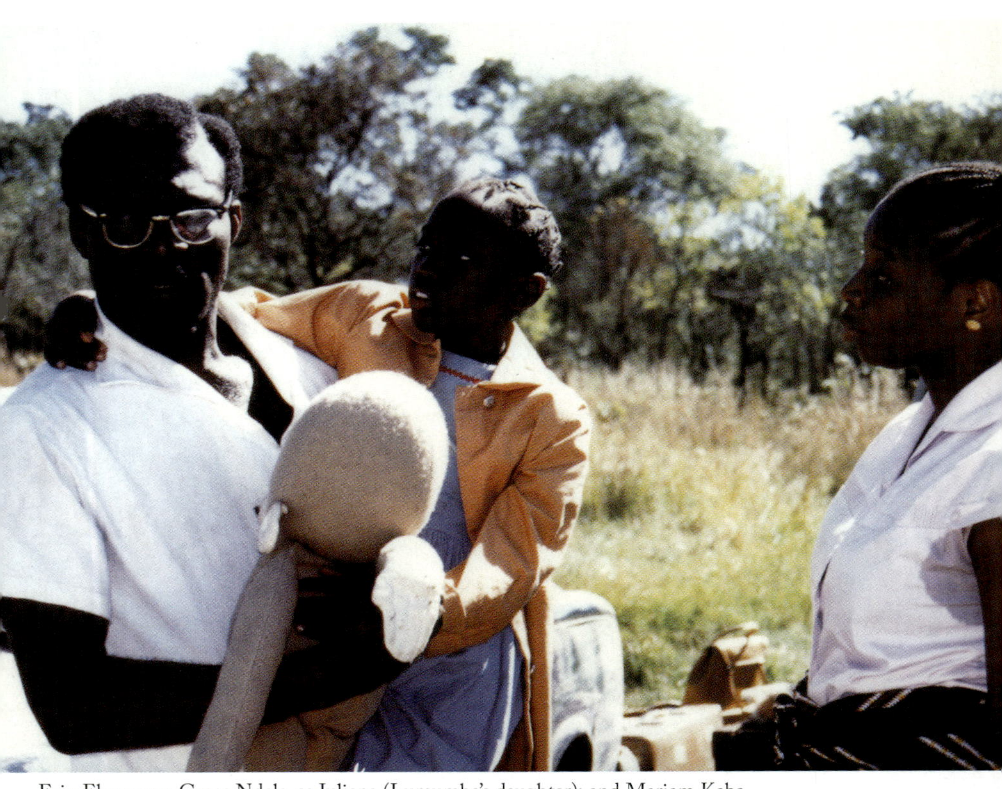

Eriq Ebouaney; Grace Ndala, as Juliana (Lumumba's daughter); and Mariam Kaba, as Pauline (Lumumba's wife).

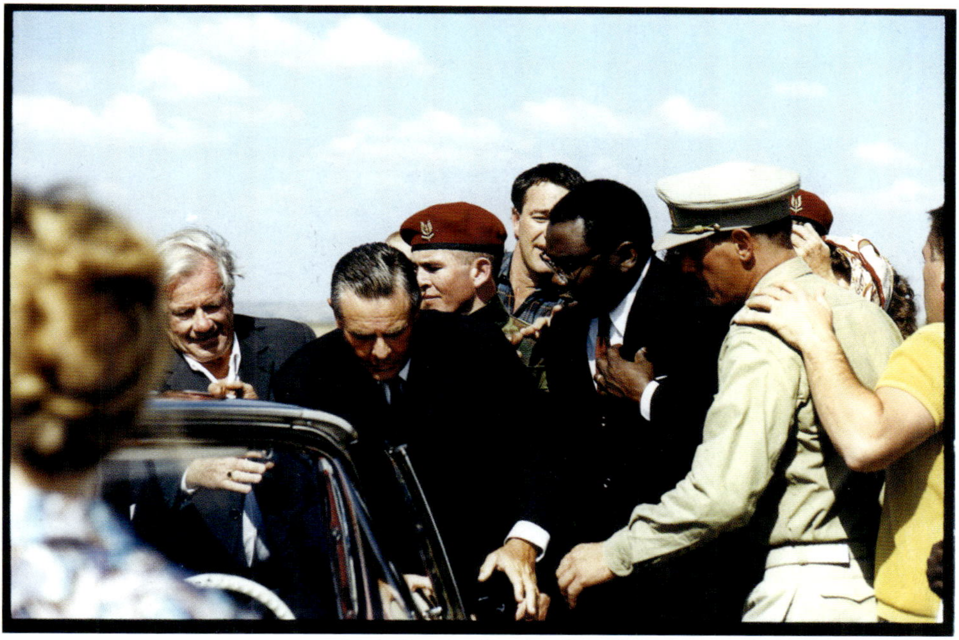

Maka Kotto, as President Kasa-Vubu, being pushed by Belgian refugees.

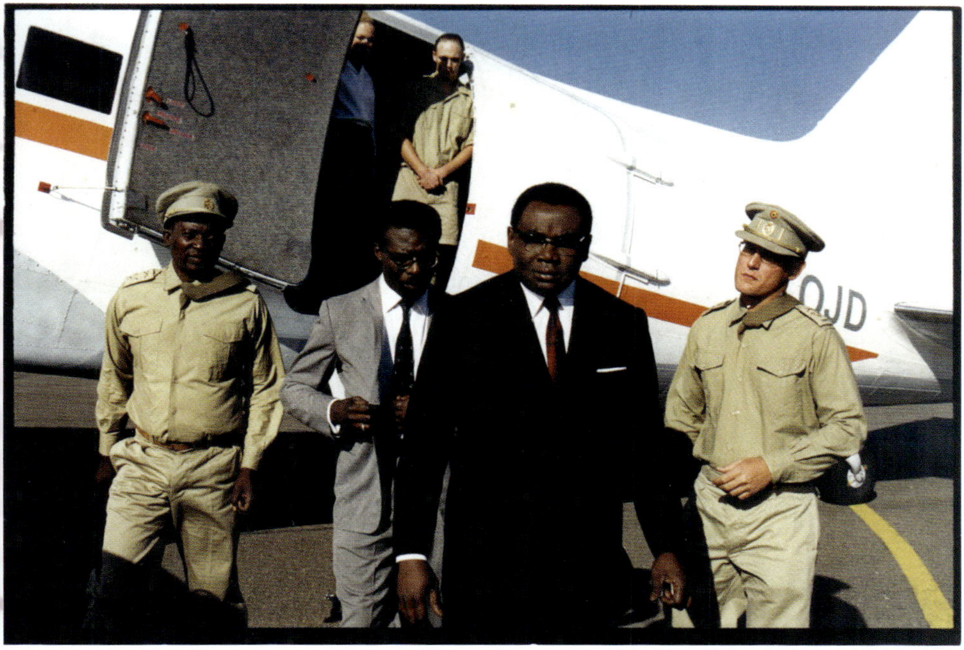

Eriq Ebouaney, as Lumumba, and Maka Kotto, as President Kasa-Vubu, landing in Njili airport.

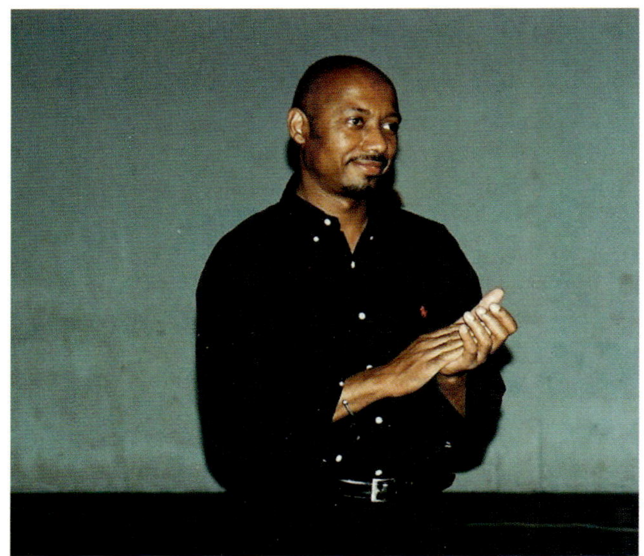

Raoul Peck at the St. Bart's Film Festival, 2001. © *Rosemond Gréaux*

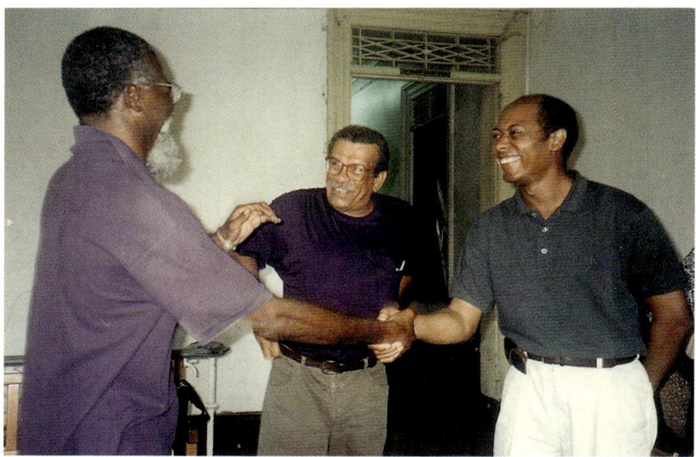

Raoul Peck with Earl Warner and Derek Walcott at
Carifesta in Trinidad, 1995. © *Georgia Popplewell*

Almost immediately, a man in uniform appears in the doorway. Because of the backlighting, his features can't be distinguished. Sarah's face suddenly lights up. This man, his silhouette, is like a strange, mystical apparition to her, possibly reminding her of her father. The man steps forward. Indeed, his features are those of François Jansson . . . Sarah smiles.

INT. SHOP—DAY

When the man enters the shop, his features are no longer those of François Jansson. It is Janvier. Acting flirtatious, he comes closer to her.

JANVIER

May I come in, charming young lady?

Silence. Sarah fans herself.

JANVIER

Did you have a good trip?
(trying on a pair of eyeglasses)
How do they look?
(pulling a face, trying on another pair)
A bit eccentric, don't you think?

Silence.

JANVIER

(coming even closer)

Here, try them on!

He puts the eyeglasses on her nose, takes a mirror, and holds it up to her face. Sarah looks comical with eyeglasses that are much too big for her.

JANVIER

Pretty funny, isn't it? You see, I'm your friend.
I'm not mean.

*Sarah clumsily removes the unwieldy glasses, manages to fold them,
and then carefully puts them down on the counter.*

JANVIER

(taking a necktie and holding it up in front of his collar)
How's your father?

SARAH

I don't know.

JANVIER

You're still mad at me?

SARAH

That's my grandmother's tie.

JANVIER

Looks good on me, don't you think?

VOICE

Give them to me, I'll wrap them up for you.

*Grandmother is standing right behind Janvier, still winded from
running.*

JANVIER

(turning around)
Oh, Madame Desrouillere!

(pause)
No, that won't be necessary.
(handing the glasses back)
I was passing by and seized the opportunity to
see this dear young lady again.

GRANDMOTHER
(to Sarah)
Go upstairs!

JANVIER
(exiting)
You didn't put up any flag? You should be celebrating like everyone else. It could be misunderstood.

GRANDMOTHER
(with innocent irony)
People bought so much black cloth that I had
none left for myself. You see—
(pointing to the shelves, walking toward him)
—with all these celebrations!

Janvier goes up to Sarah and looks at her.

GRANDMOTHER
Don't you touch her! I thought there was an
amnesty.

JANVIER
(ironic)
Oh?

GRANDMOTHER

Is there an amnesty, yes or no? Apparently, you
don't really agree with the president's orders.

Grandmother stares him down.

JANVIER

(sardonic)

You must be happy to see your granddaughters
again . . .

*Silence. Janvier reaches into the back pocket of his pants and takes
out the three passports seized from Assad. He flips through them and
taps them against the palm of his hand.*

JANVIER

The winning cards have changed hands,
Madame Desrouillere. Take good care of them.
Accidents happen so easily.

*Flipping the passports between his fingers, Janvier spreads them out
into a fan shape.*

JANVIER

Give that message to Captain Jansson for me.

*He exits. Grandmother watches him. Sarah runs into the back room
of the shop.*

EXT. STREET—DAY

A rara band is marching down the street. Sarah and her girlfriend, standing with their bicycles, watch the parade go by. Sarah motions in the direction they should go for their ride.

GRACIEUX

Beware of the beach. Don't go there.

He looks distressed and sings.

GRACIEUX

Twa fèy twa rasin o . . . Jete bliye . . . Ranmase sonje o
Twa fèy twa rasin o . . . Jete bliye . . . Ranmase sonje o
[Three families, three roots . . . Throwing is forgetting . . . Picking up is remembering]

The two girls set off on their ride. We see them go past the macoutes barracks.

EXT. BEACH—DAY

The two girls are sitting side by side.

SARAH

My father's in Cuba.

GIRL

Where's Cuba?

SARAH

It's in that direction.

(gesturing with her hand)
My father is waiting for me.

GIRL
They've disappeared my father.

SARAH
Disappeared?

GIRL
They've disappeared him. That's the word they
use. No one knows where he is. But I know where
he is. Is it true your father was a *macoute*?

SARAH
No, it's not true. And he loved me a lot.

GIRL
That's got nothing to do with it.

SARAH
Yes it does. The *macoutes* kill children too.

EXT. MAIN STREET—DAY

*Sarah's face bathed in sweat. She has just leaned her bicycle against
the wall of the shop. She stares at Gracieux still sitting in the same place
as before. Her face is expressionless. Sarah stands in front of Gracieux.
They look at each other.*

GRACIEUX
Sarah.

(beat)
You've become so grown-up! So beautiful!

Silence. He squats to be level with her.

GRACIEUX
Do you remember me?
(beat)
You don't want to say hello to me?

Sarah hesitates. She goes up to him and kisses him on the cheek. She runs off and goes inside the shop.

INT. CHURCH—DAY

Sunday. Te Deum Mass for the martyrs of the War of Independence. No one can afford not to attend. The church is jam-packed. The few city dignitaries are there with their families. Janvier, sole lord and master, is sitting enthroned next to his wife. We recognize some of the faces in the audiences. Grandmother is sitting in the back with Sarah.

THE CHOIR
. . . Kyrie, eleison . . .

The priest goes up to the pulpit. The audience stands up.

PRIEST
. . . Today is a unique day in the religious history
of our country. The meeting of two sovereign and
loving wills. The will of a great pope burning with
holy zeal for the House of our Lord. The will of a
great Head of State—

Janvier looks at his wife, with a self-satisfied expression.

PRIEST
—fulfilling the heroic dream of adding a spiritual dimension to the sacred heritage of our ancestors. This agreement with Rome is the final consecration of our clergy's "Haitization" under the authority of our natural leader. Finally there exists a deep covenant between the State and the Church . . . Amen.

The faithful line up to receive the holy communion. We see the blue shoes that Madame Janvier bought in Grandmother's shop on the tiles of the central aisle. They are too tight. Grandmother looks at Madame Janvier's feet. Sarah looks at her grandmother and smiles.

EXT. STREET—DAY

Gracieux is holding a bottle and heading up a passageway between two houses. He steps out into the street.

GRACIEUX
What a sun!

A car speeds by him just as he is about to cross the street.

GRACIEUX
Lousy bourgeois. *Macaque!*

Gracieux hums the tune of a song.

GRACIEUX

. . . Haiti dear . . . It's when I left you that I
learned to love you . . .

*Suddenly he stops and, with a pensive air, goes up to the shoemaker's
workbench, grabs his hammer, and makes hammering gestures with it.
He hangs around a bit and is reprimanded by a man who is idly sitting
in front of a house. The façades of the houses are covered with images of
Duvalier.*

GRACIEUX

I've got my eye on you . . .

THE MAN

Clear off!

GRACIEUX

(knocking on the front door of a house)
Celibra Boeuf. Show your face, in God's name.
I have something to tell you. Who invented the
macoutes?

*He drinks a glassful of liquor and chases after a woman who walks
by, whose skirt he tries to lift up. He spins around.*

GRACIEUX

God says he didn't. Satan says he didn't. What
about Duvalier?
(with a nasal accent, imitating Duvalier)
Duvalier says, "Haiti, your mother's cunt!"

Gracieux throws the empty bottle against a wall and walks on.

EXT. MACOUTES BARRACKS—BALCONY COURTYARD (FLASHBACK)—DAY

Gracieux is sitting in the dust in the middle of the barracks' courtyard. He is in a pitiful state. Tied up like a "top," his hands behind his back, he can hardly breathe. François Jansson is standing at a slight distance, not daring to intervene.

FRANÇOIS JANSSON
(annoyed, to Janvier)

That's enough now.

JANVIER

Keep out of it.

GRACIEUX

Gentlemen, have pity. What have I done to you?

JANVIER

Shut up! I'm in charge of this investigation!

JANSSON
(stepping closer to Janvier, ironically)

Investigation!

JANVIER
(pointing to Gracieux)

See that mound of flesh, Captain? It's nothing
to me.

(striking him)

I can make it disappear in a snap.

(snapping his fingers)

That goes for all subversives.

GRACIEUX

Please, Janvier. Mercy.

JANVIER

You just shut up. Who gave you permission to
speak my name?

*Janvier strikes Gracieux. It's a powerful, dull blow, immediately fol-
lowed by another. They take off Gracieux's pants. In a brusque motion,
Janvier shoves his stick into the man's anus (as previously seen from afar,
scene . . .). He cries out like an animal being slaughtered.*

SARAH

(covering up Gracieux's cry)

No!!!

JANVIER

You make her shut up. Make her shut up.

JANSSON

(rushing at Janvier)

Bastard!

The men overpower Jansson.

Gracieux's swollen and blood-drenched face.

INT. ATTIC—DAY

*Sarah, in underpants, is tying a belt around her waist. She inserts
her father's 45mm gun. She slips her dress on again.*

EXT. STREET—DAY

Sarah mounts her bicycle and rides away. Gracieux runs after her.

GRACIEUX
(almost in a whisper)
Sarah!

But Sarah doesn't hear or see him. She is already at the end of the street and nearly out of sight. Gracieux is left standing in the middle of the road.

EXT. BEACH—DAY

Sarah and her friend are bicycling down to the beach on the sand. They pass by the militiamen's barracks again. In front of the barracks, a macoute tries to stop them playfully.

MACOUTE
(whistling)
So, sweethearts, are you coming to see Uncle Jean?

Janvier is standing against a wall watching them go by.

EXT. ROAD LEADING TO BEACH—DAY

Gracieux is running to the beach so fast that he loses a sandal. Voice over of the two girls singing.

EXT. BEACH—DAY

The two girls are seen from the back, sitting together, singing, exchanging a nursery rhyme and Haitian proverbs.

TWO GIRLS

... All sea creatures eat men, but only the shark has a bad reputation ... Hit the dog, wait for his master ... Iron cuts iron ...

They set off again, on foot, holding their bicycles. They stop dead in their tracks when they catch sight of Janvier, then walk on. Janvier rushes at them. They try to run away but Janvier ends up catching Sarah's friend. He forces her into the bushes and tries to rape her. Sarah rushes to help her friend, threatening Janvier with her weapon. When he tries to prevent her from shooting she fires. Janvier, still not realizing he has been shot, falls down dead.

As the girls leave, we see Gracieux crying, on his knees, holding a pistol.

VOICE OVER (SARAH)

Many years later, whereas the demons are constantly baring their teeth, whereas the uniforms are still being stained with blood, whereas my story ceases to be just my own and has become everyone's story, I sometimes wake up soaked in sweat. Then the departed grandmother says to me: It's only a bad dream my darling, only a bad dream.

The panoramic shot comes to a standstill. The sand, some trees, the sea, the sky.

END.

Lumumba (feature; 2000)

I think of *Lumumba* as the film I would love to have seen when I was twelve, but didn't because at that time such films didn't exist: a film that would make sense of the world from a different point of view, a political one; one that would help me understand who I am and where I belong, and that doesn't conceal the complexity of my world. Instead of this, the kids of my generation were constantly decoding Hollywood in order to have any ownership of the stories we were being told over and over.

Growing up in Haiti, one could permanently feel like a kid who has to peek through windows from behind barricades, behind everyone else, with only a partial, obstructed view, to watch a movie on the screen, while everybody else—the Western world—would get to see the movies like regular paying customers. With *Lumumba*, I felt somehow that I was letting all my friends in like paying customers. We could watch a film—one that spoke to us—from a comfortable point of view at last.

We shot *Lumumba* in 1999 in Zimbabwe, Mozambique, and Brussels. My cabinet minister position had ended back in 1997.

It is impossible to talk about *Lumumba* without talking about why I became a filmmaker. I don't believe in the dogma of entertainment above all. There is no inherent contradiction between entertainment and quality content, nor is there any correlation between a boring film and one with serious content.

My documentary on Lumumba had dealt with my family and

the Haitian immigration to the Congo. In *Lumumba*, the feature film, the story is about Prime Minister Patrice Lumumba and his assassination. It was a hard story for me to find because it was complicated to understand the real story. It took me several drafts before the screenplay could dare to tell it from Lumumba's point of view. In many of the drafts, I tried to tell the story through characters other than Lumumba until I was able finally to tell it from his point of view.

Depicting human psychology, human complexity, is more difficult in film than, say, in theater. Cinema tends to contaminate true stories, to reduce their complexity and how well they capture what is true. Furthermore, the world of cinema has not been particularly integrated in its first hundred years.

In my first drafts, I, too, featured a white man, a Swiss doctor, to tell the story of Lumumba. I say "too" because this has been the only approach allowed—or financeable, which is the same thing—for films with black heroes, including many quite good films, like *Cry Freedom*, which tells the story of the great South African political thinker Steve Biko through the eyes of Donald Woods, a white journalist; or, more recently, the more caricatural *The King of Scotland*, which tells the story of Idi Amin of Uganda through the eyes of his personal physician, a white Englishman. So I was also "contaminated."

I remember how, in one of the first drafts, I had the sister of the Swiss doctor return to Congo to pick up the body of her brother and meet one of the few Congolese doctors, her brother's friend, who then tells the story of Lumumba. You see all the gymnastics I had to go through to introduce that character? And the next step was to tell the story from the point of view of that doctor, who was the closest friend of Lumumba. So I had to invent a character that did not exist to tell the story of the real character. And that storytelling character had to be white. And this is what I mean, too, when I talk about stolen images. The mainstream establishment, the Hollywood establishment especially, wants to maintain certain ways of telling stories and not others, whatever their reasons and explanations may be. So I had to find a way to steal my images back. And for me, that meant telling the story from Patrice Lumumba's point of view.

By definition, those in power tend to be the very last ones to think that things could be other than how they are. The world of the slave-owner is a totally coherent world. Those in power tend to be the ones who are the most surprised when change comes!

There isn't a list of the top ten black political films of all time. Do you know why? Because there aren't ten. There aren't even five.

After I finished *Lumumba*, I thought that I was done making films. I had made the film I had always dreamed of seeing when I was twelve. This was it.

—RP

Lumumba
Return to the Congo
A film by Raoul Peck
Screenplay by Raoul Peck and Pascal Bonitzer

CAST AND CREW

Main Cast

PATRICE EMERY LUMUMBA	Eriq Ebouaney
JOSEPH MOBUTU	Alex Descas
MAURICE MPOLO	Théophile Sowié
JOSEPH KASA-VUBU	Maka Kotto
GODEFROID MUNUNGO	Dieudonné Kapongo
MOÏSE TSHOMBÉ	Pascal N'Zonzi
WALTER J. GANSHOF VAN DER MEERSCH	Andreé Debaar
JOSEPH OKITO	Cheik Doukouré
THOMAS KANZA	Makena Diop
PAULINE LUMUMBA	Mariam Kaba
GENERAL EMILE JANSSENS	Rudi Delhem

Main Crew

DIRECTED BY Raoul Peck
WRITTEN BY Raoul Peck and Pascal Bonitzer
PRODUCED BY Jacques Bidou and Raoul Peck
ORIGINAL MUSIC BY Jean-Claude Petit
CINEMATOGRAPHY BY Bernard Lutic
FILM EDITING BY Jacques Comets
CASTING BY Sylvie Brocheré
ART DIRECTION BY André Fonsny
COSTUME DESIGN BY Charlotte David

Africa is speaking to you.
Yes! Africa says F . . . you to us . . . and they're right!
—Georges Simenon

A prisoner who was once idolized by the crowds . . . His very
existence transforms regrets into hope.
—Jean-Paul Sartre, "The Political Thought of Patrice Lumumba"

to Aimé Césaire

EXT. KATANGA—FOREST CLEARING—DAWN

Images in black and white. Elongated shapes vaguely resembling white bags. Three bags are removed from a hole by two men, one of whom is wearing a handkerchief over his mouth.

> **VOICES**
> Take the other end . . . Wait. Hold here . . . I'll pull the feet.
> Can we rest a while. I'm tired.
> We've got to finish now or we'll be at it all night.

Music: a loud requiem mass. Title, followed by credits: white letters, black background.

The two men pile up the makeshift sacks in the back of a truck. The image moves gradually from black and white to color.

> **VOICE OVER (MAN)**
> *(with a Parisian accent, over titles)*
> How did we come to this? Africa is a strange place, you know. It's Joseph Conrad's Africa . . . not Club Med . . .

EXT. KATANGA—SAVANNA ROAD—DAWN

Music.

The images are now in full color. Aerial view, wide shot: on the horizon a public works truck approaches in a cloud of dust on a savanna road. The image gets closer and circles around to the back of the truck.

There, between two barrels, along with shovels and pickaxes, lay the three long shroud-like sacks.

Music breaks up several times, failing to take form.

We continue to move closer to one of the shrouds to the point of identifying a face behind a sheet, which has come undone and is now flapping in the wind.

VOICE OVER (ANOTHER MAN)
(with a Belgian accent)

A ninety-year regime destroyed in just a few months. Scratch the surface and savagery reappears.

CROSSFADE
FROM THE
FACE TO:

EXT. LEOPOLDVILLE—STREET—DAY

Black and white: close up of a man smiling. He's big and slim with a thin moustache and a goatee beard: Patrice Lumumba is cheered by the crowd. The music continues, though now it is mixed with African rhythms.

Credits continue. The music is interrupted.

VOICE OVER
(with the sound of ice cubes clinking in a glass)

So, we should have left it all to the Russians? The uranium, the diamonds, the copper?

ANOTHER VOICE OVER

In any case we had to . . .

EXT. KATANGA—SAVANNA—DAWN

Color images again. A large metal drum inside of which burns a raging fire. Hands throw bits and pieces of something we cannot make out into the fire. Various instruments, saws, and petrol cans are strewn about.

VOICE OVER

Get rid of the bodies . . Imagine the pilgrimage
site this would have been . . .

The music starts again. Credits continue over the flames.

VOICES

Shit, it won't cut anymore.
Add some acid. It's the flesh that makes it difficult . . .
Where are you going?
I've gotta get some air . . .

EXT. ARCHIVAL FOOTAGE—DAY

The streets of Paris. Students—for the most part, black—are being beaten with batons by uniformed police. Placards with the image of the "martyr" Lumumba are trampled underfoot. Similar scenes are repeated elsewhere: Brussels, Cairo, Tunis. An embassy burns.

EXT. KATANGA—SAVANNA—DAWN

Seen from afar through a heat glaze (as in the style of Jean-François Millet's painting Angelus), two men are standing around a drum.

VOICE OVER (WOMAN)
(clinking ice in a glass)

They say Kennedy would have freed him?

VOICE OVER (MAN)
(with an American accent)

What about the CIA. Wasn't he killed just before Kennedy entered the White House?

VOICE OVER (MAN)

So what?

Music. Rest of credits. Sounds of a fire as it swells, crackling, splintering.

EXT. KATANGA—FOREST ROAD—NIGHT

Headlights illuminate a forest road. The ground is wet, sodden. An incongruous convoy of dark limousines passes through the jungle vegetation.

Caption: Congo, January 17, 1961

INT./EXT. KATANGA—FOREST ROAD—CAR—NIGHT

In the back of one of the cars, three men, faces battered, hands tied behind their backs, stare at the road ahead in silence: Patrice Lumumba, Joseph Okito, Maurice Mpolo.

Close up of Lumumba's bloodied face.

VOICE OVER (LUMUMBA)

Get rid of the bodies . . . their one obsession. As
if that would erase everything. It took me a while
to understand . . . to understand that the game was
fixed from the start. It took me a while to recognize
the good guys from the bad . . . to understand that
I arrived too soon. Forty years too soon.

EXT. KATANGA—FOREST CLEARING—NIGHT

The cars have pulled into a circle in the forest, their headlights glar-
ing. Silhouettes are differentiated, throwing monstrous shadows against
the dark curtain formed by the forest. Silent comings and goings as in a
well-planned choreography. African and European men, some in suits,
others in uniforms.

VOICE OVER (LUMUMBA)

That is something they do not forgive.

A Belgian in civilian clothes brings Mpolo, who growls something
in a language we don't understand, out of the car. He is placed in front
of a tree. Things are happening very quickly. A burst of gunfire. Mpolo
falls to the ground. A few groans of agony in the night. The crisp sound
of a coup de grâce.

VOICE OVER (LUMUMBA)

And if I had won? Perhaps I too would have
become a pathetic tyrant in a leopard-skin hat.
Maybe I would have done like all the others. Pil-
laging, work camps, waste, debt? No, in truth this

country didn't deserve that. And yet, one day . . . a
day will come. And that day . . . ahhh.

Long sigh. A calm settles against the sounds of crickets.

FADE TO:

EXT. LEOPOLDVILLE—STREET—DAY

Caption: Leopoldville, July 1957

A street in an industrial area of Leopoldville. Shopkeepers sing the praises of their goods to passersby on foot, on bicycle, and in cars. There are a lot of European faces. In short, it is daily life in a thriving colony.

A bus stops. We discover a young man, a little awkward in a suit that's a size too small for him. Patrice Lumumba. Before crossing he buys a doughnut, which he eats in one mouthful. He wipes his hands in a handkerchief that is as big as it is immaculate, while he crosses the busy street.

EXT. A LARGE BREWERY—DAY

On the facade of a big gateway, a signpost with a giant glass of beer, bubbles, foam: "Polar freshness—Coolness under the Tropics."

Patrice goes up to the security guard who checks his papers before waving him into the brewery.

INT./EXT. BREWERY—DAY

Patrice follows the general manager through the vast bottling corridors. One of the workers recognizes him and greets him with enthusiasm.

The general manager of the brewery is a cigar-smoking Belgian. He's as tall, dry, and skinny as his assistant manager is red-faced, sweaty, and pot-bellied. He rolls up his sleeves and shows a foreman how to fix the safety valve on a large funnel-shaped vat. The assistant manager shows up and introduces Patrice to the manager.

A long corridor in the basement of the brewery. The assistant manager, Beulemans, fans himself with a folded newspaper, while trying to follow the conversation.

MANAGER

You spent a year in jail?

PATRICE

That's all in the past. Now I need to work, and I know how to.

MANAGER

It seems that you're good at talking to people. That's exactly what we need. Here, in Leoville, people are very difficult. They try to undermine us by playing dirty. They spread rumors . . .

(starting to get worked up)

In short, our beer is up against a competitor who is unfair, base, and has no scruples . . .

PATRICE

The competition is Primus?

MANAGER

Yes, King Kasa's beer, as they say. Since this dirty ... since this Kasa-Vubu cleaned up in the local elections, with his party of b ... with his Abako party, their profit has skyrocketed—
(he indicates the ceiling)
—and ours has, well ...
(he points to the floor)
In a word, don't let it be heard, but our business is floundering. If you can help by firming things up again ...

BEULEMANS

You could say, ha ha!

Patrice and the manager look at him; he tries to explain.

BEULEMANS

They say our beer causes impotence.
(becoming worked up)
They'll say anything!

MANAGER

(silencing him with a gesture)
If you show me that you are capable of sorting out the situation, I'll give you the salary of an assistant manager.

They reach the end of the corridor where there is a staircase leading out to a big courtyard.

MANAGER
(*pointing his cigar*)
Like him. A decent salary, isn't that right, Beulemans?

BEULEMANS
A very decent salary, sir.

MANAGER
Yes, but you must earn it. You'll go everywhere, giving away free samples of beer, but in a month, I want things to have picked up.

PATRICE
I've a free hand?

BEULEMANS
In a manner of speaking, ha ha!

Patrice and the manager look at him. He immediately stops laughing.

EXT. BAR NA BISO—TERRACE—DAY

Patrice is in the company of two pretty girls. He has two employees stack four cases of Polar beer on the floor. He takes a case and showily puts it on the table.

The customers sit up and pay attention. Passersby begin to stop, until they form a compact circle around the terrace to hear Patrice speak.

PATRICE
Come closer, my friends, come on up. Have a taste. It's free.

PASSERBY

The girls?

(laughter)

PATRICE

The beer, smart ass, the beer!

The girls uncap the bottles and start handing them out.

PATRICE

And not just any beer! The best, the queen of
beers, Polar! Polar, the freshness of the pole right
here in the tropics! The beer of Congolese good-
will and fraternity!

ONLOOKER

Not for me, thanks. Polar beer makes you impotent. Everyone knows that!

PATRICE

Well, what do you say to that, girls?

HELENE

(wrapping her arm around his neck and kissing him)
I say that you're the best, Patrice, the strongest.
All of you there, and all the men of this town, not
one of you can match him!

PATRICE

She's quite a charmer. But drink, and you'll see,
or rather your wife will see, if Polar beer makes you
impotent. It's the jealous ones who say that, because in fact the opposite is true! Polar beer is the
beer for real men.

ANOTHER ONLOOKER
I'm for Primus! Long live King Kasa!

PATRICE
All right! The competition reveals itself! I'm all for dialogue, sir! I support democracy! King Kasa is very good! Abako is a strong party! It's the party of the Bakongo, and the Bakongo are the majority here in Leoville.

ONLOOKER
You can say that again!

PATRICE
But the Congolese National Movement is good as well, in fact, it's even better! It's the party for all Congolese, like Polar is the beer for all Congolese!

OTHER ONLOOKER
I know him! It's Patrice Lumumba! He's a Tetela.

PATRICE
And so? Tetela or Bakongo, we are all Congolese. Right, girls?

GIRL
You said it, baby . . .

OTHER GIRL (MARIE-JOSEE)
See, she's a Lulua and her, a Kikongo. We're all Congolese! All brothers and sisters in the greatest, the most beautiful country in Africa!

ONLOOKER

And the richest!

OTHER ONLOOKER

But who has the wealth? It's not us, sir, not the
poor niggers.

PATRICE

We'll see about that, but shhh—
(gesturing that somebody is listening)
—for now, let's drink! Polar for everyone! It's
on me!

ANOTHER ONE

In that case, long live the MNC!

ANOTHER

Long live Abako!

PATRICE

And I say, long live Congo! Long live a free
Congo!

A VOICE

(more confident than the others)
Long live independence!

*Patrice turns toward the direction of the voice. He finds a young,
good-looking man, with delicate intellectual glasses, who gives him a
friendly smile.*

PATRICE

What vigor, young man! Come closer, try our
Polar beer.

There is no more beer in the cases: it's all been handed out. The bottles are now being passed from hand to hand.

PATRICE

Well here, let me offer you this beer, straight
from my own personal supply.
(taking a bottle from his pocket)
Certain occasions merit a little sacrifice.

He takes the young man by the arm and leads him to the bar, while along the way he greets people and even stops to give a girl two friendly pecks on the cheek.

YOUNG MAN

(having trouble following him)
Mr. Lumumba, I . . . I'm very . . . very happy to
finally meet you . . .

PATRICE

(turning to shake his hand)
Patrice. Pleased to meet you. And you are?

YOUNG MAN

Désiré . . . Joseph Désiré Mobutu.

INT./EXT. BAR NA BISO—DAY

They reach the bar. Patrice raises two fingers in sign to the barman, who repeats his gesture.

PATRICE

Something to drink for our friend Joseph here.

The barman puts two beers on the counter, each a different brand.

PATRICE

What are you trying to do to me, brother? I act like a fool to give your dump some atmosphere and you serve me Primus.

BARMAN

There's nothing left, Patrice. Your promotion has used up all my stock.

PATRICE

You've got to order more, then! If you don't double your stock, you won't be able to hold out.
(turning to Joseph)
Only one Polar left, which one do you want?

JOSEPH

Let's have some glasses and share it.

PATRICE

Good idea! To our health!

JOSEPH

To the future!

Music. The party is going strong. Patrice surveys his work with pleasure.

JOSEPH

I read all your articles in the *Courier d'Afrique.* They are really well written. I'd like to write like that.

Lumumba (feature; 2000)   **225**

PATRICE

You want to write? It's easy . . .

JOSEPH
(embarrassed)

In fact I . . . I've already submitted some articles . . . I've done portraits of the mayor . . . the chiefs . . .

Patrice looks at him, intrigued.

JOSEPH

Published articles? Désiré Joseph . . . I don't recognize the name . . . and I read all the newspapers . . .
(laughing)
I'm competitive! If I read one that's better written than mine, I'm jealous . . . Désiré Joseph?

One of the girls has plugged in a record player and put on a 45. A cha-cha-cha starts up.

Song: Cathééérinnnn ohhh . . . Cathééérinnnn ohhh

JOSEPH

Joseph Désiré Mobutu. But my pen name is Jean de Banzy, because I'm from Banzyville.

PATRICE

Jean de Banzy. Oh yes. I get it.

JOSEPH

I can't sign my real name. I'm in the civil service. Jean de Banzy—good one, eh?

The rhythm picks up pace. One of the girls dances up to Patrice and pulls him away. The onlookers begin to clap, and some start dancing among themselves.

Song: Cathééérinn gaaaaare à toi . . .

INT. STATE SECURITY OFFICE—DAY

Caption: December 1958

We hear the sound of typewriters. Patrice is waiting in line, among many others.

> **VOICE**
> Lumumba Patrice Emery?

> **PATRICE**
> That's me.

> **VOICE**
> This way.

He enters a small office.

INT. STATE SECURITY—ANOTHER OFFICE—DAY

A government official, sitting behind his desk, is going through a thick file.

> **OFFICIAL**
> Name?

                    PATRICE

Lumumba. Patrice. Emery.

                    OFFICIAL

You have a police record.

                    PATRICE

. . . Yes.

                    OFFICIAL

And you hope to leave.

Patrice doesn't reply.

                    OFFICIAL

One thousand twenty-six francs.
                    (whistling)
A little greedy, no? Wasn't your salary as a post-
man, third class, enough?

*Prudently, Patrice remains silent. The official watches him, looking
for a weak spot.*

                    PATRICE

It was a mistake. I paid for it.

                    OFFICIAL

You paid nothing at all! . . . Be quiet!

Silence.

                    OFFICIAL
                    (sliding a passport toward Lumumba)
Here.

                         PATRICE
                       (in disbelief)
        I've got my visa?

                         OFFICIAL
        Yes, and a lot of luck. Or connections. Your
        buddy Kasa-Vubu . . .

                         PATRICE
        I've never met him . . .

                         OFFICIAL
        A manner of speaking. He was refused. So you
        should be grateful.

                         PATRICE
        Thank you.

                         OFFICIAL
        And don't go doing the nigger on us there and
        start bad-mouthing the government. We'll know
        about it. We know everything. We have ears every-
        where. For us, Ghana is very near. Accra is like
        Leopoldville. Understand? And as for your little
        party, the MNC, we can crush it in one breath, if
        we want. Got it?

INT. POOR NEIGHBORHOOD—PATRICE'S
HOUSE—EVENING

*Pauline is packing clothes into a suitcase, amid a bunch of shirts and
other linens strewn on the bed. Juliana is crying.*

JULIANA

Papa, I don't want you to go . . .

Patrice takes her in his arms and tries to console her.

JULIANA

Take me with you.

PATRICE

I can't, darling. I won't be long. Think of it: the first Pan-African conference. All the countries in Africa will be represented. And it's your daddy who's going to represent Congo, the whole Congo!

JULIANA

(opening her eyes wide)

The whole Congo?

PATRICE

The whole Congo! You see, I couldn't miss a thing like that. Pauline, don't forget my ties, all my ties!

ARCHIVAL IMAGES

Gaumont Pathé or Fox Movietone newsreels of the period on the first Pan-African Conference in Accra. Droning tone of the commentator.

COMMENTATOR

From every corner of colonial and postcolonial Africa, these young African delegates have rushed to Accra to celebrate the mass gathering that they call, a little pompously, "Pan-Africanism" . . .

The speakers, often fresh from the bush, discover the joy of the micro-phone and compete in the use of anticolonial rhetoric under the watchful eye of their pope, Nkrumah, who is today the man directing the dance (we see folk dances and a succession of illustrative images which are almost derisory).

EXT. LEOPOLDVILLE—INNER-CITY STREET—DAY

A jeep, with a white police officer and five black policemen aboard, drives slowly along a street, which is strangely deserted, and positions itself strategically across the street. Further on another car makes a wide circle and, in turn, blocks another street.

VOICE OVER (PATRICE)
We repeated, over and over, that we were against no one, only against the domination, the injustices, the abuses . . .

EXT./INT. OPEN-AIR SPACE (OR NON-DESCRIPT ROOM)—DAY

On the platform, behind a microphone, Patrice improvises, pages in his hands. The place is packed.

PATRICE
Leopold II "gave" the Congo to Belgium. How are we to understand that? If at least he had bought us! We could have a collection and refund him.
(laughter; then, in Lingala:)
We ourselves are going to organize our own independence, without regard to the Belgians . . . if one of us is imprisoned, you must all rise up! . . .

INT. POOR NEIGHBORHOOD—BACKYARD—DAY

A checkerboard, for which the opposing markers are Polar and Primus bottle tops. Two young men are playing in the open air.

RADIO (PATRICE)
(in Lingala)
If they put him in prison, you all go to prison!
(in French)
No collaboration. Civil disobedience! . . .

INT. POOR NEIGHBORHOOD—"DEVELOPED"
PERSON'S HOUSE —DAY

RADIO (PATRICE)
It's been going on for eighty years. At first it
was slave trading, then ivory trafficking, and after
that it was the destruction of our villages to export
rubber . . .

A modest sitting room, simple wooden furniture. The sound is coming from a radio on the dresser. A couple of European examiners—he's wearing a bush shirt, she a prim suit—are silently noting what they see. Seated on a sofa, a young African couple—she in an elegant native dress, he in a suit and tie. The European woman, an examiner, points to a sideboard.

WOMAN EXAMINER
Can you open it?

The man gets up to open the sideboard.

RADIO (PATRICE)

... today it's uranium, diamonds, copper, magnesium, zinc ...

The male examiner goes to the radio and switches it off, but in the background the speech continues, as it does on a thousand radios in the whole neighborhood.

RADIO (PATRICE)

... Everyone knows that independence will come soon ... but tomorrow, tomorrow, is still not soon enough for us.

INT. POOR NEIGHBORHOOD—BACKYARD—DAY

From a neighboring house, a third young man calls the checker players.

YOUNG MAN

Come on! It's Patrice! He's back! He's talking on the radio!

YOUNG MAN 2

On the radio? On Belgian radio! They let him?

YOUNG MAN

Of course not! On the BBC! Quick!

The three of them get up and go into a nearby house.

RADIO (PATRICE)

... In spite of our ethnic differences we have the same consciousness, the same soul which, night after night, is prey to anguish. In spite of the borders, we all dream of a single Africa . . .

INT. POOR NEIGHBORHOOD—"DEVELOPED" PERSON'S HOUSE—DAY

The young African woman is holding the cutlery in her hands. She is awkwardly trying to set the table.

WOMAN EXAMINER
Fork, on the left!

The young woman hesitates, looks at the examiner, mouth open, embarrassed. The examiner, in turn, puts down her clipboard on the table (on which we read, "development certificate") and shows the African woman how to do it.

WOMAN EXAMINER
(exasperated)
It's not as difficult as Flemish, just the same!

At that moment the male examiner comes back from the kitchen, holding a saucepan.

MALE EXAMINER
It's monkey! That's really something! You want to be a "developed person"? You want your registration? Do you think you're going to get it that way?

AFRICAN MAN
It's the neighbor's. He doesn't have a fridge.

EXT. LEOPOLDVILLE—INNER-CITY STREET—
MARKET CORNER—DAY.

Some young people dance while rhythmically beating on some wood planks, chanting: Dipenda, dipenda! [Independence!] A spontaneous demonstration. They try to entice some street vendors into their dance.

EXT./INT. OPEN-AIR SPACE (OR NON-DESCRIPT
ROOM)—DAY

Still on the platform, Patrice harangues the crowd.

PATRICE
Long live the Congo! Long live the Congolese
National Movement! Uhuru!

THE CROWD
Uhuru!

PATRICE
Uhuru!

THE CROWD
Lumumba! Uhuru!

Mpolo and two other militants come up behind him and lead him back behind the curtains.

EXT. LEOPOLDVILLE—INNER-CITY STREET—
MARKET CORNER—DAY

Two jeeps crammed with policemen storm in and brake hard in the middle of the square. Panic. The people, including the vendors, flee in all directions.

EXT. CIRCLE—"THE MEETING OF THE PARTIES"—DAY

A villa surrounded by a garden and woods. Under a tree, Mpolo, wearing sunglasses, is seated behind a wooden table, an intransigent look on his face. Behind him, a sign with the slogan "Independance Tout de Suite" [Independence Now].

MPOLO
(to the two guys in front of him, scratching his head)
Sure, I want to believe you, that you've already paid your subscriptions, but I say: no independence without receipts. Didn't the Belgians teach you anything?

Patrice arrives along the passageway with Mobutu beside him. He seems preoccupied and shuffles the pages he has in his hands.

LUMUMBA
(without raising his head)
Mpolo . . . stop terrorizing our militants.

MPOLO
And the other one there, the corporal with you, has he paid?

EXT. CIRCLE—"THE MEETING OF THE PARTIES"—DAY

Thirty or so men. Behind a long table, four men including Lumumba, interrupted in his speech.

MUNONGO
(getting up)
Allied to what? You went there as if you were the Congo, and your party does not represent the whole Congo.

CHAIRMAN
Lumumba has the floor, please. Let him finish.

PATRICE
. . . That's quite true, my party is not the whole Congo. Not yet . . . Neither is the Conakat of Mr. Tshombe the whole of Katanga.

TSHOMBE
Ours is the number one party . . . Yours is nothing . . .

PATRICE
There are two hundred and fifty parties across the Congo. Not counting the ones the Belgians set up. Mr. Kasa-Vubu is also disappointed that his power was not represented in Accra. What can I do? I'm not the one issuing the visas.

TSHOMBE
That's just it. How come the authorities let you go alone?

PATRICE

Go ask them.

MUNONGO

We already know. It's because you sell Polar, the
beer belonging to the minister of the Congo.

*Surprised. Patrice turns to Mpolo as if to ask confirmation of the al-
legation. He nods his head and murmurs.*

MPOLO

They say he has a 51 percent share.

PATRICE

(turning back to the others)
I didn't know.

TSHOMBE

There's a lot of things you don't know . . . and
firstly the most elementary order of hierarchy . . .

*He stops. A militant has approached the table and, on a signal from
Patrice, gives typed mimeographed sheets to Munongo and Tshombe.
Munongo glances at them and throws the papers to the ground.*

MUNONGO

Is this a joke?

PATRICE

Not at all. I would prefer that you have a full
transcript of my speech rather than the chopped-
up extracts from the newspapers. Perhaps, I should
have spoken of you and your rich province but I
do not think of the Congo as a collection of

provinces, of tribes and ethnic groups, but as a whole. Africa as a whole. We must go beyond provincialism, beyond tribalism . . .

MUNONGO

Are you still giving your speech? Do you think you are still in Accra?

PATRICE

Not quite. You are only two, even if you represent many others. I had an audience of ten thousand. I could not mention Mr Tshombe's Conakat just to make him happy. Nobody would have understood. At the next Pan-African conference, I will with the greatest of pleasure speak of your party, your huge party.

MUNONGO
(getting up)
This man is mocking us.

TSHOMBE
(also rising, to Patrice)
Your sarcasm is out of place . . . it's insulting.

PATRICE

I can only reply this: I made this speech, read it, or don't read it, in any case it's too late to rewrite it now.

As he leaves, Munongo turns, a threatening look on his face.

MUNONGO

You travel a lot promoting your beer. Just avoid my region. The Lunda people forget nothing.

Patrice looks at him. Munongo, Tshombe and some others leave with a determined gait as the rain begins to fall, creating a further sense of disorder.

EXT./INT. MNC HEADQUARTERS—DAY

A collection of grey buildings somewhere between a squat and a crumbling villa. Mobutu emerges at the corner of an alleyway, carrying several packages and a winter coat over his arm. The courtyard is buzzing with activity. The militants, excited and in good moods, busy themselves with diverse tasks. In a corner the machine that prints the pamphlets, in another, posters and banners are being finished, someone is counting money, another is distributing a pile of brochures. Mobutu sticks his head in an open window.

MOBUTU

Have you seen Patrice?

MPOLO
(without raising his head)

On the other side.

(smiling)

He's resting.

Mobutu moves on and Mpolo gets back to his radio.

MPOLO

Always the same. You can never get that damn
Deutsche Welle when you're looking for it.

MILITANT

You put the tip of the needle between Oslo and
Lisbon, just on the "n" of Sydney

MPOLO
Yeah, yeah, smartass.

EXT. MNC HEADQUARTERS—DAY

Sitting on the steps, side by side, Patrice and Hélène are telling each other stories. Hélène, holding a bottle of sparkling water in her hands, teases him.

HELENE
(laughing, in Lingala)
Stop Patrice, a little further and you're going to
be taken for a martyr . . .

PATRICE
(in Lingala)
When I think that I actually had that published.
(in French)
. . . Lost, you danced, in the moist evening . . .
and there surged, magnificent, sensual and virile . . .
like a trumpet voice . . .

HELENE
(almost choking)
. . . emerging from your pain, your powerful music
. . . Jazz, forcing the respect of the white man . . .

Hélène passes him the bottle. He drinks from it. There is an obvious familiarity between them. She sings softly.

HELENE
Do you know if the child is okay?

Mobutu arrives.

MOBUTU
(in Lingala)

So, young lovers, wish me "Bon Voyage."

HELENE
(in Lingala)

You got on your course?

MOBUTU

Chin chin to Brussels!

PATRICE

We must celebrate that.

EXT. MNC HEADQUARTERS—DAY

Lumumba and Mobutu cross the courtyard.

PATRICE

Listen, get everything you can out of it. We need people like you.

MOBUTU

Did you see the coat? A little big, but you can't look gift horses in the mouth, can you?

PATRICE

Have it cleaned first, otherwise they're going to think you use mothballs as perfume.

RADIO

The aim of our presence on the black continent
was defined by Leopold II: to bring European civilization to these backward countries, to call on
their populations to emancipate themselves, to
bring freedom and progress . . .

INT./EXT. MNC HEADQUARTERS—DAY

Mpolo pokes his head out the window.

MPOLO
(shouting)
Patrice! Patrice! The king! It's Baudouin! Come
listen! They're going to give in! They're going to
give in!

RADIO (BAUDOUIN)
Continuing these noble aims, our resolution
today is to bring, without digress nor unnecessary
urgency, the Congolese people to independence,
in prosperity and in peace . . .

PATRICE
(arriving)
I don't believe it. They're up to something.

MPOLO
No! They've lost their heads. They've lost. De
Gaulle gave in. Little Belgium has no choice. We'll
eat them alive!

PATRICE
You know Maurice, one of these days someone

will take you literally and think that you're a cannibal.

MPOLO

Can I what?

PATRICE

Cannibal. Someone who eats human flesh.

MPOLO
(laughing)

Oh, if that's what it means, then tonight, everybody better watch out, cause I'm feeling can-I can-I ball!

Laughter.

RADIO (BAUDOUIN)

Belgium intends to organize in the Congo a democracy capable of exercising the prerogatives of sovereignty and of determining its own independence . . .

Outside, a commotion grows louder.

VOICE OUTSIDE

The police! Get out of here!

INT./EXT. MNC HEADQUARTERS—DAY

Against the background of the king's speech, the police descend in formation: blows, insults, destruction, chaos.

RADIO (BAUDOUIN)

While we have no hesitation in approving, in
seconding the aspirations of our black brothers, we
cannot however forget that for eighty years . . .

*Papers fly, furniture is turned over. The radio falls to the floor. Men
and women escape through the window.*

RADIO (BAUDOUIN)

. . . through our services and efforts, Belgium
has earned the right to their friendship and coop-
eration . . .

*A white officer points to Lumumba. Two black policemen grab him
and take him away. Hélène tries to intervene but she's brutally pushed
aside.*

INT. PRISON—DAY

Caption: January 24, 1960. Coquilhatville Prison.

*Two Belgian guards are searching Lumumba's cell. He is sitting on
his bunk. One of them finds a piece of paper hidden behind the toilet.*

PRISON GUARD 1

Well, the warden was right. He's getting papers
through to the outside. Bastard!

He hits Patrice. The other guard takes the paper and reads:

PRISON GUARD 2

"Solemn protest" . . . Sure, why not. "Illegal in-
carceration." Well now. That's what they all say. "I

demand my release so that I can participate, as a delegate of the MNC, in the round table discussions taking place in Brussels." Who does he think he is? Ape!

They hit him.

PRISON GUARD 1
You think that we're stupid enough to let you out, when you're in here in the first place because of your subversive carrying-on? You're here for two years and we'll take care of you all right. Starting with this!

He hits him.

PRISON GUARD 2
You see yourself in Brussels, savage? And what would you say to the king, if you saw him?

Another blow.

PRISON GUARD 1
Well he wants to be a minister. That's what they all want. You want a decoration? You'll see how we decorate you.

He hits him again.

PRISON GUARD 2
You'd like to be called Excellency, you ape? Excellency.

They laugh. At this very moment, the cell door opens and in walks the warden. The two guards stop laughing. One of them hands the paper to the warden.

PRISON GUARD 1

We found this, sir.

WARDEN

Why is his nose bleeding?

PRISON GUARD 2

Usual thing. He was making a din. We came in. He started getting physical, sir.

The warden glances at the paper. He clears his throat.

WARDEN

Mr. Lumumba, I've just received orders from Brussels concerning you. His Excellency, the minister of Congo, has decided that as president of the MNC, you can take part in the round table discussions. You are being released provisionally. There is a Sabena flight leaving for Brussels tomorrow. Mr. Lumumba, you are free to go.

EXT. BRUSSELS—ZAVENTEM AIRPORT TARMAC—DAY

Caption: Brussels, Zaventhen. Three days later.

A plane lands and comes to a halt. Lumumba appears at the top of the stairs. Cameras flash, journalists rush forward.

JOURNALISTS

Mr. Lumumba, what is your position on the future of the colony?

Total or partial independence? Immediately or in stages?

Are you going to meet with Mr. Kasa-Vubu ?

Lumumba moves through the journalists and heads toward Mpolo. He stops in front of Mobutu, who waves to him joyfully.

PATRICE

Joseph!

EXT. BRUSSELS—ZAVENTEM AIRPORT TERMINAL EXIT—DAY

At the terminal exit is robustly accosted by an elderly Belgian woman who presents him with a bouquet of flowers.

Lumumba sits into the waiting car. Squeezed a little too closely by Mobutu, he grimaces.

PATRICE

Easy there, my ribs . . .

JOSEPH

The plane?

PATRICE

No, not the plane . . . the prison . . . I think one of them is fractured . . . Don't make that face . . . A guy like you from the Public Force must have seen plenty . . . Tell me about Brussels instead . . .

JOSEPH

It's a beautiful city ... They're building every-where ...

PATRICE

I don't give a damn about the city! What about the Round Table? How's it going?

JOSEPH
(huffing)

I've no idea. All I know is that they only talk about you.

EXT./INT. BRUSSELS STREET—ROYAL PALACE—CAR—DAY

The car turns the corner of 38 place du Trône in front of the statue of Leopold II, and drives onto the big avenue in front of the Royal Palace. Lumumba is captivated and leans over to better take in the long building over which flies the Belgian flag.

JOSEPH

Up until the last moment we didn't know whether we'd be able to get you out. Kasa-Vubu and his gang weren't too hot about the idea. We had to apply a lot of pressure. The round table without the MNC was meaningless, etc., etc ... Finally, believe it or not, it was the Belgians who tipped the balance in your favor ...

PATRICE
(laughs)

Divide and conquer ... those Flemish ... We'll sort them all right, eh, Mpolo? We've got them,

Lumumba (feature; 2000)   249

and we won't let go.

                    MPOLO
    Mmh.

EXT. BRUSSELS STREET—ROYAL PALACE—
DAY

The car drives off and turns left into rue de la Régence.

INT. BRUSSELS—PRIVATE HOTEL—
KITCHEN/STAIRCASE/LUMUMBA'S SUITE— DAY

*In the narrow kitchen, a half dozen waiters jostle each other trying
to fill their various orders.*

                FIRST WAITER
    Hey! Don't push!

                SECOND WAITER
                (to the chef-steward)
    Finish those three flamingos for twenty-six?
    And the twelve croques for the Kamitatu suite?

                MAÎTRE D'HOTEL
    Who's going up to the third?

                THIRD WAITER
    Send Mathieu. Me exclusive service for Bom-
    boko.

FIRST WAITER

What's so interesting about that clown?

THIRD WAITER

He's got class, old chap, class.

SECOND WAITER

More like big tips.

FIRST WAITER

Clear a passage, professors! There's work to be done!

We follow him through the cramped space onto a landing where two magnificent blondes are coming down the stairs. A small man, wearing fancy shoes, ushers them back up the stairs.

SMALL MAN

No, no, no, we're not finished yet . . . back up you go!

FIRST BLONDE
(sighing)

Oh la la la . . .

Mpolo appears accompanied by two journalists.

MPOLO

Mr. Lumumba will see you at 7:00 p.m., as planned. Not now . . .

FIRST JOURNALIST

Just a photo then . . .

MPOLO

... Gentlemen ... Please ...

Delegates pass by. A tribal chief dressed half-European, half-native.

MPOLO

Thomas! Over here.

We follow Thomas Kanza into Lumumba's suite.

MPOLO
(handing pages to a secretary)
Benoît, three copies before 4:00 p.m.? ...
Come, Thomas, this way ...

In the other room Patrice talks on the telephone.

PATRICE

What do you mean, "sort of independence"? It's
already a reality ...

Mpolo and Kanza come up to him.

PATRICE

... Well, yes, it's still flexible ... It's not our fault
if no date has yet been fixed ... One moment,
please.

MPOLO

Patrice ... You wanted someone who could
proofread and correct your speeches.
(pointing to the young man)
Let me introduce the first Congolese graduate
from the University of ... of ... Thomas Kanza.

PATRICE

Pleased to meet you . . . A graduate, good . . . Very interesting. Kanza? Who is Daniel Kanza to you?

KANZA

My father.

PATRICE

Very good, very good . . . The father is with Kasa-Vubu, the son shall be with us . . . excuse me, I'm in the middle of a telephone interview. We'll talk later . . .

(on the phone)

My friend. Neither east nor west . . . It's no longer a problem of blacks and whites but of building the Congo with any Europeans of good will . . . but these are only political formulae . . . tribalism, federalism . . . The federalism proposed by Conakat is the most reactionary . . . It is extreme in its separatism . . .

Suddenly the noise, the clatter of the mimeograph, and the chattering voices stop. Mpolo, Patrice, and the young Kanza turn their heads towards the entrance.

MPOLO

(to himself)

Where does he think he's going?

Surrounded by some Abako delegates, Kasa-Vubu makes a grand entrance. Patrice hangs up the phone and stands.

PATRICE

Very pleased to see you, Mr. Kasa-Vubu.

He points to an armchair in which Kasa-Vubu makes himself comfortable. He then makes a sign to Mpolo, who, in turn, addresses himself to the other visitors.

MPOLO

Please, could all those with no political mandate leave. Thank you.

The activists and the visitors leave the room. Joseph, however, has also installed himself in an armchair.

MPOLO

Joseph, did you hear me?

JOSEPH

I'm a delegate of the MNC.

One of Kasa-Vubu's men interrupts.

ABAKO DELEGATE

Aren't you a student or an intern here in Belgium?

JOSEPH

Yes, but I'm . . .

ABAKO DELEGATE
(cutting him off)
Then excuse me but your place isn't here. This meeting is only for delegates who have come from the Congo.

JOSEPH

No. I'm a delegate of the MNC. I must attend this meeting.

ABAKO DELEGATE

I'm sorry, but if you insist, we'll have to cancel the meeting.

Mpolo approaches Mobutu.

MPOLO

Joseph, these are the Common Front rules.

Joseph turns to Patrice, who remains silent. Joseph stands up and leaves. There is a brief silence.

PATRICE

Would you like something to drink? In terms of beer, the only thing in this hotel is Leffe. Neither Primus nor Polar. We're on neutral ground.

KASA-VUBU
(permitting a smile)
Not for the moment, thanks. Mr. Lumumba, I heard you speak this morning. I believe that we are in agreement on the essential issue: giving priority to the repeal of the colonial charter. The future political structures of the Congolese state are the concern of the Congolese people themselves, and not of this Round Table. Agreed?

PATRICE

Absolutely.

KASA-VUBU

On that point we shall not give in. Today is the 1st of February. What do you think of June first as a date?

PATRICE

That suits me fine.

KASA-VUBU

The Minister doesn't approve of this date and proposes June 30th for the proclamation of independence instead. Does that seem too long to you?

PATRICE

I prefer the first of June. I believe you feel the same.

KASA-VUBU

The trouble is that the tribal chiefs, Joseph Ileo's group, Tshombe's Conakat, not to mention the National Popular Party, of course . . .

PATRICE

Of course!

MPOLO

NPP, the Niggers' Paid-off Party!

KASA-VUBU

. . . All of them are in agreement with the Minister's timetable. There's the risk of splitting the Common Front. A serious risk.

PATRICE

That's what the Belgians want . . . Personally, I don't believe it.

INT. BRUSSELS—PRIVATE HOTEL—PRIVATE LOUNGE—DAY

Through a half open door someone is watching the scene from afar. He turns. In the luxurious and richly decorated room some Belgian businessmen meet with a group of politicians, among whom we see the man who will later be revealed as the resident Minister, Mr. Ganshof.

INDUSTRIALIST
(closing the door)

It's a crime, I tell you.

GANSHOF

I think that you give too much importance to one word.

INDUSTRIALIST

Independence, just one word? God is also just a word. I believe in God, and I say that we are giving the Congo and Africa away to the Communists. Like the French did with Algeria.

INT. BRUSSELS—PRIVATE HOTEL—LUMUMBA'S SUITE—DAY

KASA-VUBU

Our two groups are the most powerful. I propose that we adopt a common position.

PATRICE

Are you thinking of a compromise? Independence on the 15th of June?

KASA-VUBU

The Minister will refuse.

PATRICE

(after a moment)
You want us to give in on the date.

KASA-VUBU

Only to preserve the unity of the Common
Front.

Patrice stands up and thinks about it for a moment.

PATRICE

They want more time? Why? To prepare their
exit? Or to sabotage our future State?

KASA-VUBU

Sabotage?

PATRICE

Unified Mines in Upper Katanga. Copper, diamonds. Will they leave all this under the control
of the new government? Or . . . ?

KASA-VUBU

We don't know what the new government will
be. Let's wait for the elections.

PATRICE
(*smiling*)
In other words, we'll cross that bridge when we
come to it.

KASA-VUBU
(*smiling*)
Let's wait for the elections. Today, I ask that we
take a position, a position that is both firm and
flexible concerning the date of independence.

MPOLO
And then what? What will we give in to next?

ABAKO DELEGATE
Let's be serious. Just a year ago we imagined our
independence to be thirty years away. Now, it is
set for June: the first or the thirtieth …

EXT. BRUSSELS—STREET IN FRONT OF PRIVATE
HOTEL—DAY

*In front of the private hotel: two policemen, various Congolese and
Belgians come and go. One of the women spotted inside the hotel leaves
angrily. At the window Ganshof watches the street.*

INT. BRUSSELS—PRIVATE HOTEL—PRIVATE
LOUNGE—DAY

*Until now, Ganshof had involved himself little in the discussion. He
turns.*

GANSHOF

Chaos is a risk. We have no choice but to take it. Let them try their freedom. They will either give Africa the example we've given Europe, that of a decent, unified, and industrious people. Or, the primitive instincts will resurface, and then . . .

INDUSTRIALIST

And then?

GANSHOF

We have an army, militia, airplanes, tanks.

INDUSTRIALIST

So do the Russians.

POLITICIAN

If you are thinking along those lines . . . The Americans . . .

There is a knock on the door. Silence.

INT. BRUSSELS—PRIVATE HOTEL—KITCHEN—DAY

A waiter fixes his bow tie, a tray in his hands. He opens and enters.

INT. BRUSSELS—PRIVATE HOTEL—PRIVATE LOUNGE—DAY

The waiter enters, the discussion continues.

FIRST POLITICIAN

I ask you: what can they possibly do with independence? They are not a people, they are a bunch of tribes. The Lulua hate the Baluba, the Baluba detest the Bakongo, and the Bakongo can't stand the Bengala. The only thing that holds them together is the colonial administration.

INDUSTRIALIST

Exactly, and we're getting rid of it!

FIRST POLITICIAN

You think so? We didn't make the same mistake as the French: we didn't train any African administrators. Look at the army, the legal system, the police, the postal services. All of the higher ranks are Belgian. Without them, it's complete chaos. They'll have Congolese ministers? So what? As my wife says, let them have some fun.

They all laugh, except for Ganshof.

INT. BRUSSELS—PRIVATE HOTEL—LUMUMBA SUITE—DAY

Commotion and laughter. Delegates of both parties speak at the same time. Patrice calls for silence, then sits back down.

PATRICE

Good. Let's go for the 30th of June. Independence is now a fact. The only remaining question is whether the resulting state will be federalist, as you would like, or unified, as I want. I'll draft a press release and we'll all sign it.

KASA-VUBU
Don't forget to let me read it first.

They all laugh.

PATRICE
Mpolo, order some champagne. Good. Gentlemen, I propose that we drink to independence, to the elections, and to the future government of free Congo that is to say, to ourselves! Have you heard the latest hit? (He sings) "In - de - pen - dence cha-cha o sing o . . ."

EXT. LEOPOLDVILLE—DAY

Caption: Léopoldville, May 1960. Four months later.

A view of Loopoldville.

INT. LEOPOLDVILLE—POOR NEIGHBORHOOD—
PATRICE'S HOUSE—DAY

Patrice is feeding little Juliana in the kitchen of his house, while Pauline is cooking. There is a commotion outside and the crackling of a radio inside. Shouts and cheers: Pa-trice, president!

The door opens and in comes Joseph Mobutu.

PAULINE
No! Get out!

JOSEPH
(ignoring her) `
Patrice, we're winning! Their manipulations
didn't work!

PATRICE
We're ahead?

JOSEPH
Everywhere! We're even beating the Abako party!

PATRICE
(excited)
Even in Leoville?

JOSEPH
Well no, not quite.

*A small group of militants come in behind him and take over the
kitchen. Mpolo and Kanza are among them.*

MILITANTS
(chanting)
Pa-trice, president!

JULIANA
What is president, Daddy?

PATRICE
It's nothing! Everybody out! I have to feed the
little one!

EXT. BAR NA BISO—EVENING

The music swells: "Independence cha-cha o sing o"... The song is being played by a band inside a Leoville bar and amplified into the streets through a loudspeaker. The atmosphere is one of celebration, with singing, dancing and drinks.

> VOICES
> And one Primus! ... Two Polars!

Patrice is dancing with Hélène Bijou in the middle of an intoxicated crowd clapping rhythmically to the music.

Mpolo is dancing with another woman. He is soaked in sweat. While dancing, he accidentally bumps into Patrice and catches him by the arm.

> MPOLO
> Sorry, I can hardly stand up anymore.

> HELENE
> Quite a party!

> MPOLO
> It's not party, it's a revolution. And now, Patrice, we've got to go all the way, right to the end.

> PATRICE
> Yes, yes. To the end. You don't know what you're saying anymore ...

> MPOLO
> I know exactly. I know that a revolution can't be an half-way thing. All the Flemish have to be

kicked out of the country. Expropriate the missions, expel all these parasites, all the bureaucrats.

PATRICE

And replace them with whom?

MPOLO

We don't need any bureaucrats.

Patrice laughs. They start dancing again. The music takes over.

Music:
Round Table, independence ohhh
Lumumba, independence ohhh
Kasa-Vubu, independence ohhh
Belgium, independence ohhh

INT. MINISTER GANSHOF'S RESIDENCE—DAY

A portrait of the young King Baudouin sits on minister Ganshof's desk. Standing in front of the minister's desk, Patrice Lumumba signs several pages and then hands them to Ganshof.

GANSHOF
(getting up)
Your task won't be an easy one.

PATRICE

I'm aware of that. But I need a clarification. Am I supposed to form a government, or is my mission simply to inform? I didn't quite understand.

GANSHOF

(uncomfortable)

Your mission is to inform in order to form the government.

PATRICE

I still don't understand. The independence ceremony is set for the 30th of June. If by then the government is not formed . . . and if my mission is merely officious . . .

GANSHOF

It is official. But one of information. Please allow me to do things in the order mandated by His Majesty. Information first. Formation next. Everything in its own time.

PATRICE

I'll do my best. But time is limited, Mr. Resident Minister.

GANSHOF

I wish you the best of luck, Mr. Information Officer.

They shake hands coldly in front of the picture of King Baudouin.

EXT. MINISTER GANSHOF'S RESIDENCE—DAY

Caption: Four days later

In front of his residence, Ganshof reads a press release in the presence of Kasa-Vubu:

GANSHOF

Given the failure of Mr. Lumumba's mission, I have decided to give Mr. Kasa-Vubu the task of forming the new Congolese government . . .

INT. POOR NEIGHBOURHOOD—PATRICE'S HOUSE—DAY

Joseph, Mpolo, and Kanza are gathered with Patrice, who is pacing the floor like a caged animal.

KANZA

Patrice, calm down.

PATRICE

I know where all this is coming from! Brussels! They nominated him so as to get rid of me. They're playing Kasa-Vubu against me!

JOSEPH

They can't get rid of you. You won the elections. You have all the regions behind you! You can only be president, or prime minister.

PATRICE

I don't give a damn, Joseph! I don't want to be a puppet-minister! I don't want to be thrown a bone, I want to be able to form the government!

MPOLO

Without you, there is no government. We only have to block everything.

Lumumba (feature; 2000)   **267**

KANZA

To what end?

EXT. IN FRONT OF PATRICE'S HOUSE—DAY

On the steps in front of his house, Patrice reads his press release:

PATRICE

Given the situation, I accuse minister Ganshof and the duplicity of the Belgian government, who consider me dangerous, of not allowing me to form a government made up of men I choose. No doubt Brussels would rather have no government in place on June 30th, than have one formed by Lumumba. Under these conditions, there may not even be a Head of State by June 30th. For neither my party, nor its allies, will vote the investiture of Kasa-Vubu . . .

INT. MINISTER GANSHOF'S RESIDENCE—DAWN

Dawn. The Resident Minister has loosened his tie and collar. His eyes are blood-shot and he seems exhausted. He is shaving with an electric razor while looking into a mirror placed on his desk. The razor buzzes.

Sitting at the other side of the desk, no less exhausted and disheveled, are Kasa-Vubu and Patrice Lumumba. They read and correct a list of names, changed many times over, on a sheet of paper. A servant brings in coffee.

PATRICE

Conakat yes, but Tshombe no. The coalition wouldn't last a day.

KASA-VUBU

Even with the title of State Commissioner for the Katanga province?

PATRICE

(gesturing "no")

We can do better. For the post at the Finances, I accept your man. But I insist that Thomas Kanza be at least our delegate at the UN.

KASA-VUBU

The son of a man whom our party excluded last year. I don't like that.

PATRICE

The son is not the father. And he will do a good job.

Kasa-Vubu signals his acquiescence. Patrice adds Kanza's name to the list. The buzzing of Ganshof's razor stops.

GANSHOF

Gentlemen, I'd like to inform you that it is now day.

EXT. MINISTER GANSHOF'S RESIDENCE—DAY

In front of the house, in the presence of a now clean-shaven Resident Minister Ganshof, the two rivals solemnly shake hands before the press. The cameras click away.

PATRICE

The National block over which I preside will give its entire support to the candidacy of Mr. Kasa-Vubu as the President of the Republic. I never contested this title, a title that is rightly his.

KASA-VUBU

My first act will be to appoint Mr. Lumumba as Prime Minister of our government of national unity. Unity is what the Congo now needs.

EXT. BAR NA BISO—NIGHT

The bar terrace where all the Belgian and Congolese politicians meet, as well as journalists from all over the world. When Patrice and his friends appear, the reporters, caught off-guard, quickly aim their cameras. There is a burst of flashes as the customers stand up on their chairs to get a view of the newcomers.

Patrice, relaxed and smiling, perhaps drunk with fatigue, is lead by Hélène Bijou who is wearing a revealing flowered dress. She wants to dance with him to the music. She wraps her arms around him and presses her body against his.

HELENE

Come on . . . let's dance.

Cameras flash around them. Patrice, laughing, pushes her away gently. He is surrounded by journalists.

PHOTOGRAPHER

So Patrice! Prime Minister! Smile!

OTHER PHOTOGRAPHER

(to Hélène)

Hey darling, how about loosening a few more buttons?

JOURNALIST

(with a German accent)

Mr. Lumumba . . . Is it true that Katanga is not represented in your government? Do you not fear its secession?

PATRICE

Of course, your friends are represented. The Katanga is not just Tshombe and Munungo. But please, no more questions! The Congo is and will remain united . . . Is that enough of a declaration for you? Good.

Three soldiers from the Public Force, prostitutes hanging on their arms, push their way through the journalists to reach Patrice.

FIRST SOLDIER

United or not, what we need are stripes!

SECOND SOLDIER

And money! To no longer live in shit!

THIRD SOLDIER

We don't want to be lead by the Flemish any more! No more humiliation, no more solitary!

SECOND SOLDIER

We've had enough! On top of it, we have to cut
their grass and do dishes for their wives. Any
more, and they'd have us do the rest too.

PATRICE

Come on. Sit with us. All this won't change
overnight, you know. Patience! I've asked the king
for a general amnesty and promotions for you . . .
I promise you! June 30th will be a day of joy for
the entire population . . . without distinction for
category, province, or ethnicity . . . One people
united. That's all!

EXT. BAR NA BISO—NIGHT

*Later. The end of the night and the tail end of the party. The bar is
nearly empty. The last customers are all drunk, asleep, or in a stupor. A
slow tune has replaced the cha–cha beat of the Independence song.*

*Hélène Bijou dances languorously by herself, her eyes closed, as in a
dream.*

*At a table covered with empty glasses and bottles, Patrice is sitting
by himself, lost in thought.*

*Mpolo, drunk, is flicking pieces of bread at Mobutu. Using rolled up
paper napkins and other bits, Mobutu returns fire.*

*Kanza, exhausted, sleeps sitting on his chair, his head to one side, his
mouth open.*

At the other end of the bar, a small group approaches. We recognize Munongo and Tshombe flanked by bodyguards.

TSHOMBE

Lumumba! Patrice Lumumba!

PATRICE

(turning)

Well! The entire Conakat has arrived . . .

TSHOMBE

I'm going back to Elizabethville today. I waited the whole day yesterday for the list of members appointed to the government. You had promised to communicate it to me.

PATRICE

We have made it available to you.

MUNONGO

Liar!

MPOLO

(sitting up in a menacing posture)

What is he saying?

PATRICE

Calm down, Maurice.

(to Munongo)

You seem to know about this list, apparently.

TSHOMBE

We know that your government is a ragbag of extremists. Let it be known that we will oppose,

by any means available to us, the unitary structure
you want to impose by force on this country.

KANZA
(awakened by the shouts)
What does that mean, "by all means available . . ."?

PATRICE
You are opposing the results of a democratic
vote.

MUNONGO
We are opposed to communism.

KANZA
We're no more Communists than you are . . .

PATRICE
Let it be, Thomas. They're angry.

MUNONGO
You're going to change your tone!

*He is about to jump on Patrice. Mpolo, despite his state, is faster, and
pushes him off. Munongo pushes him back. Mpolo pushes him back.
Joseph pushes back one of Tshombe's bodyguards, who was about to intervene. A chair falls over. Some reporters wake up or have just rushed
in. The cameras begin once again to flash. Tshombe pulls Munongo by
the sleeve. They retreat.*

Patrice wipes his glasses. He smiles and exhales.

PATRICE

My friends, that's what independence is all about. It's a struggle!

MPOLO

Well, we're not done yet . . .

INT. VILLA TILKENS—DAY

June 1960. The house seems larger than it really is, as most of the furniture has been removed.

Pauline goes from one room to the next, more surprised each time as she counts the number of bathrooms.

Upstairs, two white employees are still taking pictures from the walls. Wooden boxes are filled with dishes, carpets and old paintings.

FIRST EMPLOYEE
(leaning towards the stairs)

Save yourselves. The Bantus are coming.
(taking down a painting and coughing)
Pfff, this dust! We might at least leave them these crumbs . . .

SECOND EMPLOYEE

Property of the Belgian state. Those are our orders. (He turns to face an equestrian painting of the King Leopold II and stands at attention) Sire, they will turn your Congo into a pigsty.

FIRST EMPLOYEE

And the wine cellar. They're leaving them the cellar! Man, he didn't deprive himself, the governor. Check out these Margaux!

SECOND EMPLOYEE
(putting an African mask away into the box)
Well, they won't be too bored either.

Downstairs, Patrice holds his daughter Juliana in his arms. He locates a chair, and collapses into it, exhausted. He smiles sleepily at his daughter. Juliana looks at him:

JULIANA
Tired papa?

Before he can answer, the telephone rings. He picks up the receiver.

PATRICE
No, Governor Cornelius isn't here. No, he does-
n't live here anymore. You've reached the residence
of Patrice Lumumba, prime minister of the Re-
public of the Congo.

He hangs up and adds, for the benefit of his daughter:

PATRICE
And who has not slept for five months.

EXT. VILLA TILKENS—NIGHT

The Villa Tilkens at night.

EXT./INT. VILLA TILKENS—MORNING

Thomas Kanza shows up at the villa.

INT. VILLA TILKENS HALL—STAIRCASE—
MORNING

In the lobby are camped a crowd of family heads, unemployed, mothers with children in their arms while party activists who try to organize and screen all of their demands.

A member of the secret service stops Kanza at the entrance to the main room.

KANZA
I'm Thomas Kanza, senior delegate to the UN.
Patrice . . . The prime minister summoned me.

SECURITY
I beg your pardon, Excellency.

He shows Kanza in.

INT. VILLA TILKENS—LUMUMBA'S PRIVATE
LOUNGE—MORNING

PATRICE
And my other cufflink? Where's my other cufflink?

PAULINE
Why don't you look for it instead of playing
with the child!

Joseph is closest to the door. He gestures to Kanza to come in, grimacing to show that things are getting hot.

KANZA
(in a whisper)
Domestic problems?

JOSEPH
(shaking his head)
The king refused to grant the amnesty. Patrice
is furious. He wants to shake things up.

There are others in the room. Those we know (Mpolo, Joseph, Pauline, Patrice . . .) and those we don't (Okito, the president of the Senate, who is quite ill at ease). Patrice, half-dressed in a dinner jacket, the bow tie hanging undone at his collar, is busy looking under a chair for his cufflink, while Juliana playfully grabs at his feet. Then Pauline pulls her off, and takes her away crying.

The others pass out sheets of typed paper and begin to read.

PATRICE
(spotting Kanza, seeming more malicious than angry)
Thomas, finally! We need you. Give these back
to me.
(taking the sheets away from the others and giving them to Kanza)
Read them and tell me what you think.
(to the others)
What time is it? When does the car arrive?

OKITO
(in a sweat)
I'm telling you, it's impossible, Excellency. It's

not because I'm presiding over the ceremony, but because of the consequences . . . It will be seen as a provocation . . .

MPOLO

Who started the provocation?

PATRICE

They didn't even send me the king's speech, or the president's. I'm denied amnesty, which would have been the symbolic gesture expected by the public . . . the essential gesture of this ceremony . . .

He speaks without looking at anyone as he walks around the room, scanning the carpets and parquet floor for his cuff link. Okito is following him, begging him to change his mind.

OKITO

We agree, your Excellency. But what can I do? The program says that only the king and the president are to speak.

PATRICE

I nominated you to chair the Senate because I thought you had character. Was I wrong?

MPOLO

(dunking a piece of bread in his tea)

You don't need to introduce him. The microphone stays on. When Kasa-Vubu finishes his speech, Patrice will take it. They'll just have to stay and listen . . .

OKITO

You want to offend the king, General Janssens,
the bishop . . .

PATRICE

The king, the general, the archbishop. Hmm,
I'd forgotten about him. All the better. For once
they'll hear the truth. It will be a change for them.
It will be a change for everyone. (Suddenly he gets
down on all fours and thrusts his arms beneath a
couch. He lets out a cry of triumph). At last!

He gets up on his knees, and brandishes his cuff link.

*Kanza has finished reading. He raises his head and looks at Patrice,
speechless. He holds up the pages.*

KANZA

You're really going to say that?

INT. PARLIAMENT—DAY

*At the podium, a slim young man wearing glasses reads from his speech
without once raising his head. It is Baudouin, king of the Belgians.*

KING BAUDOUIN

It's up to you, Gentlemen, to show that we were
right in bestowing our trust in you . . . Your leaders
will realize the difficulties of governing. They must
teach the Congolese people that independence does
not come through immediate fulfillment of superfi-
cial desires, but through work, respect for the freedom of others, and for the rights of the minority . . .

While he is speaking, the faces of the officials present, among them Belgians: the Resident Minister Ganshof, Ambassador Van den Bosch, General Janssens, and the archbishop, all wearing expressions that suggests a lack of emotion or just drowsiness . . .

Then the Congolese, beginning with the head of state, Kasa-Vubu, who as always, is completely stone-faced.

In the first row below, Kanza scribbles and corrects Patrice's text. Patrice in turn crosses out a word and replaces it with another. Kanza shakes his head in consternation.

This activity does not go unnoticed by the Belgians, who start looking towards Patrice. Even the master of ceremonies, Chairman Okito, is completely distracted by the two men's activities.

In the meantime, the king finishes his speech.

KING BAUDOUIN

Do not compromise the future with hasty reforms, and do not replace the systems left behind you by Belgium until you are certain to do better. Gentlemen, the eyes of the entire world are focused on you. God save Congo!

Applause.

A slight movement passes through the room as the king leaves the podium and President Kasa-Vubu rises to address the assembly.

Patrice and Kanza, not unnoticed by many of the delegates, leave their seats and go out to the corridors.

In the background we hear the beginning of Kasa-Vubu's speech.

KASA-VUBU
(*off-screen*)
Excellencies, dear compatriots . . . at this solemn occasion, when the Republic of Congo introduces itself to the world, and to history . . .

Kanza and Patrice engage in a brief discussion.

KANZA
Patrice, it's too dangerous.

PATRICE
You've corrected all you wanted to correct.

KANZA
Are you really aware of what you're doing? You really want to confront them?

PATRICE
You heard what he said. Would you leave that unchallenged? What will our children remember of this great day?

KANZA
Kasa will answer them.

PATRICE
Okay, then listen to him. Listen to his answer.

Kasa-Vubu is at the podium.

KASA-VUBU
Sire, the presence of Your Venerable Majesty at today's memorable ceremonies constitutes a bright

and renewed testimony of your solicitude for the people you have loved and protected ...

Patrice and Kanza return to the room and take their places. This time, the eyes of the entire Belgian contingent are fixed upon them.

KASA-VUBU

We shall show the world, by our actions, that we are worthy of the trust given us by the people, and of the confidence shown us already by many countries. We will not disappoint them.

Applause. Kasa-Vubu bows and takes his place. Patrice looks at Okito.

OKITO
(hesitating)
I now give the floor to the prime minister.

Slight commotion. Whispers. Patrice stands up.

PATRICE

Fellow countrymen. Freedom fighters, today victorious ... Congolese independence is proclaimed here today through the agreements made with Belgium, a country we consider a friend and treat as an equal. However no Congolese worthy of the name can ever forget the struggle that achieved this, (applause) a struggle in which we spared neither our strength nor our sacrifices, our suffering nor our blood.

We see the effect of these words on the young king and his entourage. Consultations. The king whispers to Kasa-Vubu.

PATRICE

This struggle of tears, of fire and of blood, we
are deeply proud of, as it was noble and just, a
struggle necessary to end the humiliating slavery
imposed on us by force.

*We see now, throughout the country, the effect of these words on the
Congolese, as the speech is retransmitted by radio.*

EXT./INT. BAR NA BISO—DAY

At Bar na Biso, the regulars adjust the radio for better reception.

RADIO (PATRICE)

We have known hard labor in exchange for
miserable wages . . . We have endured sarcasm, insults, and violence, morning, noon and night because we were Negros.

INT. POOR NEIGHBORHOOD—"DEVELOPED"
PERSON'S HOUSE—DAY

*In the home of a "developed" family. Absorbed interest. The husband
eats chicken with his fingers.*

RADIO (PATRICE)

We have known that in the cities whites live in
magnificent homes, and blacks in crumbling straw
huts, that blacks were not allowed in cinemas, nor
in restaurants, or in so-called European stores . . .

EXT. PUBLIC FORCE BARRACKS—DAY

At a Public Force station. Each word is greeted by cheers.

RADIO (PATRICE)
Who will forget the shootings in which so
many of our brothers died, the miserable prisons
in which were thrown those who escaped the soldiers bullets, soldiers who were the tools of the
colonialist's domination.

Applause.

EXT. LEOPOLDVILLE—MARKET CORNER—
DAY

*Reactions in Leopoldville. In the market area, reactions of joy, laugh-
ter among the women shopkeepers. One of them throws an empty can at
a scoundrel who has stolen a piece of fruit.*

RADIO (PATRICE)
All of this, my brothers we have suffered deeply
and our wounds are still too fresh and too painful
for us to chase them from our memories.

INT./EXT. LEOPOLDVILLE—RESTAURANT
REGINA—DAY

*Some whites look at each other embarrassed over their glasses of beer.
Signs of impatience and disdain.*

RADIO (PATRICE)

All of this my brothers, we say it loud and clear,
all of this is now over.

EXT. LEOPOLDVILLE—STREET—DAY

A jeep passes by. Some pedestrians, with different rapport between blacks and whites. A white woman finishes her shopping. Her "boy" puts groceries in the trunk.

RADIO (PATRICE)

The Republic of Congo has been proclaimed
and our country is now in the hands of her own
children ...

INT. PARLIAMENT—DAY

We finish inside the conference hall, where the appalled expressions of the Belgian officials contrast strikingly with the enthusiasm of the Congolese members of the audience. This contrast is both comic and troublesome.

PATRICE

We are together going to instigate a system of
social justice and ensure that our fatherland is for
the benefit of its children.

(applause)

We will accept collaboration and assistance as
long as it is fair and doesn't seek to impose its politics.

(applause)

There, Your Majesty, Excellencies, Ladies and
Gentlemen, dear compatriots, brothers in race,

brothers in struggle, there is what I wanted to say to you. Long life the Independence of African unity! Long life an independent and sovereign Congo!

Applause.

EXT. RESIDENTIAL AREA—DAY

Caption: Leopoldville. July 4, 1960. Four days later.

The air shudders in the torrid midday heat. Nobody in the streets. Silence. Bougainvillea. Silence. Heat.

EXT. VILLA TILKENS—BACKYARD—DAY

It's laundry day. Behind the house, a servant is busy with several large baskets full of clothes and soapy water. Juliana, fully dressed, slides playfully into one of them. She bursts out laughing. Pauline runs out.

> **PAULINE**
> Get out of that right away. I've had enough of your silly games.

EXT. LEOPOLDVILLE—RESIDENTIAL AREA—DAY.

Same time. Heat.

A drunken soldier waves his military belt in the air. He blabbers something in Lingala, about "politicians selling out to the Flemish." Two

*other soldiers hold him back. They are as drunk as he. They laugh. It's
not clear whether they are fighting or playing.*

*A Belgian in shorts and a t-shirt, his head shaded by a colonial hel-
met, walks his dog on the footpath across the street.*

The soldiers address him in Lingala, shouting insults.

THE SOLDIERS
(in Lingala)
We're going to eat your dog, Flemish bastard!
We're hungry!

*The man doesn't respond, but the dog begins to bark ferociously at the
soldiers. A woman steps out onto the terrace of a villa.*

WOMAN
Maxence! Maxence! Come in right now!

MAN
They don't frighten me. They're with the Public
Force. I'm going to take down their ID numbers.

*After these brave words, he pulls on the leash of his dog, who has be-
come increasingly ferocious. The soldiers, in turn, advance menacingly
towards him. The man understands. He pulls the dog around as the bark-
ing becomes more frantic. He shouts at the dog, while forcing him into
the house. The man and dog get in just before the soldiers reach them. The
woman slams the door behind them. The sound of the door being bolted.
One of the soldiers throws a rock at a window, shattering it.*

INT./EXT. VILLA TILKENS—VERANDA—NIGHT

It is night. A night full of stars.

On the veranda, Juliana sits on Patrice's lap. He is showing her the stars and constellations, telling her their names.

Pauline, sitting on the ground, is mixing some ingredients in a large bowl.

> JULIANA
> So when the sun goes to sleep, it goes under the earth? Is under the earth in Belgium?

> PATRICE
> No, darling, Belgium is on the earth . . . It's just far away . . . very far.

> JULIANA
> As far away as the moon?

> PATRICE
> *(laughing)*
> Almost.

> JULIANA
> Then on the moon are there also Flemish and Walloons?

> PATRICE
> Oh no. The moon is too far just the same.

> JULIANA
> On Mars, then. There must be tribes there, Daddy!

(counting on her fingers)
Like the Walloons, the Flemish, the Tetelas, the
Mukongos, the Balubas . . .

PATRICE

Yes, but you know, on Mars, people are green.

JULIANA
(opening her eyes wide)

Green?

PATRICE

Yes, and very small.

PAULINE
(in Swahili)
Stop filling her head with such silliness!

EXT. BARRACKS—DAY

Caption: Camp Léopold II. The next day.

In the open air, in front of the barracks, troops from the Public Force
stand in formation. In front standing to attention, the three soldiers
who had drunkenly harassed the Belgian man and his dog. They don't
look quite as carefree as last we saw them. General Janssens himself strips
them of their epaulets, one by one.

JANSSENS

Worthless . . . Sacks of shit . . . You are a shame
to your regiment . . . Oh, and you're not the only
ones. There are others of your sort throughout the
provinces . . . In Madimba, they even raped a

white woman. Execution! You dishonor the Public Force ... Immediate arrest ... take them away. Get them out of my sight.

A detachment of four soldiers leads them away to jail. General Janssens turns towards the troops standing to attention.

JANSSENS

I want to make things clear. Independence is fine for civilians. For the military, there's only discipline. Disc-i-pline. Before the 30th of June, you had white officers. After the 30th of June, you still have white officers. Perhaps the politicians have been telling you another story. They lied. I, however, have always told you the truth. And if you can't hear it, I'll write it for you.

He turns to a blackboard set up behind him, and writes in large letters: "AFTER INDEPENDENCE = BEFORE INDEPENDENCE"

A few yards away, the soldiers' wives, having witnessed the entire scene from nearby, begin to display their anger, in Lingala:

WIVES

You see!
We'll get them today
We're not dogs!
Lumumba lied to us!

Among the soldiers, we hear similar whispers.

The rumor swells: "LUMUMBA LIED TO US! DEATH TO LUMUMBA! LUMUMBA PAMBA!"

INT./EXT. ROAD IN AN INDUSTRIAL AREA—CAR—
DAY

Near the Leopold II camp, a minister's limousine rolls slowly by. The Minister consults his documents on the way to a meeting of the government. Suddenly a rock shatters the side window.

More rocks follow. They are thrown by soldiers of the Public Force, provoked by the sight of the shiny limousine. They yell in Lingala.

SOLDIERS
Death to Lumumba! Lumumba pamba!

The minister, alarmed, shouts at the driver to speed up. But the armed soldiers block the way. Some of them try to open the limousine door. They bang the windows with their fists. A barrage of rocks showers the chassis.

Finally, the driver sees an opening, and speeds away.

The soldiers throw stones after the car. One of them aims his rifle and fires.

INT. VILLA TILKENS—COUNCIL OF MINISTERS
ROOM—DAY

A group of ministers are assembled around Patrice. Among them are also two civilians and one Belgian military officer, apparently advisers. The faces are serious, frightened even.

EXT. VILLA TILKENS—STREETS—DAY

Members of the security forces are roaming around the house, armed to the teeth.

INT. VILLA TILKENS—COUNCIL OF MINISTERS ROOM—DAY

PATRICE
These are only isolated incidents . . . Let's not over dramatizes . . .

A minister, sweating profusely, arrives in the room, and in his agitation drops his briefcase from which all the files fall. Without picking them up or sitting down, he interrupts Patrice.

MINISTER
Prime Minister, forgive me . . . I've just escaped a lynching . . . Camp Hardy is also in revolt . . . They have taken their officers hostage . . . They are looking for you . . . they say they want to kill you . . .

Everyone begins to speak at the same time.

PATRICE
Be quiet! Sit down . . . Let's examine the situation calmly . . .
(pointing to Mpolo who has his hand raised)
The minister of youth and sports . . .

MPOLO
The situation? It's simple . . . There are 25,000 men in the Public Force . . . They have transmitters tuned to the same frequency. Do you under-

stand what that means? Even before their officers, they know exactly what is happening from one camp to the other across the whole country. It could spread throughout the entire country. It's a powder keg and the fuse is lit.

A MINISTER
Are they crazy? What do they want?

JOSEPH
What do they want? They want to be promoted! That's what they want! I know, I was one of them!

BELGIAN MILITARY MAN
If I may, Prime Minister, it's true the men are tired. They've been on duty for more than five months, with the festivities, the riots . . .

MPOLO
It's their Flemish general, this Janssens, who incites them against us, while he refuses as always to Africanize the officers. He should be shot.

Several ministers protest.

PATRICE
To replace him, would be simpler. I propose Senator Lundula, and you, Mpolo, I propose you be made colonel. Let's vote.

MINISTER
(standing up, his voice trembling)
I'll never vote for a man who wants to shoot everyone.

ANOTHER MINISTER
He's not even a military man!

JOSEPH
Prime Minister, I've spent seven years in the
Public Force. Without denying the qualities of my
colleague Maurice Mpolo, I believe I am more
qualified to . . .

BELGIAN ADVISOR
I believe that it's an excellent proposition. It is
important for the new commander to come from
the ranks . . . a good choice.

MPOLO
What about seniority? Mobutu is too young.
Lundula, fine! He's a veteran, he was in Burma . .
.

EXT. VILLA TILKENS—DAY

*Suddenly we hear screams and shots coming from the outside. Sounds
of glass breaking. The door to the garden is forced open. Scuffles in the
garden.*

INT. VILLA TILKENS—COUNCIL OF MINISTERS
ROOM—DAY

*A dozen rebel soldiers from the Public Force, armed and angry, break
into the room. Some of the ministers begin to panic. Patrice approaches the
soldiers. One of them walks towards him. He holds a paper in his hand.*

SPOKESMAN FOR THE SOLDIERS

Excellency . . . We mean no harm . . . We have a petition. We would like you to answer right away . . .

KANZA

We won't listen to you . . . Not under these conditions . . .

PATRICE

Give me your petition. I'll read it and give it consideration.

SPOKESMAN

No, Excellency. You'll answer right away.
(beginning to read aloud)
"Desiring to fulfill our military duties with honor, we denounce General Emile Janssens, who is attempting to disgrace the Congolese army. We want a system of justice and equality. Such a system is inconceivable as long as there are officers in the Congolese Army."

PATRICE

Officers? You mean white officers?

SEVERAL SOLDIERS

(together)
Yes, white officers! No, officers! No, no more officers! Yes, officers—black officers !

PATRICE

I understand your desire for justice and equality. But I will not comply with any demands under the pressure of the gun. I ask you to return to your barracks. The free Congo needs a strong and disciplined army.

A SOLDIER

We've heard that before! Janssens talks like that!

SPOKESMAN

We want an answer. Right now.

Some soldiers cock their rifles. The sound of snapping metal resounds throughout the room. Tension in the room.

PATRICE

I have listened to you, despite your illegal and violent intrusion. You even disagree amongst yourselves about the meaning of your petition. (whispers). But I understand your indignation. I will answer in person at the camp Leopold tomorrow, first thing in the morning. You have my word. Now, I ask you to leave and return to your barracks.

SEVERAL SOLDIERS

No!

PATRICE

Well then, shoot!

This challenge creates a certain indecision among the soldiers, and anxiety among the ministers.

SPOKESMAN
(after a silence)
You will go to Camp Leo?

PATRICE
I promise you.

SPOKESMAN
We are holding fifteen white officers and their
wives hostage. If you don't show up, we'll kill them.

The spokesman for the soldiers signals the others to retreat. They leave.

PATRICE
(sitting back down)
Gentlemen, the meeting is not over . . .

INT. VILLA TILKENS—SMALL OFFICE—NIGHT.

Patrice is working at the typewriter. On the radio, alarming news. Pauline appears, barefoot.

PAULINE
Aren't you coming to bed? It's four o'clock in
the morning.

PATRICE
I've got to finish this.

She rubs his neck with her hand.

PAULINE

You're going to fall asleep at your desk again.

He turns away from his work for a moment and turns to Pauline, whose stomach reveals her advanced state of pregnancy. He touches her stomach.

PATRICE

You mustn't worry.

PAULINE

How can I not worry? You don't sleep more than two hours a night. I'm beginning to believe that you actually have been taking dope to keep yourself going.

PATRICE

That's what they've been saying?

PAULINE

Oh, you know, if I repeated everything the servants told me . . .
(*shrugging*)
Pffff . . .

He takes her by the waist and holds her.

PATRICE

You've got to watch out for the children . . . if anything happens to me . . .

EXT. LEOPOLDVILLE—IN FRONT OF THE REGINA—DAY

In a little square in the center of town, in front of the restaurant Regina, Belgians, in police uniforms hand out rifles and pistols to civilians, men and women in a state somewhere between panic and bravado.

EXT. VILLA TILKENS—FRONT COURTYARD—DAY

Two limousines are parked in the front yard. Patrice walks down the stairs to the exit, accompanying Kanza on his way out.

KANZA
Good luck.

PATRICE
You too. Good luck at the UN.

A limousine enters the yard and comes to a stop near them. The chauffeur gets out and opens the back door. General Janssens gets out. He salutes Patrice succinctly.

PATRICE
General, have you guessed why I summoned you?

JANSSENS
I'm waiting for you to inform me.

PATRICE
I'm waiting for you to explain the meaning of
this (he brandishes a piece of paper). I received
this letter last night.

JANSSENS
It seems perfectly clear to me.

PATRICE

Excellency.

JANSSENS

Pardon me?

PATRICE

You say: Excellency. I'd like to know what you
mean by this:
(reading)
"As I don't like to contradict or to repeat myself,
I'm asking you, respectfully, to consider this a final
and solemn warning." Tell me, do you think that
in Belgium a general could address his superiors
in such a manner?

JANSSENS

Forgive me—
(emphasizing the word)
—Excellency. In Belgium there is order. Here,
we're headed for catastrophe. Chaos continues to
spread.

PATRICE

It is spreading because you cannot control your
men, who are fed up with your methods. The Public Force must change, like everything else. I want
your resignation.

JANSSENS

Mr. Lumumba . . . Excellency . . .

PATRICE

I've said all I had to say to you, General.

*The general disappears into the limousine which speeds away. Patrice
and Kanza look at each other.*

EXT. LEOPOLDVILLE—ROAD TO THE BEACH—
END OF AFTERNOON

*A car, piled high with luggage, speeds as quickly as it can in the di-
rection of the Brazzaville Beach (as indicated by a sign). A roadblock
stops the car. Other cars are already stopped there. Congolese rebels make
the occupants get out.*

> **REBEL**
>
> Wallon or Flemish?

> **DRIVER**
> *(pale with fear)*
>
> Wallon.

> **REBEL**
>
> That'll cost you one hundred francs.

*The driver's wife wants to protest, but her husband signals her to
keep quiet and to get back into the car.*

He points with his chin at a ditch where a white man lies motionless.

*Frightened, the woman moves to get into the car, but two soldiers
prevent her. The woman begins to scream. Her husband also panics and
tries to reach her: he receives a blow to the face, which knocks him out.*

*The soldiers try to silence the woman, who hasn't stopped shouting. Half
strangling her, their hands over her mouth, they tear off her clothes . . .*

INT. VILLA TILKENS—PATRICE'S OFFICE—NIGHT

In Patrice's office, a servant bursts in.

SERVANT
Excellency . . .

He hands Patrice a small card and whispers something to him.

PATRICE
At this time?
    (checking the wall clock, showing midnight)
Show him in.

INT. VILLA TILKENS—PATRICE'S OFFICE—NIGHT

*Enter a man in a three-piece suit and tie, the Belgian Ambassador
Van den Bosch. Patrice points to a chair and sits down facing him.*

PATRICE
Ambassador . . . You bring news?

VAN DEN BOSCH
Nothing you don't already know, Excellency. It
is quite bad. I know you were chased out of camp
Leopold . . .

PATRICE
(wearily)
There were some difficulties, but order will be
reestablished.

VAN DEN BOSCH

I don't know of what order you speak. In any case, I didn't come to the Congo to passively witness the rape and massacre of my compatriots. If you don't have the means to stop this, I must inform you that I do . . . They are at your disposal.

PATRICE
(calmly)

Intervention?

VAN DEN BOSCH

The situation is critical. I think that you could "solicit" Belgium's help. There is a treaty that authorizes you to do so.

PATRICE

I am of a different opinion.

VAN DEN BOSCH

If you decline my offer, we will be forced to consult our Western partners. Do you understand what I mean?

PATRICE

No, I still don't understand you. But I'll tell you what I have decided: One, General Janssens, commander in chief of the Public Force, must leave the Congo within twenty-four hours. Two, you are charged with informing the person in question, and to ensure his departure. Three, you will be held personally responsible for his activities from now until his departure.

VAN DEN BOSCH

Excellency, this officer has been of great service
to the Congo. I demand that he be treated with
the appropriate respect . . .

*At this last word, Patrice stands up so abruptly that the Ambassador
involuntarily draws back.*

PATRICE

(shouting)

Respect! All that is happening now is because of
you, you, the Belgians! Camp Thysville revolted because of a Belgian officer, camp Leopold because of
General Janssens, in Elizabethville, it was Weber!
You spread rumors of a Soviet invasion to incite
panic . . . From the beginning you have plotted
against me, against the Lumumba government, and
you dare to threaten me with the UN, with NATO!
You dare come to the Prime Minister's residence in
the middle of the night with threats and insults . . .
Tomorrow morning, I'll call a press conference to
denounce your plot, your threats, your insults! I was
advised by phone to take refuge in Brazzaville, and
here I will stay, do you hear me, here, behind my
desk, until the Belgians come to massacre me!

*The ambassador has stood up at this outburst He backs towards the
garden and tries to say:*

VAN DEN BOSCH

It is I who should be complaining, yet it is you
who are angry . . . If I may, I'd like to say I find this
quite peculiar.

PATRICE

If I may, I'd like to ask you to leave.

Without another word, Van den Bosch leaves.

Patrice, left by himself, collapses into a chair, his head in his hands. After a while, he forces himself to get back up and goes out into the garden.

EXT. VILLA TILKENS—GARDEN—NIGHT

Patrice addresses one of the guards he meets in the garden.

PATRICE
(in Tetela)

You, still here?

GUARD

Yes, sir, we decided to change the guard shift.
What with the way things are these days.

PATRICE

What could happen to me?
(nodding his head at the building across the street)
It is they who are afraid of me.

EXT. TILKENS NEIGHBORHOOD—VILLA WITH
BELGIAN FLAG—NIGHT

The Belgian flag flies at the villa across the street, where there is a lot of activity. Cars, doors opening and closing, voices . . .

EXT. VILLA TILKENS—GARDEN—NIGHT

SOLDIER
I'm not talking about them, sir.

PATRICE
Well . . . we're all brothers. We'll end up getting
along. Right?

The soldier looks at him without answering.

EXT. VILLA TILKENS—FRONT COURTYARD—DAY

*A crowd of journalists and press photographers gather in front of the
residence with cameras, microphones and tape recorders pushed towards
the prime minister. Patrice stands on the first step, his face shows the
signs of his sleepless night.*

PATRICE
. . . Under these conditions, I dismissed General Janssens. For his own good and for his security, I urge him to take the first plane for Brussels.
I nominate Major Victor Lundula commander in
chief of the Public Force, and I promote Joseph
Mobutu to the rank of colonel. Furthermore, the
Public Force now becomes the National Congolese Army.

JOURNALIST
Mr. Lumumba, is this sufficient to reestablish
order? How will you put an end to the violence?

PATRICE

Difficulties are inevitable. The unrest is caused by a minority of troublemakers and is a result of a huge misunderstanding. In order to put an end to this, and to set people's minds at ease, I have decided, with President Kasa-Vubu's agreement, to set out on a tour across the country to explain and pacify the situation.

JOURNALIST

Will you go to Katanga? And to Elizabethville?

PATRICE

I will go everywhere. To Coquilhatville, to Stanleyville, to Luluabourg, and to Elizabethville. I warn the Belgian government against any attempt to take advantage of the situation to intervene militarily or to stir more unrest. Only through work will we prosper. Those who refuse to accept this and who undermine our effort should be considered enemies of the people.

JOURNALISTS

What does Mr. Tshombe think of this? . . . Will you go to the UN?

INT. "LUMUMBA–KASA-VUBU" AIRPLANE—
CABIN—DAY

Inside a Dakota airplane, Patrice Lumumba and Kasa-Vubu sit on either side of the central aisle. Turbulence shakes the plane. Patrice holds the pages of a speech in his hands.

PATRICE
(reading)

...Katanga, your beautiful and prosperous province, one of the principal sources of our national wealth ...

(stopping)

What time is it in Elizabethville? The same as in Luluabourg?

KASA-VUBU

I don't know anymore. I only hope that Elizabethville is our last stop. Ten days of this touring. I'm fed up of the plane. The Congo is too big for us.

PATRICE

Don't say that, Mr. President. The Congo is big, and demands big things of us. But it is not too big for us. Let me go on: "Whoever says secession, says treason ..." We're going down?

PILOT
(off-screen)

Mr. President, the Elizabethville control tower refuses to let us land.

PATRICE

What?

Patrice stands up. Kasa-Vubu follows him into the cockpit. The Belgian pilot holds out the radio speaker.

RADIO (MUNONGO)

I repeat: you are not authorized to land, by order of the Katangan government.

PATRICE

What government?

KASA-VUBU

That's it. The secession is happening.

PATRICE

I want to speak with those in charge.

INT. ELIZABETHVILLE—CONTROL TOWER—
DAY

MUNONGO

We could allow a visit of President Kasa-Vubu,
but it's out of the question for the traitor, Patrice
Lumumba, to set foot on Katangan soil.

INT. "LUMUMBA–KASA-VUBU" AIRPLANE—
CABIN—DAY

PATRICE

I recognize that voice. It's Munongo.
(to the pilot)
Proceed to land.

PILOT

I can't!

PATRICE

Do as I tell you!

PILOT

I can't! They're putting trucks on the runway.
(to Kasa-Vubu)
Mr. President, we've got to turn back. There is
no other way.

EXT. BUSH AIRPORT—DAY

*The Dakota has landed on the tarmac of a small savanna airfield,
and is being refueled. The savanna stretches for miles out into the horizon. A few feet away from the plane, two men walk the tarmac while
they talk: the prime minister and the president of the Congo. Two men
lost in this immense space.*

KASA-VUBU

We weren't careful enough with Tshombe.

PATRICE

Tshombe would never have acted alone. The
Belgians encouraged him.

KASA-VUBU

What do we do now?
(smiling)
We have a choice between war, shame, resignation and the abandoning of 70 percent of our natural resources.

PATRICE

Mr. President. We have no choice. We must
break the rebellion.

KASA-VUBU

You know, the United Mines of Upper Katanga
meddles with international high finance.

PATRICE

Can you imagine leaving them a territory sixteen times larger than Belgium? We won't make a
gift of it. We must call upon the UN.

KASA-VUBU

You think that the UN is the best way? If we
must bring in the military, don't you think the
Russians …

PATRICE

The Russians? They already call me a communist
puppet. Do you want me assassinated by the CIA?

*Kasa-Vubu, instead of replying, stops and looks at the landscape
around him.*

KASA-VUBU

What peace. This silence is wonderful.

EXT. LEOPOLDVILLE—N'DJILI AIRPORT—
RUNWAY—DAY

*The Dakota lands and comes to a stop in front of a platoon of Bel-
gians paratroopers.*

INT. N'DJILI AIRPORT—"LUMUMBA KASA-VUBU"

AIRPLANE—CABIN—DAY

Inside, Patrice Lumumba doesn't wait for the plane to come to a full stop, but walks towards the cockpit, opens the door and addresses the Belgian pilot:

> PATRICE
>
> Why are we at N'djili? We told you to go to Stanleyville.

> PILOT
>
> I received other instructions.

> PATRICE
>
> You are under orders! It is not up to you to decide our priorities!

> PILOT
> *(coldly)*
> I am Belgian . . . Excellency.

Patrice slams the door behind him. He rejoins Kasa-Vubu who is about to descend the stairs to exit, but for some reason remains immobile at the doorway.

EXT. LEOPOLDVILLE—N'DJILI AIRPORT RUNWAY— DAY

Below, at the bottom of the stairway, they see a detachment of Belgian paratroops, a smiling general at their head. Belgian General Cumont approaches them and salutes Kasa.

CUMONT

Mr. Head of State, would you like to review the troops?

Kasa-Vubu and Lumumba look at each other.

KASA-VUBU

It's a set-up!

PATRICE

You are asking the head of state of an independent country to review foreign troops? Out of the question!

Cumont ignores Lumumba's interjection and addresses Kasa-Vubu.

CUMONT

Mr. President, our troops are here only to honor you and to insure your safety. I insist that you review the troops.

KASA-VUBU

We refuse your protection. You are no longer welcome here.

CUMONT

Mr. President, I beg you to listen to me. We wanted to welcome you with the honor due your rank.

KASA-VUBU

We don't need your honors. Leave, that is all!

CUMONT

Mr. President, it is inadmissible to speak to a Belgian general in this manner.

Hostile words are heard from the platoon. Lumumba turns abruptly to the troops. We now see a group of Belgian civilians moving toward the plane: pale, and near hysteria, as they wait for their flight. Suddenly another officer comes from behind Cumont and points to the refugees.

OFFICER

Look at these women! They were raped by your troops, and our men were ridiculed and mistreated. You are the shame of Africa and of the world!

Cumont again addresses Kasa-Vubu.

CUMONT

Mr. President. We are here to protect our citizens. No more blood should be shed.

PATRICE

If blood is shed this evening, you will be held responsible.

BELGIAN SOLDIER

Assassins, sadists, you rape nuns and white women!

A WOMAN

God will punish you!

Kasa-Vubu and Lumumba make their way as best they can to the waiting limousine. The people crowd in around them and soon they find themselves in the middle of a lynch mob of refugees and soldiers. Insults,

*cries of hatred, racial slurs . . . They reach the car and climb in, followed
by a barrage of spit.*

*Two soldiers climb onto the bumpers and start rocking the car with
all their strength.*

*Patrice, his teeth clenched, orders the Belgian chauffeur to take off.
The crowd presses in around the car. The thump of hammering resounds
against the body. Faces distorted by hate.*

CHAUFFEUR
I can't drive through this crowd.

PATRICE
Do as you're told.

*He is finally able to move. The crowd opens up. The soldiers jump
from the car. The car moves away from the runway, where General Cumont remains immobile.*

INT./EXT. N'DJILI AIRPORT EXIT—CAR—DAY

*Lumumba and Kasa-Vubu remain silent. Lumumba has tears of
anger in his eyes.*

VOICE OVER (LUMUMBA)
At that moment, I understood that the humiliation would never end. Not from one side, nor the
other. It's at that moment . . .

ARCHIVAL PHOTOGRAPHS

VOICE OVER (LUMUMBA)

… I finally understood that they were ready to do anything, Even sacrifice their own people. Panic fed panic. Reprisals from one side led to reprisal on the other. I understood that the real enemies weren't those poor, angry women, those children with haggard eyes …

Congolese soldiers, hands on their heads, are roughly marched off by Belgian soldiers.

VOICE OVER (LUMUMBA)

… from nightmares, nor even the soldiers, humiliated by having had to flee before their old whipping-boys …

INT./EXT. N'DJILI AIRPORT EXIT—CAR—DAY

Cut back to the silent faces of Lumumba and Kasa-Vubu.

EXT./INT. LEOPOLDVILLE—MILITARY CAMP—DAY

In a room in a military base, a group of soldiers huddle around a radio transmitter, which sends and receives intense and absurd messages over the air waves.

RECEIVER

Request for Commander Jacques, where are the rifles? Russians are landing at N'Djili . . .

TRANSMITTER

What do you mean Russians? Disguised, they are all disguised . . . They are going to massacre us! We must arm ourselves.

RECEIVER

. . . Don't panic. Lock up Matelar. The traitor.

TRANSMITTER

They're crazy, they're crazy! Kindu here. It's the Paras, the Belgian paras! They're everywhere!

RECEIVER

The white officers have locked up all the arms . . . Did the Belgians called them? . . . send troops to the airfield . . . The Russians must not land . . .

TRANSMITTER

Why are they evacuating their women and children? It's in order to massacre us! They're handing out weapons everywhere!

EXT./INT. LEOPOLDVILLE—MILITARY CAMP—DAY

Mutineers lock white officers into a room and insult them.

EXT. LEOPOLDVILLE—DOWNTOWN—CINEMA

STREET—DAY

A jeep crammed with mutinous soldiers, followed by a requisitioned car emerges from a street. Near the cinema, they shoot in any direction, without aiming. A signpost is hit.

ARCHIVAL PHOTOGRAPHS

Black and white images. The exodus of the Belgians continues. Sabena planes arrive in Brussels and unload women, children, old people, nuns, still frightened by what they have just gone through. Politicians solemnly make statements. There are calls for intervention.

VOICE OVER (LUMUMBA)
. . . We were now leaving behind a history of colonisers and colonised. It was no longer Belgium against the Congo. We were now entering the Cold War . . . The tragedy grew, while the diplomats and politicians shrunk from view, becoming characters out of a comedy . . . It seemed like chaos, but it was all planned.

EXT. MATADI PORT—DAWN

The roar of low flying planes.

Caption: The port of Matadi, July 11, 1960.

A platoon of Belgian paratroopers advance among the giant cranes of the port. They force open the hangar doors and order out the soldiers. They shoot them at the slightest sign of resistance.

EXT. MATADI PORT—DAWN

Paratroopers break down the door of a cabin where Congolese soldiers have hidden. Some try to surrender, one tries to escape. They are shot. Further on, a column of Congolese soldiers are unceremoniously marched away, hands on their heads. More planes fly over.

EXT. MATADI PORT—DAWN

Five railway carriages explode, one after the other, under an aerial bombardment.

EXT. LEOPOLDVILLE—DOWNTOWN—STATUE OF LEOPOLD II—DAY

Two bloody soldiers' corpses are displayed on the hood of a jeep.

Mpolo is standing in the vehicle, his foot resting on the windshield. He harangues the group assembled around the bloody remains.

MPOLO

Friends, comrades—this is what the Flemish have done! They tricked their way into Matadi, they machine gunned and bombed the port, massacring men, women and children. That's what the Belgians want to do to the Congo!

MEN
(in Lingala)

Death to the Flemish! Revenge!

MPOLO

And now they want to chop it up in pieces, cut it up to take it back bit by bit. That's their plan! They have started their attacks in the provinces, they have invaded the Katanga with the help of that traitor Tshombe and his bunch! Are we going to let them do it? (shouts: No!) Are we going to let ourselves be slaughtered like sheep? (shouts: No!) Are we going to allow our brothers' blood to flow without retaliation?

SOLDIERS

No! Death to the Belgians! To the white neighborhood!

MPOLO

They will pay! Long life the Congo! Long life Lumumba! Death to the Belgians!

SOLDIERS

Death to the Belgians!

ARCHIVAL FOOTAGE—NEW YORK—UNITED NATIONS SECURITY COUNCIL

Caption: UN Security Council

BELGIAN DELEGATE

...Do you think that if we had a conspiracy in mind, we would have left them, left our women, our children, and our little girls with people devoid of honor?

The debate is intense. Some are sweating, others are discussing with their neighbors. Stares, false smiles, and approving nods are exchanged.

SOVIET DELEGATE

... This foreign aggression against the Republic of Congo is a threat to international peace ... The Katanga's secession reveals quite clearly the tactic of international high finance ...

AMERICAN DELEGATE

... It is regrettable to note how the Soviet Union is obviously trying to introduce the cold war to the very heart of Africa.

KANZA

(off-screen during a wideshot)
... I would like to remind the honorable delegates that the Congo is now a sovereign state, and no longer a Belgian colony.

SECRETARY-GENERAL

I propose a vote on the resolution: the immediate departure of Belgian troops and the sending of UN troops to Congo.

ARCHIVAL FOOTAGE—LEOPOLDVILLE—N'DJILI AIRPORT

Machine guns point from a cargo plane. Soldiers in UN uniforms, Canadians, Swedes, Russians spill out onto the tarmac.

Dag Hammarskjold salutes the Katangan flag.

Other footage, documenting the scope of the UN intervention.

INT. VILLA TILKENS—LIBRARY—DAY

A strange scene, given the precarity of the moment. Lumumba, in full evening dress, stands in front of a bookcase being photographed by two westerners. The assistant finishes "stuffing" the gaps in the library that has surely seen better days.

ASSISTANT
Two medical dictionaries and the autobiography of Cecil Rhodes should do the trick, Mr. Prime Minister.

LUMUMBA
I can only regret the literary taste of my predecessors. But is this photo really necessary?

PHOTOGRAPHER
Don't worry, Mr. Prime Minister, we'll take care of it. Don't forget that there must be one in every ministry, every school, every store . . .

At this moment, Mobutu appears at the door of the library.

LUMUMBA
Excuse me.

Lumumba leaves his place and closes the door of the adjoining room behind him.

PHOTOGRAPHER
We'll never get it. We've been after him for

more than two months now.

*The photographer's assistant catches the eyes of Juliana, who watches
them quietly from one corner of the room.*

ASSISTANT
Let's take the girl in the meantime.

INT./EXT. VILLA TILKENS—
OFFICE/STOREROOM—DAY

*Adjoining office, used more for storage and for mail than business.
Mobutu stands near the door, Lumumba leans against a bookshelf.*

LUMUMBA
So, you confirm it?

MOBUTU
It's a war, Patrice . . .

LUMUMBA
The UN speaks of genocide.

MOBUTU
The UN is manipulated by the Americans . . .

LUMUMBA
Manipulated or not, hundreds died. Yes or no?
We told you to take back Kasai, not to turn the
whole region into a blood bath. And why? To
what end? Most of the leaders sought refuge in
the Katanga.

MOBUTU

We recaptured Kasai, didn't we?

LUMUMBA

You butchered it.

MOBUTU

War means killing. Or be killed . . . that's the price to pay.

LUMUMBA

Who pays? Always the same! Until now I've covered for you. But no longer! I cannot accept these horrors.

MOBUTU

Mr. Prime Minister . . .

LUMUMBA

Stop this pretense . . .

MOBUTU

Patrice . . . I'm a military man and an officer. I have proved it. I regained control of the Public Force. I follow orders, and when none are given, I make the decision alone.

LUMUMBA

One hundred people . . . women, children, old people, locked inside a church and eliminated? These are your decisions?
(beat)
Answer me!

MOBUTU

No, of course not . . . But Patrice, it's a war . . .
Wars are dirty . . . War terrifies men . . . And when
they are terrified, they do this sort of thing . . . Orders can do nothing against it . . .

LUMUMBA

You let it happen! You didn't shoot those responsible for it!

MOBUTU

Patrice . . .

LUMUMBA

Do you know this will cost us? It is I who will
be held responsible for this! You leave me more
alone than I've ever been.

MOBUTU

You're not alone. I'm at your side . . .

LUMUMBA

No. You're no longer at my side . . . you're at my
back. I have no need of an assassin, of a murderer,
at my side and even less at my back . . .

MOBUTU

What does that mean?

LUMUMBA

It means get the hell out! Is that clear?

*Lumumba, alone, seems suddenly overwhelmed. A moment of weak-
ness. He recovers himself.*

INT. VILLA TILKENS—LIBRARY—DAY

He leaves the room and watches Juliana being gratuitously photographed by two photographers. He picks up the telephone. Through the window he sees:

EXT. VILLA TILKENS—DAY

In the garden, children play.

LUMUMBA
(on the phone)
The President of the Republic. From the Prime Minister . . .

INT. PRESIDENTIAL PALACE—WAITING ROOM—DAY

Patrice is in the waiting room. He sees the American ambassador come out of the President's office. The ambassador is embarrassed, but salutes the Prime Minister.

PATRICE
Mr. Timberlake . . . Glad to see you . . . I've tried to reach you at the embassy, but without luck.

TIMBERLAKE
(with an American accent)
I move around a lot, Excellency.

PATRICE

Everyone is moving around a lot these days.

TIMBERLAKE

My government has some proposals to make you . . .

PATRICE

Proposals? I'll willingly hear them out, but allow me to doubt the reliability of American proposals. You probably know the Bantu proverb: "the hand that gives is the hand that rules." And your hand weighs quite heavily in the Congo these days. Please excuse me.

The usher opens the door for him.

INT. PRESIDENTIAL PALACE—KASA-VUBU'S OFFICE—DAY

Kasa-Vubu greets Patrice fraternally.

KASA-VUBU

Mr. Prime Minister, I must tell you what has been preoccupying me . . . The Congolese National Army . . .

PATRICE

I know, Mr. President. The Kasai massacres. I am appalled, and I communicated this personally to those responsible.

KASA-VUBU

That doesn't help the Congo's cause.

PATRICE

No. The problem of the Katanga remains the same. On one hand, our troops have no leadership and commit atrocities. On the other hand, the UN betrays its mandate and passively supports the Belgians. Ghana backs us only with words. Guinea doesn't have the means.

KASA-VUBU

Do you have a solution?

PATRICE

The Russians.
(beat)
They promise Ilyouchines, and military advisors ... They could reinforce General Lundula's troops. He could replace Colonel Mobutu, whom I no longer trust.

KASA-VUBU

I thought that the Russians scared you. That they would compromise you.

PATRICE

That was a century ago, Mr. President. We're already compromised up to our necks.

Kasa-Vubu seems to be collecting his thoughts. His eyes wander over the walls and tapestries for a moment.

KASA-VUBU

Isn't this a beautiful place? What peace. Have you noticed? No outside noise reaches us here. Have you already visited the gardens? They're magnificent.

PATRICE

I haven't had the time. Allow me to insist, Mr. President. Do I have your authorization to call in the Russians?

Kasa-Vubu is silent.

PATRICE

If you have a better solution, I am ready to listen, and to implement it.

Kasa-Vubu thinks, or appears to think for a moment.

KASA-VUBU

I don't see any.

Patrice stands and shakes the president's hand.

PATRICE

Thank you, Mr. President. We work well together. As long as we remain united, no one can break Congo.

INT. PRESIDENTIAL PALACE—WAITING ROOM—DAY

INT. VILLA TILKENS—SMALL OFFICE—EARLY MORNING

*It's very early. The sun is just rising. In his office Patrice is dozing
over his typewriter. The radio is broadcasting an English lesson.*

RADIO
(in English)
Please repeat after me: . . . to be as cold as a cu-
cumber.

Abruptly, the program stops and the voice changes.

RADIO ANNOUNCER
Dear listeners, please excuse the interruption of
our program. Here is a message from the head of
state.

Patrice raises his head.

RADIO (KASA-VUBU)
My dear countrymen . . . I have extremely important news to announce to you. The first mayor,
I mean the prime minister, Patrice Lumumba,
nominated by the king of the Belgians according
to dispositions of the provisional fundamental law,
has betrayed the office entrusted to him. He has

governed arbitrarily. And now, he is plunging to country into an atrocious civil war. That is why I have judged it necessary to dismiss him immediately . . .

Patrice, astounded, stands up.

RADIO (KASA-VUBU)

. . . I do so with the powers vested in me. I now assume the role of commander in chief of the Congolese National Army. I ask the National Army to cease, once and for all, this fratricidal war, and to temporarily hand in their weapons, everywhere throughout the republic . . .

Patrice listens no further. Without hearing Juliana, who is calling him, a globe in her arms, he rushes outside.

JULIANA

Papa!

EXT. VILLA TILKENS—COURTYARD—DAY

Patrice comes out into the courtyard.

PATRICE

Where's Justin?

GUARD

He's gone to eat.

PATRICE

And Dieudonné?

GUARD

He hasn't come back yet.

PATRICE

Then there's nobody in this bloody shanty? Go
get me the keys to the Lincoln.

PAULINE
(running after him)
Patrice, where are you going?

PATRICE

To the Parliament.

PAULINE

To the Parliament?

*She remains silent. Then she signals to two guards in the courtyard
to go with him.*

EXT. PARLIAMENT ENTRANCE—DAY

*Patrice's car arrives at the gates of the parliament. A throng of about fifty
people crowd against the gates. Lumumba's car has difficulty clearing a path.
Patrice is sitting in front. He and the two soldiers are in a tight spot.*

There is banging on the hood and windows, the antenna is bent.

CROWD

It's Patrice, it's him, let him pass! . . . Long live
Lumumba! . . . Down with Lumumba! Traitor!
Communist! . . . Death to Lumumba! . . . Sell out!
Tshombe, thief! Kasa President for life!

Patrice opens the door. The guard next to him holds him back.

FIRST GUARD

Don't do that, chief. There's only two of us.

PATRICE

What can they do to me?

SECOND GUARD

I'm not getting out in that crowd.

PATRICE

You two stay inside then, if that's what you
want.

Patrice gets out of the car. People rush forward.

CROWD

Down with Lumumba! . . . Long live Patrice! . . .
Hurrah for the MNC!

*Patrice manages to climb onto the hood of the car and gestures for si-
lence. Despite the lack of success, he starts to speak.*

PATRICE

(shouting)

What happened today is scandalous. Mr. Kasa-
Vubu cannot, and has no authority to dismiss a
deputy elected by the people. We have never re-
lented in our efforts, we work twenty-four hours
a day to defend the people who have long suffered
from the colonial Belgian's oppression. And at the
moment when the Congo should bask in world

admiration, Kasa-Vubu strikes below the belt and drags it through the mud. This will not continue!

CROWD
Down with Kasa Vubu!

INT. PARLIAMENT—DAY

Stormy debate. We are in the Congolese parliament, which is emptier than usual. The interruptions are all the more excessive.

OPPOSITION DEPUTY
Mr. Lumumba wants to instigate a dictatorship. That is why he was removed! It's because of him that all the European administrators are gone. And those Soviet planes … even the president wasn't informed about it …

ANOTHER DEPUTY
(from his seat)
Whenever it suits you, "he isn't informed." If he's never informed, he should give up his position.

Cheers of approval from a majority of deputies.

PRESIDENT OKITO
Gentlemen, gentlemen, calm please. Allow the distinguished member to finish.

OPPOSITION DEPUTY
For the moment, Mr. Lumumba is the one without a post. Parliament must not meddle in executive matters.

During these polemics, we discover deputy Lumumba, sitting in his chair. He seems at times oblivious, uninterested, annoyed, discouraged, or tired.

PRESIDENT OKITO
The floor is now given to the Prime Minister.

Lumumba climbs to the podium. He stands at the microphone, and stares out momentarily at the assembly, which is sparse in some areas.

LUMUMBA
Mr. President, distinguished members, I take the floor before you because it is my duty to inform you of what is happening today in our country. In no case did I oppose Kasa-Vubu. Furthermore, if today he is head of state, it is thanks to me, Lumumba. Some members, even from the opposition, did not support him, because they said he was a separatist. Well, the danger they feared, is here today.

Applause from the majority, noises and murmuring on the opposition benches.

LUMUMBA
If today I were to ask those elected by the nation for Mr. Kasa-Vubu's destitution, he would no longer be head of state.

ABAKO PARTY MEMBERS
Do it!

LUMUMBA

Millions of francs were used to campaign against me, on the radio and handing out daily pamphlets, all part of their psychological strategy. In order to fool the people, they call me all kinds of names: Lumumba the dictator, Lumumba the Communist, and Lumumba of Moscow, and many others. Do you think the people will let themselves be fooled?

Applause.

LUMUMBA

We do not wish to be part of any block, the Congo will never be French, Russian, or American. We don't want to be. We don't want colonialism, whether it be ideological, political, intellectual or economic. We want to remain Congolese and African. But the imperialists are very strong . . .

Applause from the majority benches.

LUMUMBA

. . . the imperialists are powerful, they have a lot of money, and we are still politically weak. We let ourselves be duped, we let ourselves be influenced by everything. But when we fought here, when I was thrown in jail because I demanded independence, was it the Russians who were advising me?

SOME DELEGATES

No! No!

LUMUMBA

When everywhere our brothers were struggling, was it the Russians who encouraged us to reclaim our independence? Who exploited us for eighty years? Was it not the imperialists? Queen Elizabeth of Belgium is the president of the Belgian-Russian Friendship Committee. Does that make her Communist?

Applause, laughter from the majority benches.

LUMUMBA

When they speak against Lumumba, know that he is only a scapegoat, for he is not their real target. They are after you and the future of Congo. Dear brothers, I call upon your wisdom, the Bantu wisdom. The situation is more serious than you imagine. Let us unite, for united you are capable of saving the country. Let us forget all that has divided us.

Extended applause as Lumumba regains his seat.

EXT. CAMP LEOPOLD—DAY

A group of soldiers practice a military drill. The Belgian officers have been replaced by officers of the UN, from North Africa.

INT. CAMP LEOPOLD—MOBUTU'S VILLA—DAY

In one of the camp's villas, Colonel Mobutu is dining with his family. He seems quite at ease, and especially happy. Also at his table sits a senior officer of the UN: the Moroccan Kettani, who is assigned to him as a "consultant." The meal is ending. The two men stand up and head towards the veranda.

KETTANI

After all, Joseph, royalty is no worse. It prevents
ambition from reaching too far.

MOBUTU

Morocco is a grand country. I dream that one
day, our officers can go to Saint-Cyr like you.

KETTANI

Colonies sometimes have their positive aspects.

MOBUTU

Of course . . . when one can choose the colonizers.

They laugh.

EXT. CAMP LEOPOLD—DAY

*Both men sit on the platform porch, from where they can see across
the entire camp. In the distance, soldiers continue to drill.*

KETTANI

Joseph, now that you have your own men . . .

MOBUTU

Well, you know, they are mine as long as they
are paid.

KETTANI

They are paid and trained. It is an investment
in the future. The future of Congo.

Lumumba (feature; 2000)   **339**

MOBUTU
(looking him in the eyes)
The future of all of us.

KETTANI
Listen, I'll be frank with you. Lumumba is as
good as dead. Kasa-Vubu is concerned only with
ousting him and letting the country rot. There's a
need for someone to take charge of things.

MOBUTU
I've thought about it. I think about it all the
time.

KETTANI
Forget Lumumba. In politics, loyalty is a weak-
ness.

MOBUTU
What are the guarantees?

KETTANI
I am empowered to guarantee you everything.

MOBUTU
Eisenhower?

KETTANI
Kennedy.

MOBUTU
What do I gain?

KETTANI

Everything.

EXT. VILLA TILKENS—COURTYARD—NIGHT

The prime minister's car enters the courtyard of the residence. Parked next to the porch is a large ambulance, its motor still running. The emergency lights sweep the area with a blood-red glare. Patrice gets out of the car without waiting for the chauffeur to open the door. A doctor and some nurses speak quietly near the ambulance. Patrice runs toward them.

PATRICE

Pauline . . . ?

He stops short. A nurse steps down, carefully holding in her arms a blanket from which escapes the crying of a newborn child. Patrice goes to her to investigate, distraught.

PATRICE

He's all yellow . . .

DOCTOR

It's a girl. Acute hepatitis. She requires immediate treatment.

PATRICE

And Pauline?

DOCTOR

Very tired . . . But she's fine, Excellency . . .

INT. VILLA TILKENS—STAIRCASE—NIGHT

Patrice rushes up the stairs.

INT. VILLA TILKENS—PAULINE'S BEDROOM—
NIGHT

He enters Pauline's room, where she is lying in bed, a hollow look on her face. He goes to her and sits on one corner of the bed. He takes her hand.

> PAULINE
> Have you seen her? She's . . .

> PATRICE
> She is very beautiful. She looks like you. What are we going to call her?

> PAULINE
> I was thinking of . . . Marie-Christine . . .

The ambulance's siren wails away into the distance.

> PAULINE
> They've taken her?

Patrice nods his head, and Pauline bursts into tears.

> PAULINE
> Oh Patrice . . . They are taking her to Switzerland . . .

PATRICE
(stunned)
To Switzerland? In Europe?

PAULINE
They said . . . Only there will she have a chance .
. . They have the supplies . . . They can save her . . .

PATRICE
But they didn't tell me a thing . . . How many
hours by plane is it? To Switzerland?

PAULINE
Do you think I could go?

*We hear the sound of an approaching engine. A car stops outside.
Patrice goes to the window.
He sees:*

EXT. VILLA TILKENS—COURTYARD—NIGHT

*In the garden, shadows move around. Soldiers are taking position
around the villa.*

PATRICE
I'll be back.

INT. VILLA TILKENS—STAIRCASE—NIGHT

He heads down the stairs, then stops halfway.

At the bottom of the stairs, in the main living room, Mobutu waits respectfully, dressed in the uniform of a high-ranking officer. He fiddles nervously with a baton.

PATRICE

I didn't see you at Parliament. What do you want?

MOBUTU

The fat man . . . I mean, the president . . . ordered me to arrest you.

(pause)

I wanted to warn you . . . and also to tell you that I wouldn't do it of course. I am a soldier, above all. I can't take sides in political disputes.

PATRICE

(after a silence)

Are these your men surrounding the house?

MOBUTU

Security measures.

PATRICE

I am not being arrested, yet the prime minister's house is being surrounded.

MOBUTU

I am only looking out for your safety. I'm your friend, Patrice. There are a lot of people after your skin.

PATRICE

Between those who want my skin, and those

who want to do me good, I don't know which to fear most. I would ask that you remove your men.

MOBUTU

You ask me, or order me?

PATRICE

I order you.

MOBUTU
(after a silence)

If I listen to Kasa-Vubu, you are no longer prime minister. If I listen to you, Kasa-Vubu is no longer president. What would you do in my place?

Patrice looks at him until he lowers his eyes.

PATRICE

I know you. You didn't make this decision alone? Who is behind you?

He turns his back on him and climbs the stairs towards Pauline.

INT. VILLA TILKENS—PAULINE'S BEDROOM— NIGHT

Pauline is feverish, and seems to be suffering.

PAULINE

Is she all right?

PATRICE

Who? The baby? Don't worry. Listen, as soon
as you're back on your feet, I'll send you to the
Guinean embassy. With Juliana. I want you both
to stay there until things return to normal.

PAULINE

And you?

PATRICE

Me . . . We'll see.

EXT. HOTEL REGINA—TERRACE—DAY

*On the almost empty terrace of a café in front of the Regina Hotel, a
small group of foreign journalists quench their thirst with rounds of
Polar beer. Two stunning black women in fluorescent green mini-skirts
and bright blonde wigs strut by.*

YOUNG JOURNALIST
(in English)
Oh baby light my fire!

VETERAN JOURNALIST
The morale reinforcements have arrived.

Laughter.

FIRST GIRL

Fake Flemish!

SECOND GIRL

Look at him. Big mouth, small dick!

YOUNG JOURNALIST
Baby, not Flemish, me American.
(in pidgin Lingala)
Na lingo yo baby . . .

EXT. HOTEL MEMLING—DAY

*An improvised press conference in front of the hotel. The journalists
and onlookers have formed a semi-circle around the speaker, Colonel
Mobutu.*

MOBUTU
. . . In order to free ourselves from this impasse,
the Congolese Army has decided to neutralize the
head of state, Mr. Kasa-Vubu, as well as the prime
minister, Mr. Lumumba. This is not a military
coup, but simply a peaceful revolution.

Commotion of the journalists trying to find out more.

*A few Belgian customers cheer. Mobutu moves away and tries to get
back to his car and escort parked further along the square.*

EXT. MEMLING REGINA SQUARE—DAY

Mobutu continues to walk, still surrounded by journalists.

MOBUTU
(above the crowd)
This is not a military coup . . . No military person will take power . . . It is not a coup d'état . . . It
is not a coup d'état . . . It is peaceful . . . peaceful . . .
We are . . .

FIRST JOURNALIST

And the new government?

MOBUTU

It is not a coup d'état . . . We shall call in neutral
Congolese experts as well as foreign ones, chosen
by ourselves to save the country from this chaos,
and to work for the country's welfare.

SECOND JOURNALIST

Who? Who are these neutral Congolese, commander?

EXT. SQUARE IN FRONT OF THE REGINA—DAY

*Mobutu has reached the center of the square. He turns a little. Kettani
draws him to the cars.*

MOBUTU
(walking)
Tomorrow I will make a solemn appeal to all
our students and to all our African experts in Europe and elsewhere. They must return as quickly
as possible to manage the country.

BELGIAN CUSTOMER

Long live General Mobutu.

MOBUTU

Oh now, not so fast.
(laughter)
That may happen, I see it.

(laughter)

But I repeat, and as General Kettani here at my side—member of the UN forces, my military counselor and a good friend—will attest: after this short revolutionary period, we will return power, with the agreement of our students, to the politicians.

Mobutu reaches his jeep. Shots of approval from a few Europeans and Congolese in the background. Mobutu, becoming bolder, climbs into the back to rise above the pack of journalists, now jostling to hold out their microphones.

EASTERN BLOC JOURNALIST

Certain sources compare the Congo to a corporation in which the stockholders with the most shares decide the direction to go.

MOBUTU
(suspicious)

So?

EASTERN BLOC JOURNALIST

What role did the Americans play in this putsch . . . in this revolution?

MOBUTU
(angry)

Look, we know all about your propaganda, Mr. Zerbrowski. This morning, we caught three Russian officers, disguised in civilian clothes, as they distributed insulting and subversive pamphlets. I'd like to take this opportunity to announce our first measure: as of tomorrow morning, all socialist embassies will be closed and they have 48 hours to leave the country. (cheers from some of the crowd).

INT. VILLA TILKENS—PATRICE'S OFFICE—DAY

The room is filled with smoke like at the end of a poker session. A few friends are gathered, two members of parliament, and a bodyguard in African garb, a secretary busily typing away in one corner. Lumumba is on the telephone. He is angry at the person on the other end of the line.

LUMUMBA

Call it what you want: a putsch, a pronunciamiento, it is a coup d'état. I'm not allowed on the radio. I tried to get in today, but was forced away with a machine gun. A Ghanaian officer, no less. It's not clear whose side they're on anymore. They haven't yet cut off my phone, but it won't be long. I don't want to wait until I'm completely paralyzed. The solution is simple. We leave for Stanleyville today, together, and take it from there . . . What?

EXT. VILLA TILKENS—STREET—DAY

In the foreground, a Congolese army jeep, soldiers, an officer drawing slowly on his cigarette. In the background to the left, UN soldiers adopt an attitude of being in control.

LUMUMBA
(off-screen)
In order for me to be able to answer you, I would need to have freedom of movement. For the

moment, and despite Colonel Mobutu's declara-
tions . . .

INT. VILLA TILKENS—PATRICE'S OFFICE—DAY

LUMUMBA
. . . of neutrality regarding the leadership, I am
a prisoner and Mr. Kasa Vubu has all the freedom
in the world to act . . . Katanga? . . . You're joking .
. . when you want to drown your dog.

*A secretary brings him a letter, which he opens while continuing the
conversation.*

LUMUMBA
(more quietly)
. . . they say he is rabid . . . Yes . . . yes I'm still here.
I'm sorry . . . I have just learned that my daughter has
just died in Switzerland. I can't even go there . . .
(pause)
I can do nothing . . .

EXT. VILLA TILKENS—NIGHT

Tropical rain falls on the residence of the Prime Minister.

EXT. VILLA TILKENS—KITCHEN—NIGHT

*Patrice comes into the kitchen. A maid is finishing the dishes. A ser-
vant rises.*

PATRICE

The car that takes the employees home . . .
what time does it leave?

SERVANT

Half past six, Excellency.

PATRICE

Tell the chauffeur to come see me . . . Let him
in through the kitchen . . . without being seen by
the soldiers.

SERVANT

Very good, Excellency.

PATRICE

Wait.
(putting the note in an envelope and handing it to him)
One hour from now, you will bring this to
Maurice Mpolo. You know where he lives. Deliver
into his hands. I'm counting on you.

SERVANT

Very good, Excellency.

INT. VILLA TILKENS—PATRICE'S OFFICE—NIGHT

*Patrice begins to sort out the papers on his desk. He stops, takes the
photos of his children from the desk, and places them carefully on the
table. He remains still, looking out through the window. The telephone
rings. Patrice lets it go on for a long while before picking up.*

PATRICE

Yes? . . . Ah, Thomas, it's you. Yes, it's decided. We must end this deadlock. I can't stay here trapped in the house while they massacre my partisans one by one. Are you safe? Good . . . Listen, one of us must be sacrificed. They'll probably end up stopping me, torturing and killing me, who knows. It will be a sacrifice for the good of the Congolese people.

(pause)

All right Thomas. Don't worry. Forget what I just said, I wasn't serious. I'll send you written instructions. Yes . . . speak to you soon.

He hangs up.

INT. VILLA TILKENS—PATRICE'S OFFICE—NIGHT, LATER

The chauffeur comes in, trembling with fear.

CHAUFFEUR

The car is ready, Excellency.

PATRICE

Don't be frightened. Everything will go fine. We'll meet at Stanleyville and go on from there.

INT. VILLA TILKENS—SERVANTS' ENTRANCE— NIGHT

Patrice leaves the villa by the servant's entrance.

EXT./INT. VILLA TILKENS—COURTYARD/CAR
PARK—NIGHT

Patrice hides in the waiting Chevrolet station wagon.

EXT./INT. VILLA TILKENS—COURTYARD/EXIT—
NIGHT

The car drives around the villa and reaches the central alley. Outside, the rain has prompted the guards to seek shelter in a neighboring building. No one is there to inspect the Chevrolet station wagon.

EXT./INT. VILLA TILKENS—CAR—NIGHT

Lumumba is lying behind the front seat. The UN guards let the car pass, but the Congolese Army soldiers stop the Chevrolet. A soldier shines a torch inside. The rain is dripping from his helmet.

CHAUFFEUR
You want me to buy you some Belgas, Alphonse? I'll be back in half an hour.

SOLDIER
I smoke American ones now. Bastard rain . . . keeps dripping down my neck.

He steps away from the car, which drives away into the night.

EXT./INT. BUSH VILLAGE—DAY

Patrice Lumumba's small convoy, now composed of the station wagon, a blue Peugeot, and a Fiat, drives through a small village. Children wave at these passing strangers.

With him now are Pauline and Juliana, some loyal colleagues, and two members of Parliament.

EXT./INT. BUSH ROAD—DAY

On the road ahead, a man on a bicycle signals them to stop.

MAN

Excellency, you must leave the main road. At Diolo they told us that they saw a convoy of soldiers.

LUMUMBA

How far behind us?

MAN

About sixteen kilometers. Perhaps fewer now.

LUMUMBA

Thank you, comrade.

EXT. SANKURU RIVER—EMBARKATION
STATION—DAY

Caption: Lodi ferry. Two days later. December 1, 1960.

The car rattles over potholes in the road. The fugitives' vehicles reach the Lodi village, on the banks of the Sankuru River. The blue Peugeot is the first to arrive. Someone gets out. It's Mpolo. He walks towards the river. Patrice's car pulls up next to him.

MPOLO

There is no ferry.

PATRICE

Let's leave the cars. We'll go by canoe.

MPOLO

And once on the other side, what will we do?

PATRICE

We'll find other cars . . . and if we don't we'll go
by foot.

There is only one canoe. Everyone is now on the riverbank, near the tied up canoe, and an argument erupts with Pauline.

PAULINE

No, Patrice! I don't want to go first. They're not
after me. I'll wait for the ferry.

MPOLO

Quickly, Patrice. They are behind us.

Patrice decides to go with Mpolo and the chauffeur. He kisses Juliana and Pauline and boards the boat. They paddle away from the shore.

During the crossing, an Opel carrying four or five militiamen arrives by the shore. The soldiers, armed with machine guns, immediately take hold of Pauline, Juliana, and the others. Screams of fright are heard across the river.

The canoe has almost reached the other side.

PATRICE

I can't . . . I'm going back.

MPOLO

Don't do that, I forbid you, it's crazy! You must go to Stanleyville, it's your duty as a leader of the revolution and as a soldier!

PATRICE

And let them seek revenge on my wife and my daughter? And later to hear that I let it happen?

MPOLO

It's suicide, Patrice.

PATRICE

No. I'll speak to them. There aren't many of them, they'll listen to me.

MPOLO

Then I'll come too.
> *(shaking his head)*
This is crazy.

They turn back.

Patrice is the first to jump to the shore. He walks towards the soldiers who point their machine guns at him.

COMMANDER

Chief, we don't want to hurt you. But if we return without you, they'll kill us.

LUMUMBA

If you bring me back, it's me they'll kill. But know that you'll never be forgiven, and you'll live to regret it. I'm the one that made you a commander, while before, in the Public Force, everything was in European hands. If this soil drinks my blood, you'll all be doomed.

FIRST SOLDIER

He's right.

SECOND SOLDIER

I'm for Lumumba! I stay with him.

COMMANDER

Stop your bullshit and shut your mouth.
(to Lumumba)
Sorry, chief, we've got orders to follow.

Suddenly a truck of backup troops arrives. Many more soldiers pour out and surround. They brutally take away Patrice and Mpolo, who are violently thrown into the truck. They protest, but are pummeled with rifle butts and kicks.

Pauline and Juliana, horrified, watch powerlessly, held back by the soldiers from the Opel. They hear the commander shout:

SECOND COMMANDER
(in a high-pitched voice)
Hit them harder! You are Balubas, and he's a dirty Communist and a Batetela! He's the one that had killed and burned alive your people, raped and drowned your women and children! Demolish him!

The truck pulls away with its cargo.

EXT. N'DJILI AIRPORT—DAY

A DC 3 with Sabena insignia lands at N'Djili and comes to stop near a large hangar.

We approach the steps of the plane. The door opens. Lumumba appears. He is made to come down first. His hands are tied with a thick rope behind his back, and his white shirt is stained with blood. His glasses are gone and a blood clot covers his left cheek.

Among the waiting soldiers is a large contingent of the international press. Lumumba and his companions are pushed without ceremony.

Before being hoisted into an ANC truck, Lumumba, quite dignified in spite of the beating, turns toward the journalists who are now uncommonly quiet.

Twenty or so soldiers pile inside the truck, where the prisoners are thrown down against the bare floor and beaten some more.

The truck leaves at high speed, followed with difficulty by a car with a film crews and press photographers.

One blow. Everything goes black.

INT. CAMP LEOPOLD—MOBUTU'S VILLA—DAY

In the dining room, gathered around a well-varnished table are Kasa-Vubu, Mobutu, an officer, two civilians, and a Belgian adviser.

Away from the group sits a man with slick black hair, wearing a wide tie and an American-cut suit.

KASA-VUBU

I think, gentlemen, that it's time we voted.

BELGIAN COUNSELOR

Those who are for, raise your hands.

The Belgian advisor who just spoke raises his hand right away. One by one, each of the participants raise their hand. After the two civilians and the officers, Mobutu raises his hand as if it weighed a ton.

Kasa-Vubu keeps his hands on the table. The others look at him. Finally, he raises his hand.

The Belgian adviser turns to the man with the slick black hair.

BELGIAN ADVISOR

Mr. C.—? Would you like to add your vote?

C.— [CENSORED NAME]
(with a heavy American accent)
My country's government is not in the habit of meddling into the democratic affairs of a sovereign nation. We'll respect your decision.

The Belgian advisor rises and goes to the phone.

BELGIAN ADVISOR

Hello? Beelzebub here: "I ask for the authorization of the Jew to receive Satan." I repeat, "ask for the authorization of the Jew to receive Satan." Thank you.

INT. THYSVILLE PRISON—CELL—DAWN

*Patrice and Mpolo are sleeping on planks, wearing only their un-
derwear. They are dirty and have several days of stubble.*

                              MPOLO
          Patrice?

                              PATRICE
          What?

                              MPOLO
          Can-I-bal . . .

They start to laugh quietly.

*A key turns in the lock. The door is unlocked and opens, revealing the
guards who jumped on them.*

                              PATRICE
          I demand—

He is silenced with a blow across the mouth.

EXT. THYSVILLE PRISON—DAWN

*They are taken out into the morning light, to a yard were a jeep is
waiting.*

*Hands tied behind their backs, they are pushed into a jeep, where they
see President of the Senate Okito tied too, his face swollen and his eyes
wide with fear.*

MPOLO

You?

OKITO

They're arresting everybody.

The jeep takes off immediately.

EXT. SAVANNA AIRPORT—DAY

The jeep arrives at a small airport in the bush. A Belgian advisor in safari clothes approaches the leading soldier.

BELGIAN ADVISOR

Hurry up, come on.

They make the prisoners get off the jeep and climb into a DC-4 waiting on the runway, its propellers already turning and the motors making a deafening sound.

INT. DC-4 AIRPLANE—DAY

Inside the plane, the prisoners are attached with handcuffs to the same row of seats. The crew is Belgian and British. The soldiers are Balubas.

PATRICE

Where are you taking us? You must be aware
of —

SOLDIER

Shut up!

He strikes Patrice on the shoulder with a rifle butt, which makes him fall into the center aisle, despite the handcuffs. This provokes a further frenzy of blows and kicks. Okito, hit in the eye, begins to scream.

PATRICE
You have no right —

The soldiers jump at him.

The British radio operator, disturbed by the sounds of beatings and the screams, glances over, then bends over, nauseous.

The commander finally intervenes.

COMMANDER
Stop that! Stop it! We must deliver them alive … Stop, I tell you, you're endangering the plane's stability …

He is forced to intervene physically. The soldiers seem possessed. They beat blindly at the mass of men on the floor.

The commander, hit on the chin, steps away and locks himself inside the pilot's cabin.

EXT. DC-4 AIRPLANE—DAY

We see the plane fly-off and disappear over the savanna.

EXT. ELIZABETHVILLE—AIRPORT—DAY

The DC-4 lands and rolls into a Katangese air force hangar. An armored car, trucks, and some jeeps surround the plane. Some Katangese constables under orders from five Belgian officers form a human rope. Not far away, a group of UN soldiers and their two Swedish officers are speaking with a Belgian officer. The sound of the engines drowns out their words. A jeep pulls up and stops.

The plane door opens. The three prisoners, covered in blood, walk unsteadily down the stairs.

The plane engines cut, we now hear the Belgian officer reply to the two Swedes:

BELGIAN OFFICER

Moreover, this part of the airport is not under your command. It's a domestic Katangese matter.

SWEDISH OFFICER
(with a heavy accent)

I don't agree. I will refer the matter to my superiors.

BELGIAN OFFICER

They know all about it.

SWEDISH OFFICER

I need the order in writing.

As if to respond, the constables push the prisoners into the jeep using their rifle butts. Patrice turns his head toward the UN soldiers. One of them turns away, embarrassed, or perhaps ashamed. In the jeep, the soldiers sit on the prisoners who have been thrown to the floor. One of the three captives begins to scream.

The jeep takes off, followed by a motor convoy, and heads toward the edge of the airport, where they go out through a hole in the fence.

INT. NEW YORK—UNITED NATIONS SECURITY COUNCIL—DAY

Kanza stands before those assembled, clutching the microphone:

KANZA
We are here discussing matters of protocol while a man is being murdered . . .

PRESIDENT OF THE ASSEMBLY
Mr. Kanza, once again, you are out of order . . . You are tolerated here under the title of observer. You no longer represent your country. For the last time, I ask you to leave the microphone.

A satisfied expression on Kasa-Vubu's face as he sits behind his desk, representing the regime.

NIGERIAN DELEGATE
Mr. Lumumba has been imprisoned for more than two months. This arrest is illegal, inhuman, and immoral . . .

AMERICAN DELEGATE
We call upon the government of the former Belgian colony to grant humane treatment to the deposed prime minister, and to ensure that he receive a fair trial . . .

We strongly object to the acceptance of Mr. Kasa-Vubu's delegation as the legitimate representative of the Congo. The United Arab Republics have decided to withdraw their troops from the UN expedition . . .

TUNISIAN DELEGATE

In the name of President Bourguiba, we demand that this tragic situation be brought to an immediate end . . .

Kasa-Vubu rises to respond to the Egyptian delegate. A paper is slipped before him. He unfolds it, and reads, his face impassive. He then begins his speech.

KASA-VUBU

As the honorable Egyptian delegate has suggested, my government and I are ready to negotiate with Mr. Lumumba . . . but I cannot, as head of state, intervene in the judicial process. I am the political adversary of Mr. Lumumba, but not his enemy.

On the paper before him, we see: "PATRICE AKUFI [PATRICE IS DEAD]"

EXT. ELISABETHVILLE SUBURBS—BROUWEZ HOUSE—JANUARY 17, 9PM

Brouwez residence. A car drives into the courtyard where several others are already parked. The president of Katanga, Moïse Tshombe, gets out the car, accompanied by his interior minister, Godefroid Munungo, and several others, including a Belgian captain and a doctor. As a rainstorm begins, they all go into the house. Tshombe is uncomfortable, Munungo impatient.

TSHOMBE
I hope that they were not too . . .

EXT. BROUWEZ HOUSE—BATHROOM—DAY

In the bathroom, we discover the prisoners, still tied-up and covered with blood. Mpolo shakes with convulsions. Only Lumumba seems conscious, his eyes turned inward, frozen with pain.

The doctor leans over and examines him. Then he stands back up and approaches Tshombe, who holds a handkerchief over his mouth, close to fainting.

DOCTOR
There is internal bleeding . . . The stomach is
most likely punctured . . . Several ribs are broken.
If we don't immediately transfer them to a hospital
for operation, they probably only have a few hours
left.

While he is talking, a soldier hits Lumumba over the head with his rifle butt. Tshombe turns his head away.

Munongo takes the rifle from the soldier, but only to strike Patrice himself.

MUNONGO
I warned you. Never set foot in my country.

Patrice's broken glasses lie on the tiled floor.

EXT. KATANGAN FOREST—SAVANNA ROAD— NIGHT

A long convoy of several black limousines and two jeeps full of soldiers plow their way through the savanna until the edge of a forest.

INT./EXT. KATANGAN FOREST—ROAD/CAR INTERIOR—NIGHT

Lumumba's face. He is sweating, his face swollen, but almost serene.

EXT./INT. KINSHASA—PRESIDENTIAL PALACE— DAY

1990. A group of female entertainers dance and sing in front of the large building. Some of them, dressed in the "boubou" with "great leader" motifs, echo the chorus with lively professionalism. At the end of the garden, viewed from below, an enormous bust of Joseph Désiré Mobutu, marshal, looks on imperiously. At the railings, poorer onlookers good-naturedly follow the ceremonies.

In the courtyard, the ceremony celebrating the thirtieth anniversary of independence begins. The faces of the foreign diplomats, European ministers, French, Belgian, are all marked with a silent, almost obscene complicity.

Mobutu, in his leopard-skin hat, begins his speech.

MOBUTU

Mr. Prime Minister, Ministers, Ambassadors, Citizens . . . On this memorable day, the day of the thirtieth anniversary of our country's independence, it is with great joy and pride that we welcome you all.

Among the faces of those in attendance, some well known.

MOBUTU

In the name of the government, we now ask for a minute of silence, in memory of he who we now officially proclaim a national hero: Patrice Emery Lumumba.

In the silence, the sound of a clock counting away the seconds until . .

.

EXT. KATANGAN FOREST—NIGHT

The ground is sodden wet. A small group of Katangan ministers and Belgian advisors, some still wearing dinner jackets, exchange few words. One of them approaches the car in which the prisoners are held.

ADVISOR

You may pray, if you wish.

LUMUMBA

You are going to kill us?

The advisor doesn't answer. Okito is the first. The advisor removes his handcuffs. He is trembling slightly. He brings Okito before the group of ministers, among them Tshombe and Munongo.

One of them mutters something incomprehensible. Okito is taken to a large tree. A burst of gunfire rings out.

Then it's Mpolo's turn. He is unconscious. They drag him to the same place. A short burst. He doesn't move; he might have been already dead prior to the shots.

Lumumba is left alone in the car. He has seen his comrades die. He is serene and sad. He sees the Belgian advisor approach him.

ADVISOR

Mr. Lumumba . . . it's . . .

Lumumba gets out of the car. He stumbles, and the man holds him up. He is led to the tree.

They have stretched Mpolo and Okito out side by side on the grass. Patrice looks briefly toward them, as if afraid he might lose courage.

They stand him back against the tree.

He looks straight before him, but seems no longer to see his executioners.

A burst of gunfire. A long silence. The ticking of a clock.

INT./EXT. KINSHASA—PRESIDENTIAL PALACE—DAY

1990. We return to the large ceremonial hall. A heavy silence, much too long. Pale faces.

MOBUTU

Thank you.

Applause.

EXT. KATANGAN SAVANNA—NIGHT

We see the two men about to finish their task of cutting up the corpses. Two Belgians, dripping with sweat and whiskey, on the brink of nausea, hold handkerchiefs over their noses to keep from vomiting from the stench.

They throw petrol over the debris. One of them strikes a match.

> **VOICE OVER (LUMUMBA)**
> . . . No, in truth, we did not deserve that. And yet one day . . . and that day will come. And then . . . ahhh . . .

Long, menacing sigh.

Extreme close-up of the match that spins into the air and falls on the deformed heap. An immense blaze takes over the screen.

Music.

END.

ABOUT RAOUL PECK

Raoul Peck's feature films and documentaries explore internationalist themes of inequality and offer compelling depictions of Haiti under political duress. In addition to filmmaking, Peck has served as Haiti's minister of culture. In 2001 he received the Human Rights Watch Lifetime Achievement Award. His most recent film is *Moloch Tropical*. Peck is the president of France's cinema school, "La Fémis."

ABOUT BERTRAND TAVERNIER

Director of over thirty films, including *Death Watch*, *Round Midnight*, and *Life and Nothing But*, filmmaker, screenwriter and film producer Bertrand Tavernier won the John Huston Award from The Film Foundation in 2004.

ABOUT CATHERINE TEMERSON

Catherine Temerson's translations include Amin Maalouf's *Origins*, Elie Wiesel's *The Sonderberg Case*, Florence Noiville's *Issac B. Singer: A Life*, and Hiner Saleem's *My Father's Rifle: A Childhood in Kurdistan*.